U.S. v. Darby Lumber

LANDMARK LAW CASES & AMERICAN SOCIETY

Julie Novkov and Victoria Woeste
Series Editors

Peter Charles Hoffer
N. E. H. Hull
Founding Series Editors

For a complete list of titles in the series go to www.kansaspress.ku.edu.

JOHN A. FLITER

U.S. v. Darby Lumber

The Triumph of Fair Labor Standards

UNIVERSITY PRESS OF KANSAS

Published by the University Press of Kansas (Lawrence, Kansas 66045), which was
organized by the Kansas Board of Regents and is operated and funded by Emporia State
University, Fort Hays State University, Kansas State University, Pittsburg State University,
the University of Kansas, and Wichita State University.

Library of Congress Cataloging-in-Publication Data

Names: Fliter, John A., 1959– author
Title: U.S. v. Darby Lumber : the triumph of fair labor standards / John A. Fliter.
Other titles: US v. Darby Lumber
Description: Lawrence : University Press of Kansas, 2025. | Series:
Landmark law cases and american society | Includes bibliographical
references and index.
Identifiers: LCCN 2025008548 (print) | LCCN 2025008549 (ebook) |
ISBN 9780700640584 cloth
ISBN 9780700640591 paperback
ISBN 9780700640607 epub
Subjects: LCSH: Wages—Law and legislation—United States | Minimum
wage—Law and legislation—United States | Hours of labor—Law and
legislation—United States | Overtime—Law and legislation—United States |
Child labor—Law and legislation—United States | United States.
Fair Labor Standards Act of 1938 | Darby Lumber Co—Trials, litigation, etc.
Classification: LCC KF3489 .F565 2025 (print) | LCC KF3489 (ebook) |
DDC 344.7301/21—dc23/eng/20250307
LC record available at https://lccn.loc.gov/2025008548.
LC ebook record available at https://lccn.loc.gov/2025008549.

British Library Cataloguing-in-Publication Data is available.

Authorised Representative Details: Easy Access System Europe
Mustamäe tee 50, 10621 Tallinn, Estonia | gpsr.requests@easproject.com

CONTENTS

ACKNOWLEDGMENTS

After completing my book *Child Labor in America: The Epic Legal Struggle to Protect Children*, for the University Press of Kansas, my editor, David Congdon, suggested that I write a book on *U.S. v. Darby Lumber* for the Landmark Law Cases and American Society Series. The idea piqued my interest because the project would allow me to explore the other part of the story in the fight for fair labor standards. That missing narrative includes the movement for a forty-hour workweek, a federal minimum wage, and time-and-a-half wages for overtime. After committing to the task, however, work and family obligations during the Covid-19 pandemic intervened and delayed the completion of the manuscript. I appreciate David's confidence and patience in awaiting the final product.

I would like to thank Autumn M. Johnson, assistant professor and Special Collections librarian at the Zach S. Henderson Library of Georgia Southern University, Statesboro Campus, for assisting me with a local file on the *Darby Lumber* case. Patrick Novotny, Department of Political Science, Georgia Southern, provided local background material on the *Darby Lumber* case, including an article that he published. I am also grateful to David S. Tanenhaus and an anonymous reviewer for providing helpful suggestions that improved the manuscript.

This book would not have been possible without the support of my department and the College of Arts and Sciences at Kansas State University. My former department head, Sam Bell, and current head, Nate Birkhead, offered encouragement throughout the process. Several political science graduate students assisted with various aspects of the research, including Jessica Wilkus and Jahan Masjidi. I appreciate their help tracking down books, articles, obscure reports, and other materials. University funds supported field research at the Library of Congress Madison Building Law Library, Manuscript Division, and Newspaper and Periodical Reading Room. The helpful staff in the Manuscript Reading Room eased my access to the public papers of former chief justice Charles Evans Hughes and justices Hugo Black, William O. Douglas, and Harlan Fiske Stone, and numerous databases. The staff at the National Archives in Atlanta, Georgia, also assisted me in obtaining the original transcripts in the federal trial of Fred Darby.

This is my third book with the University Press of Kansas, and it is always a pleasure to work with their excellent staff. I want to thank David Congdon for his helpful advice and support through some difficult years. I also appreciate the assistance of my production editor, Erica Nicholson, for managing the final stages of publication, and Michelle Asakawa for her expert copyediting. Finally, I want to thank Andrea Laws and others in the marketing and sales department for the design and promotion of the book.

I wrote this book in honor of my father, John "Jack" A. Fliter Sr., who passed away in 2009. Neither of my parents attended college, but they worked hard and provided me and my siblings with educational opportunities and a comfortable middle-class lifestyle. My father was a printer, specifically a linotype operator, and a member of the International Typographical Union/CWA for nearly his entire working career. In 1906 the ITU became one of the first unions to secure an eight-hour workday. For over forty years, my father commuted to work in downtown Cleveland, Ohio, and earned his union wages and benefits. When computers made linotype machines obsolete, he had to learn how to do his job using the new technology. With no computer experience, it was difficult for him, but he made the adjustment and continued to support our family. I probably did not say it often enough while he was with us, but I appreciated everything my father did to make our lives better. Thank you, Dad.

John A. Fliter
Manhattan, Kansas

{ *Acknowledgments* }

INTRODUCTION

In late 1965 a band named the Vogues released a song, "Five O'Clock World," that became a top-five hit in the United States and Canada. The tune describes the drudgery of the workday, where our personal time is traded for a paycheck. When the factory whistle blows at 5:00 p.m., however, no employer owns a piece of our time. The following year, the Australian pop rock group the Easybeats had an international hit song entitled "Friday on My Mind," with lyrics that express the Monday through Friday work grind and how workers look forward to partying on Friday night and relaxing on the weekend. Dolly Parton also had a huge hit in 1980 with her song "9 to 5," which was written for the comedy film of the same name. The song became an anthem for office workers in the 1980s. In 1985 the band Alabama had a number-one country hit with the single "Forty Hour Week (For a Livin')," which was their salute to America's blue-collar workers.

These song titles and lyrics illustrate how the eight-hour day, Monday through Friday work schedule, and recreational weekend have become deeply ingrained in American culture. The lives of many workers are defined by this weekly routine. But that has not always been the case. For most of American history, adults and children toiled more than ten hours a day, six days a week, with only Sunday for rest. When the federal government first began keeping statistics on work hours in 1890, a sixty-hour week was common, but some employees in manufacturing jobs and sweatshop industries worked over a hundred hours a week. In the last decade of the 1800s, labor protections, such as maximum hours, minimum wage, and overtime pay laws for private-sector employees, were nonexistent, and the percentage of children in the workforce steadily increased, peaking in 1910.

Workers faced a long, difficult, and sometimes violent struggle to secure fair labor standards under law. Between 1877 and 1937, a period that includes the railroad uprisings of 1877, the Haymarket Square protest and bombing, the Homestead Steel Mill lockout, and the Ludlow massacre of striking coal miners, an estimated six hundred people were killed in labor strikes by police, National Guard units, the US Army, or private security forces. Thousands more were injured in various labor protests.

This book is not a comprehensive history of organized labor in America. Most labor scholars differentiate between employment law and labor law, and that distinction is a useful conceptual approach to our subject. Employment law is based on legislative mandates and applies to the individual worker. The foundation of employment law is the Fair Labor Standards Act of 1938, with its guarantees of maximum hours, a minimum wage, time and a half for overtime, and restrictions on child labor. Labor law is more about the rights of workers to organize and join unions, engage in collective bargaining, and exercise the right to strike. Labor law is centered on the National Labor Relations Act of 1935, also known as the Wagner Act, which protects the rights of workers to organize into unions and collectively bargain to improve their wages, benefits, and work conditions. The Taft-Hartley Act of 1947, which restricts union activities, is also part of the corpus of labor law.

There is some overlap between the two areas, but our story is mostly confined to employment law under the Fair Labor Standards Act (FLSA) and the landmark decision in *U.S. v. Darby Lumber Co.* (1941) that affirmed the constitutionality of the law. My previous book, *Child Labor in America: The Epic Legal Struggle to Protect Children*, covers the child labor issue extensively. Although the child labor provisions are an important part of the FLSA and are included in this study, my goal with this volume is to examine the broader social and legal movement for national fair labor standards that ultimately triumphed with the *Darby Lumber* decision.

Any historical analysis of fair labor standards in the United States is challenging because different groups of workers often fought their own battles and had diverse goals and strategies for achieving them. For example, the union activity of skilled white male workers and the demands they sought under law were often separated from those for unskilled laborers, women, children, and Black Americans. The most important labor union in the late 1800s, the American Federation of Labor (AFL), opposed protective labor legislation, preferring instead to advance workers' rights through unionization and collective bargaining. However, Samuel Gompers, the long-time leader of the AFL, supported labor protections for women and children because both groups lacked the political power to improve their position. There were even disagreements between labor organizations, such as the AFL and Congress of Industrial Organizations (CIO), that threatened to derail efforts to pass the Fair Labor Standards Act. Moreover, federal and state courts often treated the groups differently, at least initially, in reviewing protective labor legislation. Laws limiting work hours for women and children, for example, were often upheld based on paternalistic notions of state power while similar restrictions for male employees were overturned by the courts.

The political-economic struggle over fair labor standards embodied in *U.S. v. Darby Lumber* involves important constitutional issues concerning government regulation of market transactions, the power of Congress under the Commerce Clause, the development of the administrative state, and the relationship of the national government to the states within our structure of federalism. Probably more than any other aspect, competing visions between dual federalism and cooperative federalism influenced the fight over fair labor practices.

Since the earliest debates over labor standards, adherents of dual federalism claimed that the Constitution created a strict division of powers between the national government and the states, with the federal government limited to its enumerated powers. Those specified powers, they argued, said nothing about regulating local labor conditions. Reformers, however, argued that Congress had both enumerated and implied powers to regulate maximum hours, minimum wages, and child labor as integral features of interstate commerce and to tax products made with child labor. Under cooperative federalism, federal and state governments share responsibility for policy problems, and the US government may intervene to bring about needed uniformity in labor laws in order to prevent unfair competition. States may still regulate commercial activity, but if state law conflicts with federal requirements, federal law is supreme. These contrasting views of federalism affected every major congressional debate and federal court decision on fair labor standards.

The social movement for fair labor standards in the United States originated in the late 1700s when some of the first associations of working men demanded fair wages and maximum work hours. In seeking fair labor standards, workers and labor unions had to overcome not only opposition from powerful business groups but also legal doctrines that challenged the very idea of labor unions and deeply held beliefs that workplace regulations were local economic issues reserved to the states under the Tenth Amendment of the Constitution. At first, unions were alleged to be unjust combinations in restraint of trade. After securing their right to exist as organized unions, workers initially focused on labor issues within their specific trade or locality. There was limited success at that level. In the early 1800s labor groups sought a ten-hour workday, and New Hampshire enacted the first ten-hour law in 1847. The law was largely unenforceable because it permitted longer hours if the employer and worker consented by contract. Several associations of skilled tradesmen in cities along the east coast also achieved demands for higher wages of $1.50 to $2.00 a day, although those wage rates were not legislatively mandated.

By the 1840s, trade and mechanical associations, alarmed by the long hours children worked in textile mills, supported restrictions on child labor. In 1842 Massachusetts established a maximum day for children ages twelve and under at ten hours, and in 1848 Pennsylvania set a minimum age for factory and mill work at twelve years. By the start of the Civil War in 1861, seven states had passed legislation concerning minimum age and maximum hours to protect children. These laws were fundamentally flawed because they lacked enforcement mechanisms. Fair labor standards for children and adults in other regions of the country—particularly the South, where slavery was not abolished until the Thirteenth Amendment—were nowhere to be found.

The battle over workers' rights intensified after the Civil War as the economy was transformed during the Industrial Revolution. Increased immigration produced a cheap supply of labor, and factory conditions were largely unregulated, harsh, and dangerous. By the late 1800s, national unions and pro-labor interest groups pressed their political demands, first in state legislatures. Several state governments responded with protective labor legislation during the Progressive Era (about 1890 to 1920). These laws limited employment in some industries to ten hours a day and six days a week, and states like Massachusetts and Oregon enacted the first minimum wage laws. Employers vigorously opposed these reforms because maximum hours and minimum wage laws could increase production costs and reduce profits. Additionally, employers in states with protective labor laws operated at a competitive disadvantage compared to companies in states with lax labor standards.

There were numerous legal challenges to these state labor laws. Some were struck down under a "liberty of contract" doctrine recognized by the Supreme Court under the Due Process Clause of the Fifth and Four-teenth Amendments. The language of the amendments, which prohibits government from denying life, liberty, or property without due process of law, was given a substantive interpretation. Using the doctrine, em-ployers challenged labor protections as a violation of the liberty of a business owner to negotiate the terms of employment with workers. Most state labor laws, however, were eventually upheld by the courts if they were deemed a reasonable exercise of police powers to protect public health, welfare, safety, and morals.

Following World War I, the nation turned inward, and conservatism reigned. The first two federal child labor laws were struck down by the Supreme Court in *Hammer v. Dagenhart* (1918) and *Bailey v. Drexel Furni-ture Company* (1922). Those adverse decisions led to an unsuccessful at-tempt in 1924 to ratify a child labor amendment to the Constitution. Progressive reforms stalled during the 1920s. The decade was character-ized by the Red Scare and laissez-faire policies toward market regula-tion. Described as the "lean years" for the labor movement by political scientist Irving Bernstein, the "liberty of contract" doctrine reached its jurisprudential peak in *Adkins v. Children's Hospital* (1923), where the Su-preme Court struck down a minimum-wage law for women and children within the District of Columbia.

During the Great Depression the demand for fair labor standards moved to the national level. At the height of the economic crisis, about 25 percent of the labor force was unemployed, and wages were so low that many found it impossible to make a living. Some children worked in factories at reduced pay while their jobless fathers stayed at home. The election of Franklin D. Roosevelt in 1932 promised a New Deal for America, but economic conditions worsened over the next few years. There were numerous protests and strikes throughout the country be-tween 1933 and 1935.

The National Industrial Recovery Act (NIRA) of 1933, enacted during the first hundred days of the Roosevelt administration, improved wages for some workers and imposed child labor restrictions, but the law was struck down by the Supreme Court in 1935 as an unconstitutional delega-tion of legislative power to the executive branch. Determined to improve the situation of the working class, Roosevelt made a wages-and-hours law a central issue in his 1936 reelection campaign. His landslide victory and huge Democratic majorities in Congress emboldened FDR to act in support of his agenda. Frustrated with the Supreme Court overturning his economic programs, in February 1937 President Roosevelt unsuccessfully attempted to pack the Court with New Deal justices. Subsequent events made the plan unnecessary.

Several groundbreaking decisions by the Supreme Court in the spring of 1937 changed the whole debate over government regulation of the market and held the potential for federal legislation on fair labor standards. In what is widely known as the Constitutional Revolution of 1937, Justice Owen Roberts switched to the liberal bloc, and with the support of Chief Justice Charles Evans Hughes, the Supreme Court in *West Coast Hotel Co. v. Parrish* and *National Labor Relations Board v. Jones and Laughlin Steel Corporation* abruptly shifted its view of economic regulation. *West Coast Hotel* dealt a major blow to substantive due process. In rejecting a freedom of contract challenge to a Washington State minimum wage law, Chief Justice Hughes stressed that the Constitution neither mentions liberty of contract nor recognizes "an absolute and uncontrollable liberty."

Two weeks later, on April 12, the Supreme Court handed the Roosevelt administration a landmark victory in five consolidated cases involving the National Labor Relations Act. In *National Labor Relations Board v. Jones and Laughlin Steel Corporation*, Chief Justice Hughes argued, "Although activities may be intrastate in character when separately considered, if they have such a close and substantial relation to interstate commerce that their control is essential and appropriate to protect that commerce from burdens and obstructions, Congress cannot be denied the power to exercise that control." In upholding Washington State's minimum wage, the National Labor Relations Act, and other New Deal programs in a span of a few months, the Court applied a new deferential stance to government regulation of economic activity. States now had significant authority to regulate intrastate commerce using their police powers, and Congress had broad powers under the Commerce Clause to regulate the market and enact social welfare programs, including maximum work hours, a minimum wage, and child labor laws.

The goal of federal employment protections was not realized, however, until Congress passed, and President Roosevelt signed, the Fair Labor Standards Act of 1938, popularly known as the wages and hours

law. Historians have described the law as one of the most bitterly contested pieces of legislation ever enacted by Congress. Considered the
last major piece of New Deal legislation, the FLSA established a national minimum wage of twenty-five cents per hour, an eight-hour workday, overtime compensation, and child labor restrictions. Initially, the
maximum workweek was set at forty-four hours, but that was reduced
to forty-two hours after the first year and to forty hours by the second
year of implementation, thus establishing the forty-hour workweek in
1940. Employees could always be told by employers to work more than
forty hours, but they were to be paid time and a half for overtime. Extra
compensation for overtime discouraged business owners from requiring
their employees to work excessive hours.

After the first year that the law was in force, the minimum wage rose
to not less than thirty cents an hour, and by October 1944 the minimum increased to at least forty cents an hour. To provide flexibility for
regional wage variations, industry committees—appointed by the administrator for the new Wage and Hour Division of the Department of
Labor and staffed by representatives of employers, employees, and the
public—had the discretion to adjust the minimum wages depending on
industry rates and practices. Also, a committee could shorten hours to
forty a week faster than the graduated plan provided by the law. Under the original act, certain types of workers were exempted from its
provisions, including employees engaged in administrative, executive,
and professional jobs, local retail and service positions, fishermen, and
agricultural workers. The service industry and agricultural exemptions
disproportionately hurt Black workers and women.

Like other provisions in the FLSA, the child labor sections had limitations and exemptions. The law defined "oppressive child labor" as employment of a minor under the age of sixteen years, unless the employer
is the child's parent or guardian. Even a parent or guardian, however,
may not employ the child in manufacturing or mining operations. For
children under age sixteen, employment in manufacturing and mining
is banned in all circumstances. Children aged fourteen or fifteen years
who are employed in other occupations are not engaged in oppressive
child labor if the chief of the Children's Bureau determines that such
work does not interfere with a child's education or health and well-
being. If minors between the ages of sixteen and eighteen are working

in industries that the chief of the Children's Bureau determines to be hazardous, that is oppressive child labor. But the FLSA did nothing to protect children in service and domestic occupations that were purely intrastate, and it exempted child laborers in commercial agriculture unless the work disrupted the school year. The original law covered less than 10 percent of working children.

Despite the limitations, President Roosevelt described the Fair Labor Standards Act as a monumental achievement: "Except for the Social Security Act, it is the most far-reaching, farsighted program ever adopted here or in any other country." Almost eighty years later, an article in *Time* magazine recognized that the act "changed the entire employment culture in the United States and easily rivals Social Security in its importance." The FLSA became effective on October 24, 1938. Within a year, the pro-labor legislation was challenged by Fred W. Darby, owner of a lumber company in Statesboro, Georgia, but the Supreme Court unanimously upheld the FLSA in *U.S. v. Darby Lumber Co.* (1941). In a companion case, *Opp Cotton Mills, Inc. v. Administrator Wage and Hour Division*, the Court affirmed the administrative procedures used to determine representation and wage levels under the committee system.

The historic decision in *Darby Lumber* had three important consequences. First, it firmly rejected a narrow interpretation of congressional power under the Commerce Clause. Under Article 1, Section 8, Clause 3 of the Constitution, Congress shall have power "to regulate Commerce with foreign Nations, and among the several States, and with the Indian Tribes." Those few words, "and among the several States," provide Congress with the power to regulate interstate commerce. Several Supreme Court precedents had prohibited federal action on labor standards and workplace conditions under the theory that such activities were part of *intrastate* commerce left to state authority. These decisions were often supported by distinctions between manufacturing or production and interstate commerce, which is defined as the movement of products across state lines. The *Darby Lumber* decision affirmed the power of the federal government to regulate goods produced or manufactured under substandard labor conditions.

Second, the Court said that it would no longer examine the motives behind congressional regulation of commerce and that the Tenth Amendment did not limit federal power over commercial activity. In his opinion, Associate Justice Harlan Fiske Stone, who would become chief justice a few months after the *Darby Lumber* decision, famously wrote,

> Our conclusion is unaffected by the Tenth Amendment which provides: "The powers not delegated to the United States by the Constitution, nor prohibited by it to the States, are reserved to the States respectively, or to the people." The amendment states but a truism that all is retained which has not been surrendered. There is nothing in the history of its adoption to suggest that it was more than declaratory of the relationship between the national and State governments . . . or that its purpose was other than to allay fears that the new National Government might seek to exercise powers not granted, and that the States might not be able to exercise fully their reserved powers.

This interpretation significantly enhanced federal power with respect to the states.

Finally, the *Darby Lumber* decision overturned the *Hammer v. Dagenhart* (1918) precedent and upheld the child labor provisions of the FLSA. As previously mentioned, the *Hammer* precedent had declared invalid the first federal child labor law, the Keating-Owen Act, and the decision had frustrated the efforts of child labor reformers for over twenty years. Two more federal laws—a child labor tax law and child labor restrictions under the National Industrial Recovery Act industry codes—were also struck down. After three unsuccessful attempts to restrict child labor exploitation through national legislation, the *Darby Lumber* ruling established firm constitutional authority for federal child labor laws.

The following chapters proceed along a thematic historical approach that facilitates understanding of the three great social movements for fair labor standards—maximum hours, minimum wages, and child labor restrictions—that spanned two centuries and culminated in passage of the Fair Labor Standards Act. Chapter 1 covers the movement for a ten-hour workday, and then for an eight-hour workday. State maximum hours laws for male workers in dangerous occupations and for women and children were the most successful reforms prior to the *Darby Lumber* decision. A few federal laws established an eight-hour workday for public employees and contractors. Chapter 2 chronicles the century-long struggle to end child labor exploitation. The Supreme Court overturned the first three federal child labor laws, and a proposed constitutional amendment failed ratification. Chapter 3 covers the fight for a minimum wage for women and children during the Progressive Era. By the 1920s, fifteen states had enacted minimum wage requirements, but the *Adkins v. Children's Hospital* decision placed those laws on unstable constitutional ground. Chapter 4 examines the contentious congressional debate over the Fair Labor Standards Act. Nothing like it had ever been passed by Congress. The FLSA involved extensive government intervention into business practices and provided criminal penalties for violations of its labor provisions. A new administrative unit within the Labor Department, the Wage and Hour Division, had to be created from scratch to implement the law.

Chapter 5 identifies the problems with enforcing the FLSA, discusses the legal challenges that ensued, reviews the briefs on the merits filed in the *Darby Lumber* case, and highlights the oral arguments made by both parties before the Court. The conference deliberations and Supreme Court decision in *U.S. v. Darby Lumber* are analyzed in chapter 6. Reaction to the opinion and its impact are discussed. One consequence of the decision, the federal trial of Fred Darby and his lumber company, is described in the chapter as well. Finally, chapter 7 covers the post–World War II period through the contemporary era. Amendments to the FLSA expanded coverage to public employees and renewed a battle over federalism in the courts. The chapter also discusses more recent clashes over right-to-work laws, the $15 an hour movement, and attempts to weaken child labor laws during the Great Recession and following the Covid-19 pandemic.

Although the Fair Labor Standards Act still provides employment protections for over 150 million workers, the purchasing power of the federal minimum wage, adjusted for inflation, peaked in 1968 and has since lost 31 percent of its value. As of this writing, the federal minimum wage is $7.25, and it has not been raised since 2009—the longest period without an increase since the law was enacted. Today, thirty states plus the District of Columbia, Puerto Rico, and the US Virgin Islands have a higher minimum wage than the national minimum. New technology and the Covid-19 pandemic have also transformed the nature of work and the number of hours Americans are laboring. From rethinking the forty-hour workweek to indexing the minimum wage to inflation, a host of reforms have been proposed to reinvigorate fair labor standards, with the goal of improving the quality of life for workers and strengthening the American middle class. My hope is that this volume will help inform that public discussion.

CHAPTER ONE

"Eight Hours for Work, Eight Hours for Rest, Eight Hours for What We Will"

Throughout history, thousands of labor conflicts have centered on the issue of "maximum hours" per day and week. In their comprehensive study of the shorter hours movement in the United States, David Roediger and Philip Foner argue that "the length of the working day has been the central issue for the American labor movement during its most vigorous periods of activity, uniting workers along lines of craft, gender, and ethnicity." While maximum hours have been at the heart of many labor demands, workers have not always agreed on the ideal number of hours per working day or week. The issue is more complicated than it first appears.

The demand for shorter hours is often connected to wage levels, good citizenship, technology and efficiency, employee health, workplace accidents, and unemployment. For example, a reduction in hours will result in lower pay if wage levels are not at least held constant or increased. Early trade unions argued that a shorter workday was necessary for laborers to educate themselves and fulfill their duties as citizens in a representative democracy. As technology increased efficiency, workers sought fewer hours and more leisure time, arguing that employers would see no decline in productivity or profits. Excessive hours, it was also claimed, contributed to poor health and fatigue, and made absenteeism and industrial accidents more likely. Reducing work hours might also create more jobs and increase employment during times of recession.

One of the most important achievements of the Fair Labor Standards Act is the establishment of an eight-hour workday and forty-hour workweek with time and a half for overtime. Although the concept of an eight-hour workday has its origins in sixteenth-century Spain under a royal decree by King Philip II that applied to workers in Spanish fortifications and factories, the modern movement can be traced to the early years of the Industrial Revolution in Great Britain. In 1810 Robert Owen, a Welsh manufacturer and labor rights activist, implemented a ten-hour workday at his mill, and in 1847 women and children in the United Kingdom were granted the ten-hour workday. But Owen did not stop there. In 1817 he pushed for an eight-hour workday and coined the phrase "Eight hours' labor, Eight hours' recreation, Eight hours' rest." The idea of reducing the workday to eight hours made limited progress in England at the time, but skilled workers in Australia and New Zealand won the eight-hour workday by the 1850s. Over a period of decades, Owen's slogan arrived in America and influenced the labor movement.

From the colonial period through the mid-nineteenth century, the traditional work schedule was sunrise to sunset, six days a week. During summer months, however, that resulted in fourteen-hour workdays. Some scholars are skeptical of the "first light to dark" schedule and argue that work hours increased by the 1850s as more workers shifted from agricultural labor to factories. It is fair to say that many Americans worked long days. Workers initially pushed for a ten-hour workday, but following the Civil War, labor groups began pressing for an eight-hour day. By the time of the first modern May Day parade and strike in 1886, laborers had adopted a variation of Robert Owen's slogan by demanding "Eight hours for work, eight hours for rest, and eight hours for what we will." The phrase was also featured on the inside cover of *Proceedings*, an 1800s publication of the American Federation of Labor. It would take almost a century to secure the eight-hour day under the Fair Labor Standards Act.

The Ten-Hour Movement

Early workingmen's associations began advocating a ten-hour workday in the 1820s. In 1822, journeymen millwrights and machinists passed a resolution asserting that "ten hours of labor were enough for one day, and that work ought to begin at 6:00 a.m. and end at 6:00 p.m." Boston carpenters struck in 1825 and 1832 for a ten-hour workday, in part making an argument that the long hours prevented them from educating themselves and being good citizens. Both strikes failed. A circular defending the Boston strike, written by Seth Luther, a Rhode Island carpenter and labor activist, received wide distribution and generated more support for the reduced workday. A section of Luther's "Ten Hour Circular" read: "We have been too long subjected to the odious, cruel, unjust, and tyrannical system which compels the operative mechanic to exhaust his physical and mental powers. We have rights and duties to perform as American citizens and members of society, which forbid us to dispose of more than ten hours for a day's work."

The ten-hour workday became a primary issue for many labor organizations in the 1830s. According to labor historian Brian Greenberg, "about a quarter of the 172 recorded turnouts (strikes) between 1833 and 1837 revolved around the issue of hours." Workers often complained about the lack of leisure time. If a person worked twelve or more hours a day, as many did, and slept for eight hours, that left four hours or less for family time and recreation.

In 1835, coal heavers in Philadelphia, who were responsible for loading and unloading coal on ships, pushed for a ten-hour workday. "From Six to Six" became their rallying cry. Specifically, they demanded a twelve-hour workday starting at 6:00 a.m., with an hour off for breakfast and another hour for lunch, with the day ending at 6:00 p.m. Employers responded by hiring replacement workers, prompting the nation's first general strike, which involved over twenty thousand workers in Philadelphia. The employers believed that work hours should be determined by the natural dynamics of a competitive free market. Workers argued that the benefits of labor should go to those who create the wealth. The strike for a ten-hour workday and increased wages was a success, and it encouraged a wave of ten-hour protests throughout the country.

Organized labor won a major victory in the case of *Commonwealth v. Hunt* (1842). The notion that a labor combination to limit hours and raise wages was per se illegal under common law doctrine had been weakened over the years by state court decisions. In the *Hunt* case, Chief Justice Lemuel Shaw of the Massachusetts Supreme Judicial Court made it explicit that raising wages was not illegal and that a labor organization with the intention of setting wages was lawful, provided workers used legal means to achieve their goals. Although *Hunt* was a significant precedent, courts continued to attack some of the tactics used by labor unions, including strikes, picketing, and boycotts. Court-issued injunctions became an effective tool used by employers to oppose organized labor.

A few gains were made on the ten-hour front during the 1840s. In response to a strike in a Philadelphia naval yard, President Martin Van Buren issued an executive order on March 31, 1840, establishing a ten-hour workday for federal employees on public works. Two years later, Massachusetts and Connecticut enacted laws prohibiting children under age twelve from working more than ten hours a day. The state laws were ineffective, however, because they lacked enforcement mechanisms. Children could still work if parents approved, and many of them did. In 1847, New Hampshire became the first state to fix the legal workday at ten hours, but the law became dead letter because it allowed employers to contract with employees for longer hours.

In 1814 a group of Boston businessmen recruited thousands of young, unmarried New England farm girls to work the machines in their factories. Some of the young girls brought in to work the mills were as young as ten, but most were in their late teens or early twenties. The Boston associates preferred young girls because they could pay them less than men, although the wages were generally good for the period. As an incentive to sign a year-long contract, the girls, who were called operatives because they operated the machines, were paid in cash daily.

The most well-known of these mill towns was Lowell, Massachusetts, established in 1823, and named after Francis Cabot Lowell, who had died in 1817. Known as "Lowell Girls" or "Mill Girls," the young women lived in company boardinghouses under the supervision of matrons. Although they worked more than seventy hours a week, many of the girls enjoyed their freedom from parental authority and an opportunity for education. By 1840, as many as eight thousand girls worked in Lowell's textile factories. As the number of mills increased, overproduction led to pay cuts and rent increases, and the Lowell girls turned out in 1834 and 1836. These were some of the first strikes of cotton factory operatives in the United States.

The Lowell Female Labor Reform Association organized in 1844 under the leadership of Sarah G. Bagley, a mill operative and militant labor reformer. The association petitioned the Massachusetts legislature for a ten-hour workday. At the time, textile workers in Lowell spent an average of 12.5 hours working plus time commuting to work, six days a week. Some operatives worked fourteen-hour days. Operatives wrote that the hours of work were "sufficient to impair health, induce disease, premature old age, and death . . . to say nothing of the intellectual degeneracy which must necessarily result from want of mental recreation."

In response to the petition, the Massachusetts House of Representatives Committee on Manufacturing appointed a committee to investigate conditions in the mills. The committee concluded that Lowell workers enjoyed conditions superior to those in England and that the health of the operatives was fine. The remedy for excessive hours and low wages, it was claimed, was not the responsibility of the legislature: "Experience has taught us [that wages] can be much better regulated by the parties themselves than by the Legislature." The committee even suggested that in the United States, unlike Europe, labor was on an equal footing with capital. Despite the setback, Sarah Bagley continued to advocate for ten-hour reform until 1847, when she took a job as supervisor in a telegraph office.

Increased immigration from Europe in the 1840s and 1850s complicated demands for fair labor standards, especially work hours, and led to tensions within the labor movement. Brian Greenberg notes that by 1860, immigrants composed a majority of skilled workers in many large cities. Native-born workers reacted with hostility and nativism. The recently arrived Americans, desperate to succeed in their new country in a competitive labor market, seemed willing to work fourteen- to sixteen-hour days. American workers criticized Irish immigrants and others as "all day men" and continued their demand for a ten-hour workday. By the 1860s there was a trend toward shorter hours and better wages, and in most areas, the workday had been shortened to ten hours (six days a week).

––––––––

Demands for an Eight-Hour Workday

The two decades following the Civil War were an important formative period for the American labor movement. Reductions in the workweek reemerged as a prominent issue for labor, with the new goal of an eight-hour workday. Ira Steward, a machinist and social reformer, began agitating for the eight-hour workday in the 1850s. Steward opposed strikes as counterproductive, and he did not think that unions could be the agents for labor reforms because they were not well-organized or representative of all workers. Rather, he wanted an eight-hour workday mandated at the federal and state levels. He spent more than twenty years writing about and advocating for that goal. By the 1870s, however, Steward's ambition of eight-hour laws throughout the country had not been realized.

Boston was the hub of labor activism, and Grand Eight Hours Leagues were established there and around the country between 1865 and 1866. In response, by 1868 eight states had adopted general eight-hour laws. Like many early labor provisions, however, the statutes were weak and never seriously enforced. They allowed employers and employees to mutually consent to workdays longer than the "legal day." In 1867, workers in Illinois, exhausted by twelve- to fourteen-hour workdays, pressured the legislature to enact a law mandating an eight-hour day for work. The legislature responded with an eight-hour bill, but one that contained a loophole that permitted employers to demand longer hours. Angered by the provision, a large strike took place in Chicago on May 1. Connecticut's law, passed in 1868, merely suggested that eight hours be considered a day's work unless more than eight had been agreed to by contract.

Several national unions organized by the middle of the nineteenth century. In 1866 the National Labor Union (NLU), a new union composed of skilled and unskilled workers, formed with the goal of uniting the various national labor unions and eight-hour leagues to press for an eight-hour workday. Led by labor pioneer William H. Sylvis, the organization's slogan was "Whether you work by the piece or by the day, decreasing the hours increases the pay." In 1868 the NLU successfully called on Congress to enact an eight-hour workday for mechanics and laborers employed by the federal government. In response, many employers cut pay by 20 percent, effectively nullifying any benefits from a shorter workday.

The following year, President Ulysses S. Grant issued a proclamation that no federal employee would receive a reduction in wages because of the new workday, but his order was ignored by many federal agencies. With federal employees on an eight-hour-day schedule, many labor unions demanded an eight-hour day as well. By 1872 the NLU had evolved into the National Reform and Labor Party. The new party, however, did not survive the "Panic of 1873" and resulting economic collapse. Other labor organizations emerged to continue the fight for maximum hours. The Federation of Organized Trades and Labor Unions, which would become the American Federation of Labor, held its national conference in Chicago in 1884, and declared that "eight hours shall constitute a legal day's labor from and after May 1, 1886."

The Knights of Labor became the most prominent—and perhaps the most radical—organization advocating fair labor standards in the 1880s. Formed in 1869 in Philadelphia as a secret society of garment cutters, the Knights became more openly militant after the great railroad strike of 1877. When Grand Master Workman Terence V. Powderly assumed leadership in 1879, the Knights flourished, growing to seven hundred thousand members. Powderly ended the earlier rules of secrecy and committed the organization to seeking the eight-hour day, equal pay for equal work, and the abolition of child labor.

The organization's labor activism suffered a major setback following the Haymarket Square riot of May 4, 1886. The Knights of Labor were unfairly blamed for a bombing and violence that killed seven police officers and injured sixty others. The media castigated the labor leaders, and public scorn followed. Several activists were arrested, quickly tried, and hanged. Although it was never determined who threw the bomb, the violence impeded the eight-hour movement for years. With the fallout from the riots, combined with internal leadership conflicts and strong resistance from employer associations, by 1890 the Knights' membership had dropped to below one hundred thousand.

As the influence of the Knights of Labor waned, the American Federation of Labor (A.F. of L., or AFL) became the voice of organized labor. Led by Samuel Gompers, head of a cigarmakers' union, the AFL was a collection of smaller craft unions. Less radical than their predecessor, the organization was not primarily concerned with protective labor laws. Gompers believed that government should not do anything for labor that labor could not do itself through its trade unions. However, he favored a role for government in protecting women and children, whose vulnerability undermined the standards for adult male workers. Gompers was never a committed socialist, although according to his biographer, Bernard Mandel, he came close to that position in 1894 when the country reeled from a serious depression. More of a realist, Gompers had no vision to unite the entire working class under a socialist utopia. Adhering to a philosophy of "pure and simple unionism," the AFL focused on the eight-hour workday, collective bargaining rights, higher wages, and better working conditions for skilled tradesmen.

In an address to the American Federation of Labor in 1887, Gompers used the "make-work" argument to defend the eight-hour workday. He proclaimed that "so long as there is one man who seeks employment and cannot obtain it, the hours of labor are too long." The make-work argument was also a response to the thousands of workers who were displaced by new technology and the mechanization of the factory. If hours were shortened, more jobs would be available, and those who lost their jobs to machinery could find employment. That argument resonated with the labor movement well into the twentieth century.

An early study by historian Samuel Yellen revealed that by 1886, nineteen states and one territory had maximum-hour laws. Those statutes, however, were basically useless because of clauses permitting contracts for longer days. Consequently, the average day for many workers was ten to twelve hours. By the turn of the century, some states enacted tougher maximum-hour laws, but those legislative mandates were often challenged in the courts.

———

Maximum Hours, Liberty of Contract, and the Courts

For most of the 1800s, state courts played a prominent role in adjudicating the scope of fair labor standards. Prior to the 1890s, the Supreme Court addressed the constitutionality of labor legislation in only one area: employers' liability for workplace injuries under common law doctrine. The absence of Supreme Court review on many labor issues was due in part to provisions in the Judiciary Act, which until 1914 prohibited appeals of state supreme court decisions that held labor laws unconstitutional. Outside the area of employers' liability, no cases of this type happened until the Supreme Court granted review in *Holden v. Hardy* (1898), a case involving maximum work hours. Almost twenty years later, the Court reviewed a state minimum wage law in *Stettler v. O'Hara* (1917). One year later, the Court struck down the first federal child labor law in *Hammer v. Dagenhart.* Both the *Stettler* and *Hammer* decisions are discussed in subsequent chapters.

During the Progressive Era (1890 to 1920) state governments enacted legislation to limit the number of hours that men worked in dangerous occupations and imposed maximum hours for women and child laborers in sweatshops and factories. Some of these laws were reviewed by the Supreme Court under the "liberty of contract" doctrine. Originally ratified during Reconstruction to protect the rights of freed slaves, the Fourteenth Amendment Due Process Clause declares that a state cannot deny any person "life, liberty, or property without due process of law." A similarly worded provision is found in the Fifth Amendment, which applies to the national government. Prior to the adoption of the Fourteenth Amendment in 1868, judges interpreted the due process guarantees in the Fifth Amendment as procedural limitations on government power. Procedural due process meant that people were "entitled" to fair and orderly proceedings, especially in criminal cases, where a citizen's life or liberty is at stake. Under procedural due process, government can deny citizens life, liberty, or property only when it provides fair and proper procedures.

After the adoption of the Fourteenth Amendment, lawyers representing business interests opposed to expanding state regulation during the Industrial Revolution began to emphasize substantive due process arguments. Substantive due process focuses on the *reasonableness* of legislation. If a court determined that a state regulation of property rights was unreasonable, arbitrary, or "class legislation" that discriminated between citizens, the court could declare a violation of the Fourteenth Amendment. Substantive due process arguments were heavily influenced by an 1868 legal treatise entitled *Constitutional Limitations*, by Thomas Cooley. Cooley emphasized limits on legislative authority to protect personal liberty and private property.

In the first litigated case involving restrictions on the work hours of adult females in factories and workshops, the Supreme Judicial Court of Massachusetts in *Commonwealth v. Hamilton Manufacturing Company* (1876) ignored substantive due process arguments. Massachusetts enacted a law in 1874 prohibiting the employment of all minors under age eighteen, and of all women, in laboring more than ten hours a day or sixty hours per week in any manufacturing establishment. The Hamilton Manufacturing Company, a cotton textile mill, employed Mary Shirley (who was over twenty-one years old) sixty-four hours a week. The company argued that the law was unconstitutional, that it impaired an implied contract under the corporate charter, and that it denied Mary Shirley the right to work as many hours as she desired.

Rejecting all these arguments, the state supreme court upheld the law by deferring to the police powers of the state. "There can be no doubt that such legislation may be maintained either as a health or police regulation," the court argued, and that "the principle has been so frequently recognized in this Commonwealth that reference to the decisions is unnecessary." As to Mary Shirley's liberty to work as many hours as she preferred, the court said that the law only prohibited her employment continuously in the same service more than a certain number of hours a day or week. She was still free to find a second job if she wanted to work longer.

Although the opinion in *Commonwealth v. Hamilton Manufacturing Company* upheld a ten-hour day regulation, supporters of fair labor standards viewed the decision as somewhat disappointing because it failed to address the issues of discrimination between men and women, the concept of class legislation, and the liberty of contract doctrine. Moreover, the opinion cited no precedents. Opponents of the ten- or eight-hour movement continued to attack the laws. But there appear to be no adjudicated cases involving maximum-hour legislation between 1876 and 1894. A 1909 study by law professor Andrew A. Bruce, who helped enact and enforce child labor and sweatshop laws in Illinois and Wisconsin, identified only three commentaries on the subject in the nearly two-decade period. Two of the essays used the *Hamilton Manufacturing* case to support maximum hours legislation while the third followed arguments from Cooley's *Constitutional Limitations* to criticize the labor laws.

The Illinois Supreme Court applied many of the substantive due process concepts in *Ritchie v. People* (1895), when it struck down an eight-hour law for women in factories. On June 17, 1893, the Illinois legislature enacted the Illinois Factory and Workshop Inspection Statute. Section 5, known as the Eight Hour Law, prohibited persons from employing any "female . . . in any factory or workshop more than eight hours in any one day or forty-eight hours in any one week." Florence Kelley, the chief factory inspector for Illinois, found William E. Ritchie, the manager of a paper box factory, in violation of the law. Ritchie was convicted and fined $5. On appeal, he claimed that the law violated both the state and US Constitutions. Kelley and her staff wrote a brief defending the law.

The brief cited scholarly experts and government reports regarding the negative health effects of long work hours on women. A legal brief with social science findings was a precursor to the famous "Brandeis brief" some fifteen years later. Unfortunately for supporters of the law, the court was not swayed by the factual evidence.

In declaring Section 5 unconstitutional, Justice Benjamin D. Magruder argued that the privilege of contracting is both a liberty and a property right: "In this country the legislature has no power to prevent persons . . . from making their own contracts, nor can it interfere with the freedom of contract between the workman and the employer." Magruder acknowledged that the right to contract may be subject to limitations grounded in the duties an individual owes to society and government. For example, government may protect the public from contracts that are fraudulent or cause injury. The power of the legislature, however, to limit the right of contract must be exercised on a reasonable basis and cannot be arbitrary. Section 5, according to Justice Magruder, did not meet those requirements.

First, he characterized the Illinois law as partial and class legislation because its provisions applied only to employers and women working in the clothing industry. Section 5 violated the Fourteenth Amendment Equal Protection Clause because it "discriminates against one class of employers and employees and in favor of all others." This formalistic argument ignored the fact that sweatshop conditions were particularly egregious in the garment industry and it might be reasonable to target those practices. Second, Magruder asserted that the law violated the liberty of contract by depriving women the right of private judgment over work hours. Finally, the law was not a reasonable exercise of state police powers because it had no relation to public health or safety. "There is nothing in the nature of the employment contemplated," Justice Magruder said, "which is in itself unhealthy or unlawful or injurious to the public morals or welfare." The law was not based on the nature of the work but the sex of the person doing the labor. The court concluded that no reasonable ground existed for "fixing upon eight hours in one day as the limit within which women can work without injury to her physique."

Historian Nancy Woloch noted the connection the court made between freedom of contract and women's rights. Justice Magruder cited several Illinois laws that expanded employment opportunities for women: an 1867 law that guaranteed women a right to work overtime, an 1872 measure that prohibited employers from excluding a person from an occupation because of sex, and an 1874 law that entitled married women to sue and be sued. In a bit of constitutional irony, a state law designed to protect women from the evils of the sweatshop system was overturned on the basis of women's rights. Florence Kelley, who had lobbied for the maximum-hour law, was "dismayed" by the court's "perverted" interpretation of the Fourteenth Amendment. "The measure to guarantee the Negro freedom from oppression," she said, "has become an insuperable obstacle to the protection of women and children."

Several years after the *Ritchie* decision, the US Supreme Court adjudicated its first maximum-hour case. In *Holden v. Hardy* (1898), the Court upheld a Utah law setting a maximum of eight hours for a working day in the mining and smelting industries. The Court determined that the law was a valid exercise of the state's police power to protect the public health: "While the general experience of mankind may justify us in believing that men may engage in ordinary employment more than eight hours per day without injury to their health, it does not follow that labor for the same length of time is innocuous when carried on beneath the surface of the earth, where the operative is deprived of fresh air and sunlight and is frequently subjected to foul atmosphere and a very high temperature or to the influence of noxious gases generated by the processes of refining or smelting."

Applying a rational basis test, the Court found the Utah law to be a reasonable workplace regulation because of the dangerous work environment. "The law in question," the Court argued, "is confined to the protection of that class of people engaged in labor in underground mines and in smelters and other works wherein ores are reduced and refined." The Court recognized the hazards of work in this area: "This law applies only to the classes subjected by their employment to the peculiar conditions and effects attending underground mining and work in smelters, and other works for the reduction and refining of ores. Therefore, it is not necessary to discuss or decide whether the legislature can fix the hours of labor in other employments." Although *Holden* was the first victory for the eight-hour workday in Supreme Court jurisprudence, the holding was limited to male workers in a specific occupation.

By 1900 the average American worked fifty-eight to sixty hours, six days a week. In some industries, however, employees worked substantially longer hours. Most steel mill workers labored for twelve hours or more because it took that long to process a batch of steel in one day. When employers proposed three eight-hour shifts, many workers objected to the reduced hours and smaller paychecks. Subsequently, the twelve-hour workday was common in many steel mills until 1923. In all industries, skilled and organized (union) workers usually labored shorter hours than unskilled and unorganized employees.

In July 1902 a unanimous Nebraska Supreme Court upheld a maximum-hours law that was very similar to the one overturned in *Ritchie v. People*. The act prohibited the employment of females for more than sixty hours a week or ten hours in any one day in any manufacturing, mechanical and mercantile establishments, hotel or restaurant. The only difference was the ten-hour maximum. Wenham owned a laundry that employed a female for fourteen hours a day and eighty-four hours per week. In *Wenham v. State*, the state supreme court held that the law was a reasonable exercise of the police power that provided sufficient due process. The court also denied that the law was class legislation. The act applied to all women, and no discrimination was made based on "age, condition, or situation." Overall, state courts had a mixed record on maximum-hour laws.

Lochnerism, Liberty of Contract, and Maximum Hours

The battle between liberty of contract doctrine and protective labor legislation had been brewing for years, but it came to a head in *Lochner v. New York* (1905), which is widely viewed as one of the most controversial substantive due process cases. In *Lochner*, the US Supreme Court invalidated a provision of the 1895 New York Bakeshop Act, a law passed unanimously by the legislature. This act contained provisions that addressed sanitation in bakeries and biscuit factories to ensure "unadulterated bread"; the only controversial section was the one that limited the number of hours that someone could work in a "biscuit, bread or cake bakery" to ten hours a day or sixty hours a week. In his study of the *Lochner* case, Paul Kens notes that many tenement bakers worked seventy to one hundred hours a week. Before the Supreme Court, New York justified the law by arguing that the police powers gave the state the right to regulate working conditions and to protect workers and consumers from sickness. Joseph Lochner, owner of a tenement bakery, argued that employees and employers have a right to agree on wages and hours and that state regulation of such terms violates the Fourteenth Amendment.

A majority of the justices agreed with Lochner, concluding that the law violated his liberty of contract because it lacked a reasonable relation to public health, safety, or welfare. Justice Rufus Peckham wrote: "We think the limit of the police power has been reached and passed in this case. There is, in our judgment, no reasonable foundation for holding this to be necessary or appropriate as a health law to safeguard the public health or the health of the individuals who are following the trade of a baker." Wholesome bread, the Court claimed, does not depend on bakers' working hours.

Justice John Harlan dissented, joined by Chief Justice Edward Douglas White and Justice William R. Day. Justice Harlan believed that the law was a valid health measure. The regulation, he said, "applies only to work in bakery and confectionery establishments, in which, as all know, the air constantly breathed by workmen is not as pure and healthful as that to be found in some other establishments or out of doors." Harlan suggested that the majority had substituted its judgment of the efficacy of the law for that of the legislature.

In a famous separate dissenting opinion, Justice Oliver Wendell Holmes urged deference to the legislature, and argued that the case was "decided upon an economic theory which a large part of the country does not entertain" and that "the Fourteenth Amendment does not enact Mr. Herbert Spencer's *Social Statics*." Justice Holmes was referring to Herbert Spencer's book published in 1851. Spencer applied an extreme form of economic and social laissez-faire to society, which he later called "survival of the fittest" and critics called Social Darwinism. Advocates of the theory believed that government should not help the poor or enact protective labor legislation.

As a consequence of the *Lochner* precedent and other cases, the liberty of contract doctrine potentially limited a state's authority to enact protective labor legislation if the courts determined that the laws were an *unreasonable* exercise of the police power. The liberty of contract doctrine was criticized then (and now) because it essentially placed courts in the role of assessing whether a statute was reasonable and, therefore, necessary to solve a social problem. Because that determination is primarily a policy decision best left to a legislature, courts were vulnerable to charges of judicial activism. In fact, the *Lochner* decision spawned the term "Lochnerism" to describe conservative judicial activism in defense of business interests. The extent to which Lochnerism characterized federal court jurisprudence during this period has been a matter of academic debate for years.

The reasoning of the *Lochner* decision was reinforced in *Adair v. United States* (1908). Congress passed a law in 1898 making it illegal for employers to fire a worker solely because of their membership in a union. The law made what were called "yellow dog" contracts illegal. In striking down the law, Justice Harlan, speaking for the Court, said: "The right of a person to sell his labor upon such terms as he deems proper is, in its essence, the same as the right of the purchaser of labor to prescribe the conditions upon which he will accept such labor from the person offering to sell. . . . In all such particulars, the employer and employee have equality of right, and any legislation that disturbs that equality is an arbitrary interference with the liberty of contract which no government can legally justify in a free land."

By 1900 more than five million women earned wages, with one-fourth employed in manufacturing. Oregon passed a law limiting the number of hours for women in sweatshops, laundries, and factories to ten hours a day, six days a week. The National Consumers' League (NCL), now led by Florence Kelley, fought for limits on working hours. Curt Muller owned the Lace House Laundry. Muller's laundry workers (all women) worked more than ten hours a day. The state of Oregon charged Muller with violating the maximum-hours law in employing laundresses. He challenged the law as a violation of the right to contract because it differentiated between men and women. At the suggestion of Florence Kelley, Oregon invited a progressive lawyer from Boston, Louis Brandeis, to help defend their labor law. Brandeis wanted facts on work conditions and women's health. Josephine Goldmark, chair of the NCL's committee on labor laws, and the National Consumers' League collected material for a brief that consisted of several pages of legal arguments and over 100 pages of social science data that detailed the negative health consequences of having women work long hours in sweatshop conditions.

By a vote of 9 to 0 the Court in *Muller v. Oregon* (1908) upheld the progressive labor legislation. Clearly influenced by the arguments of the "Brandeis brief," the Court reasoned that women's physical structure and the maternal functions they perform justified special legislation restricting or qualifying the conditions under which they should be permitted to toil. Justice David J. Brewer wrote: "While the general right to contract is protected by the Fourteenth Amendment, liberty is not absolute." A state may, without conflicting with the provisions of this amendment, restrict in many respects the individual's power of contract. "Repeating work every day and being on their feet hurts the body and therefore to save mothers, and ultimately the race, the restrictions are justified. Regulations are for the benefit of women as well as for society as a whole. For these reasons, and without questioning *Lochner*, we are of the opinion that this law does not violate the Constitution." The *Muller* decision was a major victory for Brandeis and the Progressive movement, but the arguments made by the Court have been criticized by modern feminists and progressives for promoting an ideology of sexual difference and paternalism.

In 1913, Oregon prescribed a ten-hour workday for women *and men*, expanding the law regulating women's hours upheld in *Muller v. Oregon*. The measure also required time-and-a-half wages for overtime up to three hours a day. The overtime pay provision was designed to deter employers from working employees more than ten hours. Oregon claimed that the law was an appropriate exercise of its police powers. Franklin Bunting, manager of a flour mill, worked an employee thirteen hours in one day and failed to comply with the overtime regulations of the statute. He was convicted and fined $50.

Because Louis Brandeis was appointed to the Supreme Court in January 1916, Felix Frankfurter, a Harvard law professor and future Supreme Court justice, took over the task of defending the Oregon law. Frankfurter knew that the *Lochner* precedent presented an obstacle. He believed, however, that he could distinguish the Bakeshop decision while emphasizing the *Holden v. Hardy* precedent. The majority in *Lochner* had rejected the ten-hour law for bakers based on a "common understanding" of the bakery profession. With the assistance of Josephine Goldmark and the NCL, Frankfurter assembled a massive "Brandeis brief" that was full of facts emphasizing the industrial context and the power of the state to promote public health and safety.

In *Bunting v. Oregon* (1917), the Supreme Court upheld the law in a 5 to 3 decision with Brandeis not participating. Justice Joseph McKenna deferred to justifications made by the Oregon court and legislature and dismissed Bunting's contention that the law did nothing to preserve the health of employees. The Court found that the law did not provide an unfair advantage to certain types of employers in the labor market since it regulated the hours of service for workers and not the wages that they earned. Under the Oregon statute, workers and their employers were still free to implement a wage scheme that was agreeable to both of them. Curiously, Justice McKenna's opinion made no mention of the *Lochner* precedent.

Beyond the Supreme Court, the push for maximum-hours legislation continued. In testimony before the US Commission on Industrial Relations on May 22, 1914, Samuel Gompers said: "I am in favor of the legal enactment for the maximum hours of labor for all workmen in direct Government employment, and for those who do work that the Government has substituted for Governmental authority. I am in favor of the—and the federation . . . is in favor of the maximum number of hours for children, for minors, and for women." Organized labor at this time still wanted shorter hours and higher wages to come through collective bargaining rather than government mandate.

Although only a handful of states had maximum-hours legislation on the books in the first quarter of the twentieth century, the trend was toward an eight-hour workday. According to a Women's Bureau Bulletin, by 1920, eight states—Arizona, California, Colorado, Montana, Nevada, Utah, Washington, Wisconsin—one territory, Puerto Rico, and the District of Columbia (DC) had laws that limited the working day for women in certain occupations to eight hours. Of these, only California, Utah, DC, and the territory of Puerto Rico limited daily hours to eight and the workweek to forty-eight. Two states, Arizona and Nevada, limited daily hours to eight but allowed fifty-six hours weekly. In other words, women could work eight hours, seven days a week, with no day of rest. In Kansas and California, an Industrial Welfare Commission ruled that female employees working beyond eight hours must receive an increased hourly rate. Most of these laws applied to manufacturing and mercantile establishments, laundries, hotels, restaurants, telegraph offices, and transportation companies. Only five states—California, Connecticut, Missouri, New York, and Pennsylvania—had laws declaring that eight hours shall constitute a day's work for men and women in all occupations unless otherwise agreed. Five other states limited the workday to eight hours in specific occupations.

On May 1, 1926, the Ford Motor Company announced an eight-hour workday and forty-hour workweek. Henry Ford believed that workers should have more free time to spend with their families, but he also expected them to be more productive on their eight-hour shifts. Productivity increased following the policy, and various manufacturers followed suit. Although some conservatives like to give Ford credit for establishing the eight-hour workday and forty-hour workweek, that claim is not historically accurate. As our preceding discussion illustrates, labor unions had been demanding an eight-hour day since the early May Day protests of the 1860s; additionally, the International Typographical Union in 1906 became one of the first labor organizations to secure the eight-hour workday. Ford's policy, while progressive for the period, was limited to workers in one industry and not mandated by law. Any employer who voluntarily established an eight-hour workday could just as easily rescind the policy. Moreover, the increased leisure time was strictly monitored by representatives from Ford's Sociological Department, who arrived at employee homes to observe the personal lives of workers.

Toward National Maximum-Hours Legislation

At the national level, little was accomplished on maximum-hours legislation until 1916. Almost four hundred thousand railroad workers who moved freight trains sought an eight-hour day and higher wages, but railroad owners refused to meet their demands. The impasse threatened to bring much of the nation's economic activity to a halt and impact US preparations for World War I. In response to a proposed nationwide strike by the workers, President Woodrow Wilson asked Congress for legislation to avert the strike and "protect the life and interests of the nation." Congress responded quickly by passing the Adamson Act. The law established an eight-hour day, with additional pay for overtime, for railroad workers. It was the first federal law that limited the hours for workers in private companies and set a standard for wages.

The Adamson Act was challenged, but a closely divided Supreme Court (5 to 4) upheld the constitutionality of the law in *Wilson v. New* (1917). Writing for the majority, Chief Justice Edward White dismissed any notion that an eight-hour standard was unconstitutional: "We put the question as to the eight-hour standard entirely out of view on the ground that the authority to permanently establish it is so clearly sustained as to render the subject not disputable." Unlike previous decisions upholding state maximum-hour provisions, the Adamson Act was not upheld as a protection for the worker or employer but as a protection of interstate commerce under the Commerce Clause. If commerce is threatened by management and labor failing to agree on hours and wages, Congress may impose terms on both parties.

No progress was made on restricting hours in other occupations until the Great Depression. The 1932 election of Franklin D. Roosevelt and huge Democratic majorities in Congress provided an opening for the passage of federal labor protections. American workers actually came close to securing a thirty-hour workweek in early 1933. As President Roosevelt took office, Senator Hugo Black (D-AL) introduced a bill in the Senate for a thirty-hour workweek. Drafted by the American Federation of Labor, Black's bill prohibited the sale or distribution in interstate commerce of manufacturing, mining, mill, or cannery goods produced by workers employed more than six hours a day or thirty hours a week. Senator Black claimed that the reduced hours would create six million jobs. The Senate passed the bill on April 6 by a vote of 53 to 30. The House Labor Committee reported a similar bill, sponsored by William Connery (D-MA), and the legislation was expected to pass quickly if it reached the floor. Speaker Henry Rainey (D-IL), however, said that the bill's progress in the House depended on "President Roosevelt's wishes." Roosevelt and his secretary of labor, Frances Perkins, believed that an inflexible thirty-hour workweek would not solve the nation's labor problems. The president asked that the bill be stopped because he was going to introduce broader legislation in May that covered hours, wages, child labor restrictions, and other business practices. That bill was the National Industrial Recovery Act.

As part of FDR's New Deal for America, Congress passed the National Industrial Recovery Act (NIRA) during the first hundred days of the Roosevelt administration, and President Roosevelt signed the NIRA on June 16, 1933. The law directed companies to write industry-wide "codes of fair competition" that established standards on prices, work hours, wages, and production quotas, and imposed restrictions on other business practices, including a sixteen-year minimum age for employment. Committees representing business, labor, and the public were responsible for writing the codes and submitting them to the president for approval. If a business sector did not develop codes, the president was authorized to draft codes himself using legislative authority delegated by Congress. As an incentive for self-regulation, industries that worked under the codes would be exempt from antitrust prosecution.

The National Recovery Administration (NRA) was created separately by executive order to implement the program, and President Roosevelt appointed General Hugh S. Johnson as head of the agency for industrial recovery. There were numerous patriotic appeals to the public, and companies participating in the NRA program were awarded the Blue Eagle, a poster that was often prominently displayed in storefronts and on packages. Favored by workers, any business not displaying the symbol might be boycotted. Viewed as "emergency" legislation, the codes were temporary, only remaining in effect during the economic crisis, which by law was two years, unless the president declared an end to the emergency earlier.

More than five hundred codes of fair practice were established in various industries, with the first code adopted in July 1933 by the cotton textile industry. At the historic opening meeting on June 27 in the auditorium of the Commerce Department, hundreds of people watched as management, labor, and consumer leaders negotiated codes of fair competition, with General Johnson presiding over the hearings. Most of the focus was on wages and hours, but representatives of the National Child Labor Committee (NCLC) and US Children's Bureau were on hand to advocate for child labor regulations. The initial proposal from the textile manufacturers included a forty-hour workweek and a minimum weekly wage of $11 for the North and $10 for the South.

William Green, president of the American Federation of Labor, pushed for a thirty-hour workweek, although thirty-two hours was acceptable, and a minimum weekly wage above $14. Because the draft code contained no minimum age for employment and there was no mention of child labor, the NCLC protested the omission and urged other groups and individuals to contact General Johnson to ask for a child labor ban. The media responded with strong editorials in favor of the NCLC's position. On the second day of hearings the cotton industry offered to the NRA a voluntary plan for the abolition of child labor. When T. M. Marchant, president of the Cotton Manufacturers Association, read the statement in the auditorium, several hundred spectators erupted in cheers.

Negotiations continued for about a week, until the final code was announced on July 9. The textile code contained a provision favored by the NCLC that banned the employment of children under age sixteen in cotton textile mills. The mill owners, however, did not agree to this position out of goodwill for children. Desperate to curb overproduction, representatives of the textile industry were prepared, in exchange for restricting mills to two forty-hour weekly shifts, to accepting the elimination of child labor and a $13 minimum weekly wage ($12 in the South). The Code of Fair Competition for the textile industry became effective on July 17.

Support for the thirty-hour workweek had waned by August 1933. NRA administrator Johnson had planned to make a thirty-five-hour week standard in all the industry codes, but that did not happen. Economist Robert Whaples has estimated that "about half of employees covered by NRA codes had their hours set at forty per week and nearly 40 percent had workweeks longer than forty hours." Those hours are close to what would be mandated under the FLSA five years later.

President Roosevelt understood that the Supreme Court could be a stumbling block for his New Deal programs. Although the 1932 elections gave Democrats control of the White House and Congress, the political composition of the Supreme Court did not change. During this period, the US Supreme Court was led by Charles Evans Hughes, a former governor of New York and unsuccessful nominee for president, who served as chief justice from 1930 to 1941. The Hughes Court was closely divided between liberal and conservative leaning justices, with Chief Justice Hughes and Justice Owen Roberts somewhere in the middle. Three justices constituted the liberal bloc: Louis Brandeis, Harlan Fiske Stone, and Benjamin Cardozo (who replaced Oliver Wendell Holmes in 1932).

The conservative bloc of the Hughes Court consisted of Willis Van Devanter, James McReynolds, Pierce Butler, and George Sutherland. Sutherland and Van Devanter were Republicans; McReynolds and Butler were Democrats. These four justices shared an unquestioned faith in rugged individualism, limited government, and free markets. Federal judge Learned Hand called the four conservatives "the mastiffs" based on their eagerness to bite into and overturn the New Deal's major initiatives. The media occasionally dubbed them the "Four Horsemen of the Apocalypse" or the "Four Horsemen of Reaction" because their strident warnings about the evils of government intervention seemed to prophesize the imminent demise of capitalism and republican government.

As President Roosevelt feared, the permanency of the gains under the NRA codes was threatened on May 27, 1935, a day known as "Black Monday," when the Supreme Court overturned the NIRA system in *Schechter Poultry Corporation v. United States* and struck down two other New Deal efforts. Sometimes called the "sick chicken" case, *Schechter* involved a constitutional challenge to NIRA codes adopted for the poultry industry and applied in New York, the country's largest chicken market. The industry suffered from graft and terrible health and sanitation conditions. The Live Poultry Code approved by the president established a maximum workweek of forty hours and a minimum hourly wage of fifty cents. Health inspections, regulations on slaughterhouses, and compulsory record keeping were also required by the code. Government regulators found the Schechter Poultry Corporation, owned by four brothers, in violation of the Poultry Code on several counts, including selling unsanitary poultry unfit for human consumption. The government obtained a sixty-count indictment against the brothers, and a jury found them guilty on nineteen. The Schechter brothers claimed that the NIRA system was an unconstitutional delegation of lawmaking power to the executive branch and that

Congress had no authority under the Commerce Clause to regulate intrastate commerce.

In *Schechter*, a unanimous Court concluded that the NIRA was an attempt by Congress to delegate its legislative power to the president and private groups without any standards to limit their discretion. Reading the opinion from the bench, Chief Justice Hughes stated that such delegation was beyond the constitutional power of Congress. Justice Cardozo, one of the more liberal members of the Court, referred to the NIRA as "delegation running riot." More importantly, the Court concluded that Congress could not regulate under its Commerce Clause powers because the Schechter firm was employed in a local trade. The "stream of commerce" rationale, which had been articulated in *Swift and Company v. U.S.* (1905), was held not applicable because the flow had ceased. Applying the direct-indirect test of precedents, Hughes argued that the company's wages and hours had no direct effect on interstate commerce. To rule otherwise, the Court warned, would be to practically subject all activities of the people and state authority over domestic matters to the power of the federal government. The chief justice concluded that the US Constitution did not provide for such a centralized economic system. The *Schechter* decision ended the initial effort of the Roosevelt administration to address high unemployment and depressed wages, and it was the third defeat of federal child labor legislation at the hands of the Supreme Court.

The *Schechter* decision and its unanimity stunned the courtroom audience. Even the three reliable liberals on the Court had voted against the New Deal. In *FDR v. the Constitution*, Burt Solomon describes a meeting between Justice Brandeis and Tommy Corcoran in the Court's chambers following the decision. "This is the end of this business of centralization," the justice told Corcoran, "and I want you to go back and tell the president that we're not going to let this government centralize everything. It's come to an end." The absence of dissent rattled President Roosevelt, and he worried about the fate of other New Deal programs. Attorney General Homer Cummings was frustrated and angry with the Court. "If this decision stands and is not met in some way," Cummings said, "it is going to be impossible for the government to devise any system which will effectively deal with the disorganized industries of the country, or rout out, by any affirmative action, manifest evils, sweatshop conditions, child labor, or any other unsocial or anti-social aspects of the economic system."

Roosevelt did not publicly react to the *Schechter* decision for several days, but when he did comment during a press conference on May 31, he sharply criticized the opinion. The decision was an anachronism, he suggested, that took the country back "to the horse-and-buggy days of 1789." In his opinion, the Court had ruled "in effect that the Federal government was powerless to cope with the tremendous social and economic problems that came as by-products of our growth from a strip of seaboard colonies to a great industrial nation." Roosevelt's strong comments did not go over well with many press correspondents, who viewed the Constitution as a "divine parchment" and who believed that it was bad politics or strategy to criticize the Court.

In response to *Schechter*, Congress in 1936 passed a more limited law called the Walsh-Healey Public Contracts Act. The law required that under all contracts with the federal government of at least $10,000, workers must be paid no less than the prevailing local minimum wages for that industry and work no more than eight hours a day or forty hours a week; contractors would not employ boys under age sixteen, girls under age eighteen, or prisoners; and work would not be done under hazardous or unsanitary conditions. The Supreme Court upheld the law four years later in *Perkins v. Lukens Steel Company*.

The economic forces of the Great Depression, demands of organized labor, and government policy combined to shape the standard workday and workweek. By the time Congress began its historic debate over the Fair Labor Standards Act in 1937, an eight-hour workday was established under federal law for employees and contractors of the US government and railroad workers in the private sector. Several states had laws restricting the workday to eight hours, but these were often limited to women and children, or they allowed employers and workers to mutually consent to longer days. Labor unions had secured eight-hour days in some industries through collective bargaining, and various employers voluntarily moved to eight-hour shifts. As for child labor restrictions or minimum wage laws, those fair labor standards had their separate history, to which we now turn.

CHAPTER TWO

Ending Child Labor Exploitation

In addition to the maximum hours and overtime pay provisions, the Fair Labor Standards Act imposed national restrictions on child labor (for the fourth time) and established a nationwide minimum wage for the first time in US history. Prior to passage of the FLSA, child labor exploitation had been a prominent policy issue in American politics for almost a century, although efforts to enact federal prohibitions did not begin until the early 1900s. All attempts to address child labor at the national level were unsuccessful. The Supreme Court overturned the first three laws, and a proposed constitutional amendment failed ratification. This chapter describes the long struggle to curb oppressive child labor.

During the early American colonial period, child labor was considered a public good and something to be encouraged. Religious beliefs strongly influenced the positive image of children's work. The Puritans and Quakers viewed idleness as a sin and valued the discipline of work for children. John Wesley, founder of Methodism, believed that work was virtuous, and he advocated child labor to prevent youth from idleness and vice. Court records and provincial laws document the attempts to promote a Puritan work ethic among children.

As early as 1640, the Great and General Court of Massachusetts directed town magistrates to explore "what course may be taken for teaching the boyes and girles in all towns the spinning of yarne." A year later the Court expressed its desire and expectation that heads of families see to it that their children and servants were industriously employed "so as the mornings and evenings and other seasons may not be lost as formerly they have bene." Similarly, the Great Law of the Province of Pennsylvania provided that all children "of the age of twelve years shall be taught some useful trade or skill, to the end none may be idle." The aptly named Boston Society for Encouraging Industry and Employing the Poor formed in 1751 to "employ our own women and children who are now in a great measure idle." In other writings of the period, the employment of poor women and children in early manufactories was encouraged because it provided a means of support and lessened the community burden of caring for them.

In the years prior to the American Revolution, women and children were put to work making textiles. Most households had a spinning wheel and loom. From Massachusetts to Virginia, there are accounts of young children spinning and carding in their homes or in spinning schools. If not busy with textiles, many children worked family farms. There was much work to be done to maintain a functioning farm. Children milked the cows, fed the chickens, planted seed, gathered water, chopped wood, and did other chores to contribute to the family economy. These tasks were essential to family survival, especially on the frontier. Agricultural labor was viewed as beneficial because it instilled a strong work ethic and kept children out of trouble.

After the American Revolution, prominent leaders endorsed the employment of children. Impressed by machinery and its potential to promote industry, George Washington observed a new threshing machine in operation and recounted in his diary; "Two boys are sufficient to turn the wheel, feed the mill, and remove the threshed grain. Women, or boys of 12 or 14 years of age, are fully adequate to the management of the mill or threshing machine." In a report to Congress in 1791, Secretary of the Treasury Alexander Hamilton marveled at the invention of the cotton-mill in England and noted how it contributed to progress in the manufacturing of cotton fabrics. Hamilton, seeing the potential of manufacturing institutions to employ persons who would otherwise be idle and a burden on the community, commented that "in general, women and children are rendered more useful . . . by manufacturing establishments, than they would otherwise be." He estimated that four-sevenths of those employed in the cotton mills of Great Britain were women and children, "of whom the greatest proportion are children, and many of them of a tender age." As the British people would soon discover, however, there was a dark side to the widespread use of children in the mills.

When the Industrial Revolution began in England in the middle eighteenth century, children were used as a source of cheap labor. In 1769 Richard Arkwright developed a machine for spinning cotton yarn, and the invention revolutionized the production of cotton. The manufacturing of cotton moved from the cottages and farms of England to mill factories. The first rural textile mills were built near rivers for a source of power, and child apprentices were hired as the main workers. Unlike the apprentices of the guild system, these new child apprentices often did not enjoy the benefits of an education, skilled trade, or social standing. The concept of child labor changed as thousands of children were forced to work far from home with little or no protection for their well-being from employer, parents, or the state.

By 1810 an estimated two million school-age children worked in the mills and factories in England. The mill factories were damp, grim, and unsanitary. Children, many under ten years old, were removed from the poor houses in London, Birmingham, and other cities to work the machines in the textile mills. Charles Dickens called these establishments the "dark satanic mills," and he helped publicize their evils in his novel *Oliver Twist*. With a seemingly inexhaustible supply of paupers from the city, no one at first noticed the appalling sickness and death rate among the child workers. Poorly clad children as young as four or five worked from twelve to sixteen hours a day, around dangerous machinery, under brutal supervision. Through the abuses of this kind of "pauper apprenticeship" came the first child labor laws. The Factory Act (1833) and Mines Act (1842) set minimum ages for work in the United Kingdom and curbed some of the worst forms of child labor exploitation.

The Industrial Revolution quickly spread throughout Western Europe and to the United States. The latter not only lagged behind England in the industrialization of its economy, but also Americans were slow to learn the lessons about child labor exploitation from the British experience. By the time Americans began to view child labor as a serious social problem in the 1870s, Great Britain had been addressing the issue for almost a century. Whether out of greed, ignorance, or indifference, the United States repeated many of the same mistakes faced under British industrialization.

Over time, public perceptions of child labor in America changed from viewing it as a social good to recognizing it as a moral and social evil. The transition in public attitudes toward working children, however, came slowly and was not shared by everyone. During the early Industrial Revolution, many employers and citizens seemed oblivious or indifferent to the impact of mechanization on working conditions and the growing use of children in factories and mills. According to Hugh Hindman, author of *Child Labor: An American History*, the turning point in public opinion followed a shift in the household economy from production for family consumption to production for markets where children worked outside the family. Before industrialization, people made things in or around the home using hand tools and basic machines. The introduction of the factory system transformed the production process, changed the apprenticeship system, and increased the use of child laborers.

Because the conflict over slavery dominated American politics in the first half of the 1800s, child labor reforms were few and far between. In antebellum America, New England trade associations were the first social groups to express concern about child labor on the basis that long hours at arduous tasks injured the health and education of future citizens. The trade-offs were obvious. When children worked twelve to fourteen hours a day, six days a week, there was no time to attend school. Some of the earliest calls for reform noted that child labor resulted in masses of illiterate children who, when grown to adulthood, would not be able to contribute to representative democracy. In 1818 the governor of Rhode Island spoke about factory children in a message to the legislature: "It is a lamentable truth that too many of the living generation, who are obliged to labor in these works of almost unceasing application and industry, are growing up without an opportunity of obtaining that education which is necessary for their personal welfare as well as for the welfare of the whole community."

Although they did not seek an end to child labor, trade-unionists urged restrictions on the excessive hours children were employed, and campaigned for universal education. Their efforts helped secure the first compulsory school attendance laws. School programs and facilities, however, were inadequate at the time. In the 1830s, the system of common schools was not reaching the masses of poor working children. A cultural preference for individualism, suspicion of state paternalism, and concern over the teaching of sectarian religious values slowed the development of free common schools and allowed child labor to continue unabated. As common or public schools became more widely available, opponents of child labor argued that children should be in school rather than working.

Reformers recognized early on that there was no single solution to the problem of child labor. It was a multifaceted issue that had to be attacked from different angles: (1) a minimum age below which children should not be permitted to work; (2) a maximum number of hours of employment; (3) a minimum education as a prerequisite for starting work; and (4) some regulations prohibiting children from dangerous and unhealthful occupations. Over time, these four requirements resulted in detailed laws specifying occupations where children were banned, compulsory school attendance laws, and provisions for documenting proof of age and issuing employment certificates. All four elements are related and necessary for successful child labor reform. But they were not easy to achieve. Opposition from employers, parents, and politicians, combined with a mostly apathetic public, necessitated a decades-long struggle to secure effective standards in law.

In 1836 the National Trades' Union, a collection of skilled tradesmen that had formed two years earlier, proposed that states establish a minimum age for factory work, and by 1860 several states had responded with legislation. Massachusetts limited children under twelve years of age to ten hours of work a day in 1842. The law is widely considered one of the first child labor laws in the country. In 1848, Pennsylvania set a minimum age for factory and textile mill workers at twelve years, and violators could be fined $50. The age requirement was increased to thirteen years in textile and paper mills the following year. New Jersey established a minimum age of ten years for manufacturing in 1851, and Rhode Island followed in 1857 with a twelve-year minimum for factory work. In 1855 Connecticut set the age minimum at nine years in manufacturing and factory establishments; a year later, it was increased to ten years.

These few laws enacted prior to the Civil War were limited in scope and generally ignored and ineffective. The laws applied only to factory work and textile mills, and the minimum age standards were low. Moreover, there was no proof of age required, and the laws lacked enforcement mechanisms. In Massachusetts, New Jersey, and Rhode Island, employers could be punished for child labor abuses only if they "knowingly" violated the law. This placed a difficult burden of proof on local officials in obtaining prosecutions. Employers and parents consistently evaded the laws. In many states, children could legally work if underage or beyond maximum hours if their parents consented, which they often did. Consequently, in both states with rudimentary laws and those with no protective legislation, children were employed at a young age, and they worked long hours, including overtime and at night.

Reformers had achieved some success on child labor in state legislatures and courts in the late 1800s, but by 1900 only twenty-eight states had laws protecting children working in manufacturing, and only ten more had any legislation prohibiting child labor in mining. The four leading textile states—Alabama, North Carolina, South Carolina, and Georgia—had no child labor laws. An estimated twenty-five thousand children under age sixteen worked in the mills, with some starting at eight years of age. In many southern states, the absence of compulsory school attendance laws exacerbated the problem. In the first few years of the new century, a big push by school officials, reform advocates, and the General Federation of Women's Clubs led to major improvements in compulsory education. By 1905 all but eleven states had passed laws requiring school attendance for the entire session. Seven of the states required education up to age sixteen while the others compelled attendance up to age fourteen. Of the eleven states without any compulsory school attendance laws, all but one was in the South.

Even in those northern states with child labor laws on the books, most laws were limited to factory work, full of loopholes, and not strictly enforced. Only nine states had a minimum age requirement as high as fourteen years. Omissions and exemptions in southern states and the lack of effective enforcement of many state laws spurred efforts to pass national legislation to curb child labor. Financial motives certainly played a part as well. Northern textile manufacturers, for example, complained that weak child labor standards in southern states created competitive advantages for southern mill owners that could only be addressed by uniform federal regulation.

Initially, reformers and organized labor disagreed over the need for national legislation. When the National Child Labor Committee (NCLC) formed in 1904, it expressly rejected the goal of a federal child labor law. The largest national labor union, the American Federation of Labor, also staunchly opposed child labor—but it favored state legislative remedies. Concerned about maintaining states' rights within the federal system, many activists preferred to seek tougher state child labor laws. During the Progressive Era, however, public attitudes shifted in favor of using federal power to limit the excesses of industrial capitalism. Disappointed with the pace and effectiveness of state reforms, the NCLC changed its original position and endorsed national legislation.

Persuaded by NCLC studies and other accounts, national periodicals began to report and editorialize on the problem of child labor. Dozens of articles appeared in prominent publications such as *McClure's*, *The Independent*, *The Arena*, and *The Outlook*. A series of articles written by Elizabeth Van Vorst for the *Saturday Evening Post* exposed much of middle-class America to the conditions of child labor and generated support for reform. In the spirit of muckraking journalism, Edwin Markham published a series of articles for *Cosmopolitan* beginning in September 1906 entitled "The Hoe-Man in the Making," which created a stir because of its strong indictment of child labor. The series generated so much interest from readers that the magazine formed the Child Labor Federation with the slogan "Child Labor Must Go."

Although smaller in membership, the National Consumers' League (NCL) often worked with the National Child Labor Committee on child labor issues. Founded in 1899 by Jane Addams (a famous Progressive Era reformer) and Josephine Lowell, the NCL initially used the buying power of consumers to press for better working conditions and fair wages, especially for women and children. But consumer pressure resulted in few reforms, so the NCL shifted its strategy toward state-mandated labor protections. The organization's first general secretary, Florence Kelley, also served on the board of the NCLC. For thirty years she worked tirelessly to expose child labor and promote fair labor practices.

A new leader emerged during this time to champion the cause of federal child labor reform. Republican Albert J. Beveridge had been first elected to the US Senate from Indiana in 1899. A successful lawyer and effective speaker, the freshman senator began his political career as a traditional Republican who supported tariffs, defended honestly earned wealth, and encouraged American expansion abroad. During his 1906 reelection campaign, Senator Beveridge made child labor reform a central issue of his campaign. Child labor, he believed, stunted the physical and intellectual growth of children, which in turn produced future generations of degenerates that threatened the health of the nation.

On December 5, 1906, the Hoosier senator introduced the first federal legislation on child labor in the Senate, and the next day Representative

Herbert Parsons (R-NY) introduced a similar measure in the House to prohibit employment of children in factories and mines. The language of Beveridge's bill prohibited common carriers (railroads and steamboats) from transporting the products of factories and mines unless the business owners could produce a certificate stating that no child under fourteen years of age was employed at the establishment. Federal district attorneys were responsible for prosecuting violations.

In support of his measure, the senator spoke passionately on the floor of the Senate chamber for three days in late January about the evils of "child slavery" and the constitutionality of his bill. Child labor, he said, was "as brutal and horrible in its inhumanity as anything the pen of Dickens ever painted." He traced the history of the child labor problem in Great Britain, described the practice's debilitating impact on the population, and compared the British experience in the early 1800s to America in 1907. Beveridge emphasized that child labor was not just a matter of states' rights. Rather, it was a national problem that required a uniform federal law. "Not only . . . is there inequality of business opportunities," he argued, "but by that inequality the ruin of citizens in any one State, the murder of the innocents in any one Commonwealth, affects the entire Republic as much as it affects the State." The Indiana senator's tone was angry and dramatic.

For the first time, child labor received serious consideration by national representatives. However, Beveridge's three-day speech failed to move most of his Senate colleagues, including many in his own party. Senate Majority Leader Nelson Aldrich of Rhode Island; John C. Spooner of Wisconsin, widely considered the Senate's constitutional authority; Charles Fulton of Oregon; and Philander Knox of Pennsylvania led the Republican opposition to the bill. Meanwhile, Southern Democrats, even the more progressive-minded, were wedded to the dogma of states' rights and viewed child labor as a local problem best left to the states. Senator Benjamin Tillman of South Carolina opposed child labor but believed "that the good sense and the love of humanity in any State, where it is pointed to properly, will redress this wrong or cure the evil, or kill it, if the facts are ever presented to the people."

Although federal legislation made little progress during the first decade of the twentieth century, a growing societal consensus on the evils of child labor—thanks in part to the lobbying efforts of the National Child

Labor Committee, National Consumers' League, Women's Federation Clubs, and other groups—prompted states to enact more laws restricting child labor in factories and mines. From 1902 to 1909, forty-three states passed significant child labor legislation: either new laws, including in many southern states, or strengthening existing statutes. The laws varied widely in their stringency and enforcement. While a fourteen-year age minimum for factories was standard in northern states, opposition from southern textile mill owners prevented serious consideration of the age minimum until 1909. Exemptions for work outside school hours, during vacation, and for children of dependent parents seriously weakened the fourteen-year minimum. As the nation headed into the second decade of the twentieth century, all the states had child labor laws. The problem was that the laws were not uniform, and in some states enforcement was lax. Laws were on the books, but factory inspections were sometimes prohibited, and often there were no financial or administrative resources for enforcement.

Despite the *Lochner* precedent and liberty of contract doctrine, both state and federal courts sustained most child labor laws by acknowledging a state interest in the welfare of children. In a California case, *In re Spencer* (1906), the state court upheld the child labor law by declaring: "The legislature may undoubtedly forbid the employment of children under the age of fourteen years at any regular occupation if the interests of the children and the general welfare of society will thereby be secured and promoted." Likewise, the state supreme court of Oregon affirmed a 1905 child labor law that prohibited children under age sixteen from working before 7:00 a.m. or after 6:00 p.m., or for longer than ten hours a day of more than six days a week. In upholding the law, the court rejected the liberty of contract doctrine of *Lochner* and applied the concept of *parens patriae*, or state as parent: "They [children] are wards of the state and subject to its control. As to them, the state stands in the position of *parens patriae*, and may exercise unlimited supervision and control over their contracts, occupation, and conduct, and the liberty and right of those who assume to deal with them. This is a power which inheres in the government for its own preservation."

Other decisions recognized the same governmental interest in the welfare of children. *Inland Steel Co. v. Yedinak* (1909) involved an under-age injured boy employed at a steel plant in violation of Indiana state law. The company tried to avoid liability by claiming that the boy's own youthful negligence caused the injury. In rejecting that argument, the state court wrote: "The employment of children of tender years in mills and factories not only endangers their lives and limbs, but hinders and dwarfs their growth and development physically, mentally and morally. The State is vitally interested in its own preservation, and, looking to that end, must safeguard and protect the lives, persons, health and morals of its future citizens." In addition to California, Oregon, and Indiana, child labor laws were upheld in Louisiana, Minnesota, New Jersey, and New York. The NCLC and other reformers were effective in convincing legislatures and courts that states had an obligation to protect children under their broad police powers.

Another Supreme Court decision in early December placed state child labor laws on solid constitutional ground. In *Sturges and Burn Manufacturing Co. v. Beauchamp* (1913), the Court unanimously rejected a Fourteenth Amendment due process challenge to an Illinois law prohibiting the employment of children under the age of sixteen in various hazardous occupations. Beauchamp, who was under age sixteen, had been injured while working a punch press stamping metal, and he sued to collect damages (financial compensation for his loss). The company claimed that the law was a deprivation of liberty of contract or property without due process of law. The Court held that the state "was entitled to prohibit the employment of persons of tender years in dangerous occupations" and that the legislation "was reasonably related to that purpose." The *Sturges* decision is often cited by contemporary revisionist constitutional scholars to demonstrate that the "liberty of contract" doctrine used in *Lochner v. New York* (1905) was not uniformly applied to defend the economic rights of business. Using a rational basis standard, the Court found that state child labor laws were a reasonable exercise of police powers. The *Sturges* decision, however, was to be the only victory for child labor reform in the Supreme Court for almost thirty years.

The First Federal Child Labor Law

Congress, meanwhile, tried again to enact a federal child labor law that would garner majority support and pass constitutional muster. In an attempt to regulate child labor indirectly under Article 1, Section 10 authority to regulate commerce between the states, the Keating-Owen Act prohibited producers and manufacturers from shipping in interstate commerce any product, in which thirty days prior to the removal of such product, was made by children under age fourteen, or merchandise that had been made in factories, mills, canneries, or manufacturing establishments where children between ages fourteen and sixteen had been permitted to work more than eight hours a day, six days a week, or at night. The Department of Labor was authorized to enter and inspect any establishment defined by the statute to determine violations of the law. Enforcement of the law was delegated to the Child Labor Division of the Children's Bureau, headed by Grace Abbott, a long-time advocate for child labor reforms and workers' rights.

The Keating-Owen Child Labor Law was in force for nine months and was being effectively implemented before the Supreme Court declared it unconstitutional. The Children's Bureau worked cooperatively with state commissioners and factory inspectors to enforce the law. Roland H. Dagenhart, who worked in a cotton mill in Charlotte, North Carolina, with his two sons, ages thirteen and fifteen, challenged the Keating-Owen Act with the support of the Executive Committee of Southern Cotton Manufacturers. Under state law, both of Dagenhart's sons were permitted to work as much as eleven hours a day. Court records indicate that Roland Dagenhart was a "man of small means" whose family needed the compensation from the work of the two boys. Under the Keating-Owen Act, however, the older boy was limited to working only eight hours, and his younger brother could not work at all. William C. Hammer, US attorney for the Western District of North Carolina, charged the Fidelity Manufacturing Company with violations of the Keating-Owen Act.

In defense of the child labor law, the federal government argued that the statute fell within congressional authority to regulate interstate and foreign commerce. The Commerce Clause, it claimed, played a vital part in the history of the Constitution and in the nation because it addressed one of the worst evils of the government under the Articles of Confederation—conflicting commercial regulations of the various states. Citing *Gibbons v. Ogden*, the government's brief asserted that the power conferred on Congress was plenary and embraced all the power the states previously held. Any manufacturer may employ children provided the products of that labor remain within a state. Only when a manufacturer transports goods made by children to another state does the law take force. Congress, the government argued, has the power to prevent the evil of child labor that attends such commerce. Working around machinery, night work, and excessive hours all had a deleterious effect on a child's physical development and well-being by stunting growth and decreasing resistance to disease. States, the government acknowledged, had criminal statutes against child labor, but they were not uniform, and many did not meet the due standard necessary for the protection of children. As the conviction grew that child labor was socially undesirable, it came to be viewed as an unfair discrimination in interstate commerce.

Lawyers for Dagenhart argued that Congress did not have the power under the Commerce Clause to regulate child labor. Congress, they claimed, was attempting to regulate labor conditions *prior* to transportation, rather than the actual transportation of products across state lines. Moreover, any consequences of child labor involved local conditions, and the regulation of intrastate commerce was reserved to the states under the Tenth Amendment. Congress, they contended, had no authority in this area.

In *Hammer v. Dagenhart*, decided June 3, 1918, Justice William Rufus Day, joined by Chief Justice Edward Douglas White, and Justices Mahlon Pitney, Willis Van Devanter, and James Clark McReynolds, wrote that Congress lacks the authority to regulate commerce of goods manufactured by children, and therefore the Keating-Owen Act was unconstitutional. Justice Day distinguished previous cases where the Court upheld federal attempts to control lotteries, impure food and drugs, prostitution, and intoxicating liquors by arguing that the manufacture of cotton was not a moral evil. In *Champion v. Ames* (1903), the Court held that Congress can pass a law keeping the channels of commerce free from the flow of lottery tickets. In *Hippolite Egg Company v. United States* (1911), the Court upheld the Pure Food and Drug Act, which prohibited the introduction in interstate commerce of impure foods and drugs, in this case adulterated eggs containing boric acid. And in *Clark Distilling Co. v. Western Maryland Railway Co.* (1917), the power of Congress over the interstate transportation of intoxicating liquors was affirmed. In each of these areas, the Court noted, the use of interstate transportation was necessary to accomplish harmful results, and regulation was required to prohibit the intended evil. According to Justice Day, that "element is wanting in the present case" because "the goods shipped, are of themselves, harmless." The key to distinguishing the precedents was a focus on the character of the goods.

Moreover, it was argued, the regulation of child labor within states is purely a state authority. Production of goods precedes interstate commerce and is a matter for local regulation. There is no power vested in Congress, Justice Day claimed, to force the states to exercise their police powers to prevent unfair competition. He used the Tenth Amendment to support his argument, although he misquoted the provision with regard to powers delegated to Congress. Under the Tenth Amendment, he argued, the powers "not expressly delegated to the National Government are reserved" to the states and to the people. Justice Day warned that to allow Congress such authority would end "all freedom of commerce" and eliminate the power of the states over local matters and thus "our system of government [would] be practically destroyed." The majority reasoning was based on the same concept of dual federalism that over a decade earlier had helped defeat the Beveridge bill.

Reading his dissent from the bench, Justice Oliver Wendell Holmes, joined by Justices Joseph McKenna, Louis Brandeis, and John H. Clarke, argued that the Keating-Owen Act was clearly within Congress's constitutional power. The law did not preempt state authority to regulate child labor within a state. Congress can regulate commerce that crosses state lines even though it may have an indirect effect on the activities of the states. "It does not matter," he said, "whether the supposed evil precedes or follows the transportation." Justice Holmes viewed child labor as a proper subject for congressional regulation: "The notion that prohibition is any less prohibition when applied to things now thought evil I do not understand. But if there is any matter upon which civilized countries have agreed—far more unanimously than they have with regard to intoxicants and some other matters over which this country is now emotionally aroused—it is the evil of premature and excessive child labor." Justice Holmes did not believe that the Tenth Amendment restricted congressional power over interstate commerce. "The act does not meddle with anything belonging to the States," he argued. They can still regulate their internal affairs and commerce as they desire. Holmes concluded that the "public policy of the United States is shaped with a view to the benefit of the nation as a whole," and Congress may enforce its policy by all means at its command.

Using Federal Taxing Power to Curb Child Labor

In the months following the *Hammer* decision, opponents of child labor searched for a new strategy. At the urging of the secretary of labor, the chief of the Children's Bureau, Julia Lathrop, called a conference to discuss options for more permanent child labor legislation. On August 21, 1918, representatives from the American Federation of Labor, National Child Labor Committee, Women's Trade Union League, National Consumers' League, and various government officials who were responsible for enforcing the Keating-Owen Act met to draft a new child labor bill. After numerous meetings and discussions, the group coalesced around a plan to levy an excise tax on the products of any mill, cannery, workshop, factory, or manufacturing establishment in which children under the age of fourteen were employed, or children between ages fourteen and sixteen years had worked more than eight hours in any day, or more than six days a week. President Woodrow Wilson approved the proposed legislation, and it was attached to a pending revenue bill.

Shortly after returning from the Paris Peace Conference, President Wilson signed the Revenue Act of 1919, which at the time was described as "the greatest revenue bill in the history of nations," on February 24, 1919. Title XII, Tax on Employment of Child Labor, commonly called the child labor tax law, was scheduled to take effect on April 25, 1919. Under the law, companies employing children under fourteen years of age would be assessed an excise tax of 10 percent on their annual profits. The law defined "child labor" as the use of minors "under the age of sixteen in any mine or quarry, and under the age of fourteen in any mill, cannery, workshop, factory, or manufacturing establishment." Additionally, the definition applied to the use of children in these age ranges for more than eight hours a day or six days a week, or during certain evening hours.

In September 1921 the Drexel Furniture Company was found in violation of the law and was required to pay over $6,300 in taxes. During 1919 the company had employed children under the age of fourteen. The company paid the taxes under protest and filed a lawsuit challenging congressional power to tax the profits of child labor. Drexel Furniture claimed that regulation of child labor in the states was an exclusively state function under the federal Constitution and within the reserved powers of the Tenth Amendment.

In *Bailey v. Drexel Furniture Company* (1922), the Supreme Court overturned the child labor tax law on the grounds that it intruded on the jurisdiction of the states to adopt and enforce child labor codes. Chief Justice Howard Taft drew a jurisprudential line in the sand and concluded that Congress had gone too far. "Out of proper respect for the acts of a coordinate branch of the Government, this court has gone far to sustain taxing acts as such," he stated, "even though there has been ground for suspecting from the weight of the tax it was intended to destroy its subject." But he found the child labor tax to be dangerously different: "Grant the validity of this law, and all that Congress would need do, hereafter, in seeking to take over to its control any one of the great number of subjects of public interest . . . would be to enact a detailed measure of complete regulation of the subject and enforce it by a so-called tax upon departures from it." Taft feared that upholding this law would destroy state sovereignty and devastate "all constitutional limitation of the powers of Congress" by allowing it to disguise future regulatory legislation in the cloak of taxes. Associate Justice John Clarke, a Wilson appointee, was the lone dissenter, but he did not write an opinion. Justices Holmes and Brandeis, who dissented in *Hammer*, joined the majority.

In the aftermath of *Bailey v. Drexel Furniture Company*, the disappointment and anger of many people opposed to child labor was palpable. Samuel Gompers denounced the *Bailey* decision as yet another example of the Court's class bias: "The Supreme Court deals with childhood exactly as it would deal with pig iron. . . . It observes all the technicalities, weighing the lives of our little ones as so much inert material," he wrote. Gompers could not understand why the Court failed to follow the precedent of the oleomargarine case. "Perhaps there is some legal technicality which makes proper and constitutional a tax on colored oleomargarine to keep it off the market, but improper and unconstitutional a tax on child labor to keep child labor products off the market." The courts, he suggested, "were unable to comprehend and deal properly with human problems according to modern concepts." Given the decisions in *Hammer* and *Bailey*, Gompers argued that it was now up to unions to prohibit child labor, and organized labor demanded a constitutional amendment to eliminate child labor.

With the adverse decisions in *Hammer* and *Bailey*, proponents of child labor restrictions had run out of federal legislative options. If Congress lacked the authority to pass a child labor law under the Commerce Clause or taxing power, as the Supreme Court declared, the only way to give Congress that authority, short of the Court overturning its precedents at some point, was passage of a child labor amendment to the US Constitution. A campaign to use Article V to alter the Constitution began in Congress just days after the *Bailey* decision.

Congress Sends a Child Labor Amendment to the States

By the 1920s, the fracturing of the Progressive coalition presented challenges for supporters of the amendment, but they succeeded in getting a measure through Congress. After two years of congressional hearings and debates, a child labor amendment passed by large majorities in Congress in 1924. The proposed Twentieth Amendment was endorsed by the national platforms of the Republican and Democratic parties, and it had the backing of presidents Warren Harding and Calvin Coolidge, as well as future president Franklin D. Roosevelt. Others who supported the amendment included Republican senators Henry Cabot Lodge and Robert La Follette, and Secretary of Commerce Herbert Hoover, who headed the American Child Health Association. Although Hoover believed that an age eighteen restriction was too high, he nonetheless favored the amendment to eliminate a condition that was "more deplorable than war" and "poisoning the springs of the nation at their source." Public opinion surveys in the 1930s, though rudimentary at the time, also indicated that a majority of citizens favored the amendment.

On May 17, 1922, Representative Roy G. Fitzgerald, a Republican lawyer and World War I veteran from Dayton representing Ohio's Third District, introduced a resolution for an amendment that would empower

Congress to regulate the employment of children under age eighteen. The proposed amendment read: "The Congress shall have the power to regulate throughout the United States the employment of persons under 18 years of age." Republican senator Hiram Johnson of California, who was Theodore Roosevelt's running mate for the Progressive Party in 1912, introduced a similar resolution in the Senate two days later. Claiming that the amendment was needed to protect children, Senator Johnson asserted that the national government must "slightly invade state [sic] rights" when the welfare of children was at stake. "Ordinarily I would not wish to invade the prerogatives of the states," Johnson said, "but if the welfare of little children requires it, I would not for an instant hesitate."

According to press reports, Johnson's proposed amendment precipitated a sectional fight between northern and eastern senators and those from southern and western states over constitutional principles similar to slavery, states' rights, and secession. Senator Less Overman, Democrat from North Carolina, "bitterly condemned" the proposal as a "clear attempt to wipe out state lines." Other senators warned that the amendment would create a "paternalistic super-structure of a federal government." Johnson's amendment, it was argued, would give Congress the authority to enact anti-lynching laws and usurp state police powers. Although public pressure to respond to the *Bailey* decision was growing, the battle lines were drawn, and Congress adjourned without taking action on the amendment.

By the time the Sixty-Eighth Congress reconvened in early December 1923, fourteen resolutions for a child labor amendment had been introduced in the House, as well as four in the Senate. Support coalesced around a new measure introduced early in the session by Representative Israel Moore Foster of Ohio and Senator Samuel Shortridge of California. From February 7 to March 8, 1924, the House held hearings on various changes to the amendment. At this point, opposition voices became more resolute and alarmist with their arguments. Representatives from the American Farm Bureau Federation (AFBF) testified against the amendment in a House committee hearing. Gray Silver, legislative representative for the AFBF, argued: "The farmers will be among the first to resent the activities of the Federal bureau if it tried to take the place of the parents by telling the children what duties they should or should not perform and what kind of work they should do." Several state-level Granges joined the AFBF in fighting the amendment, and the National Grange voted to oppose the amendment at its annual convention that year.

After the hearings, the "Children's Amendment," as it was called by supporters, was offered by Representative Foster on April 26 1924, in the form of House Joint Resolution No. 184. The opposition was unable to derail support for the amendment. It passed the House with bipartisan support by a vote of 297 to 69 on April 26, 1924. The Senate debated the issue for another month.

By an overwhelming majority, the Senate voted down a proposal to use state ratifying conventions under Article V and rejected a time limit on ratification. Both of those votes impacted the ratification battle in the years to come. Attempts to limit the scope of the amendment by setting the age at sixteen years, exempting farm labor, or by specifying that the power applied only to commercial employment of children in mills, factories, and mines, were also turned back. At 10:00 p.m. on June 2, 1924, the Senate voted 61 to 23 in favor of the amendment, five more than the required two-thirds majority. The proposed constitutional amendment was submitted to the state legislatures for ratification pursuant to Article V of the Constitution. With forty-eight states in the Union, thirty-six were needed for ratification. The text of the amendment read:

Section 1. The Congress shall have power to limit, regulate, and prohibit the labor of persons under eighteen years of age.

Section 2. The power of the several States is unimpaired by this article except that the operation of State laws shall be suspended to the extent necessary to give effect to legislation enacted by the Congress.

The only state delegations to vote against the amendment in both the US House and Senate were Alabama, Florida, Georgia, Louisiana, Maryland, North Carolina, and South Carolina. Although proponents recognized that there would be a battle over ratification, they were optimistic about the chances for success. Florence Kelley expected swift ratification. The size of the congressional majorities in favor of the amendment and perceived support in Midwestern states were encouraging signs. A vote in favor of ratification in Arkansas at the end of June, just weeks after the amendment had been sent to the states, also raised hopes among reformers. Moreover, all three major political parties—Republican, Democratic, and Progressive—and their respective presidential candidates, backed the amendment.

The Political Battle over Ratification

In fact, the campaign for ratification started off well. In addition to Arkansas, two other states, Arizona and California, ratified by January 1925. Wisconsin joined the list the following month. Believing that their cause was just and that the child labor amendment was the solution to a national problem, supporters of the amendment felt that most opposition would collapse once the inflammatory rhetoric and misrepresentations were corrected by reasoned arguments. Suddenly, however, the ratification campaign faced a series of defeats in the states and growing public opposition nationwide.

Debate over the amendment in the states was passionate and acrimonious. A study of the propaganda over the amendment identified over seventy-five organized groups involved in the campaign to defeat or ratify the amendment in the twelve years (1924 to 1936) that it had been a prominent issue. The National Child Labor Committee served as a clearinghouse for all groups in favor of the amendment. Proponents included the American Association of University Women, the National Federation of Teachers, Camp Fire Girls, American Legion, the Young Women's Christian Association, and Northern Baptist Convention.

There was less coordination among opposition interests, but they were unified by the common goal of defeating the measure. The National Association of Manufacturers (NAM), under the direction of David Clark and James A. Emery, corporate counsel for NAM, led the opposition. Some organizations were created solely to defeat the amendment while others were strongly opposed to any kind of federal social or welfare legislation. NAM was joined by the National Farm Bureau Federation, the Grange, and various farm journals. Other groups included those who had fought against the Eighteenth and Nineteenth Amendments, such as the National Association Opposed to Woman Suffrage, renamed the Woman Patriots, and the American Constitutional League. The Nebraska and Missouri Synod of the Lutheran Church, the Chamber of Commerce of New York, and the Catholic Diocese of Boston were all vocal critics.

Opponents often dubbed the proposal the "So-called Child Labor Amendment" or referred to it as the "Disingenuous Amendment" to suggest a hidden agenda of socialism and federal encroachment on states' rights, parental authority, and liberty. Others said that the amendment would replace the authority of parents with federal authority and that it would threaten parochial schools. One dissenter writing in the *Manufacturers' Record* claimed that if adopted, the "amendment would be the greatest thing ever done in America in behalf of the activities of Hell. It would make millions of young people under 18 years of age idlers in brain and body, and thus make them the devil's best workshop." One slippery-slope argument drew a connection between the amendment and potential federal regulation of all aspects of education, public and parochial.

By March 1925 the momentum was clearly against the amendment. Six states had voted down the amendment, often by wide margins: Georgia, Kansas, North Carolina, South Carolina, Oklahoma, and Texas. Amendment supporters remained confident that once the people truly understood the meaning of the amendment, it would obtain ratification. But after eight years, only six state legislatures had ratified the amendment. During this period the amendment was rejected in one or both houses in thirty-two states, and by 1932 it was largely thought to be defeated.

The stock market crash in October 1929 led to the worst economic crisis in the nation's history. When unemployment increased during the early years of the Great Depression, many child laborers were discharged from work. In 1932, however, manufacturers increased employment of children because it was simply cheaper than paying adult wages. Child labor in the mills and sweatshops became commonplace again. Though the child labor amendment was believed to be dead, public opinion on the relationship between government and the economy shifted, and the 1932 elections breathed new life into the amendment. Concerned that children should not be competing with adults for scarce jobs, fourteen states ratified the amendment in 1933 alone. Even with the spate of new ratifications, the child labor amendment never came close to becoming part of the Constitution.

Reformers turned their attention to federal restrictions under the National Industrial Recovery Act. The hundreds of codes formulated under the NIRA contained restrictions on child labor, but they were short-lived because of the Supreme Court decision in the *Schechter Poultry* case. The Constitutional Revolution of 1937 set the stage for new child labor regulations under the Fair Labor Standards Act. As the FLSA was being debated, the numerous exemptions and restrictive provisions upset many child labor reformers, and some wanted a renewed focus on ratifying the child labor amendment. That goal was never attained. Kansas was the last state to ratify the amendment, on February 25, 1937.

CHAPTER THREE

The Fight for a Minimum or Living Wage

The demand for minimum wage laws began much later than the child labor reform movement. Although wage issues had been part of the labor movement's agenda since the colonial period, it was not until the Progressive Era that minimum wages were mandated at the state level, and no gains were made on a federal minimum wage until the Constitutional Revolution of 1937. Consequently, for most of US history, wage rates were determined either by individual negotiations between employer and worker or through collective bargaining agreements secured by unions. Those labor dynamics still play out today but within the context of federal and state minimum wage laws.

The idea of a "living" or "just" wage has been around for centuries. New Testament verses allude to a just wage in Matthew 10:10, "for the worker is worth his keep"; in Luke 10:7, "for the laborer is worthy of his hire"; and in I Timothy 5:8, "the worker deserves his wages." Despite the long history of the concept of a living wage, a clear definition remains elusive. A living wage is often described as compensation sufficient to maintain a person in good health and provide the basic necessities of life such as food, clothing, and shelter. This concept is very different from a legislative minimum wage, which is defined as the minimum pay per hour a worker is entitled to receive. Minimum wages, like those provided for in the Fair Labor Standards Act, are not necessarily living wages, but they represent a floor that wages should not fall below. A just wage is like a living wage, but it has a moral and ethical dimension—that a worker has a natural right to a fair wage that is independent and superior to human laws and institutions.

Various church doctrines, both Catholic and Protestant, have argued that an honest worker deserves more than merely a subsistence wage. In the Middle Ages, Catholic theologians like Thomas Aquinas advocated for a just wage. There were few attempts to explain the precise contours of a just wage, however, because workers, either in town or country, did not earn hourly pay. Their compensation was based on the value of the goods they produced rather than the hours they worked, so a just wage was embodied in a just price for a finished product. In *Summa Theologica*, Aquinas wrote that justice demands that a fair price be paid for a material commodity, so it demands that a fair price be given for human labor. A just wage or price for the product of a laborer was one that allowed him to support his family according to the standards of his social class. A person's social class was rigidly determined by cultural traditions.

In the late medieval period, from 1349 to 1563, payment of unskilled laborers in England was regulated by various "Statutes of Laborers." These laws generally worked to the benefit of employers. The earliest law was a response to the high wages that were prevalent following the Black Death of 1348, when labor was in short supply. In just five years the bubonic plague killed an estimated twenty million people in Europe alone. For most of the period the legal wage rate was a maximum that both master and laborer could not exceed. In England, local justices of the peace were empowered to set not a minimum wage, but the *actual* wages to be paid. A benevolent employer who paid a laborer too much for the type of work performed could be prosecuted.

With the emergence of capitalist economies, classical economic thinkers replaced the medieval standard of a just wage with laissez-faire theory. A just or fair wage for labor was determined by market competition and supply and demand. David Ricardo, in *The Principles of Political Economy and Taxation*, argued: "Like all other contracts, wages should be left to the fair and free competition of the market, and should never be controlled by the interference of the legislature." In *The Wealth of Nations*, Adam Smith wrote that wages freely bargained for, without physical or government coercion, would be just wages. But even Smith acknowledged that a society is "flourishing and happy" only when the workers are "tolerably well fed, clothed, and lodged" and not when they are "poor and miserable." He worried that the capitalists "are always and every where in a sort of tacit, but constant and uniform combination, not to raise the wages of labor above their actual rate. . . . Masters too sometimes enter into particular combinations to sink the wages of labor even below this rate." Adam Smith opposed combinations by both workers and capitalists (employers) under a theory of free competition.

Classical theory assumed that the bargaining power between employer and worker was based on free and equal competition affected only by conditions of supply and demand. Labor markets, however, are not perfect, and workers rarely bargained on equal terms.

Market forces during the late nineteenth-century Industrial Revolution led to growing criticism of the laissez-faire theory of wages. In England, where the Industrial Revolution began, the "obvious and simple system of natural liberty" promoted by Smith and other classical economists resulted in what is known as the period of English wage slavery. In negotiating wages, employers were almost always in a better position to increase their wealth. Labor competition disadvantaged workers and resulted in low pay. With men earning starvation wages, women and children were forced to work in the mills and factories.

In the United States in the 1800s, technological changes in production, increasing immigration, and population concentration in urban areas created a labor surplus. Job seekers, especially unskilled workers, were in a vulnerable position. For many employees, the market competition principle resulted in wages that did not provide for essential living expenses. In industries that used the sweating system, workers were paid by the piece rather than an hourly wage, and they had to work excessive hours just to earn enough to meet basic needs. The government largely maintained laissez-faire policies during this period. In 1869 President Ulysses S. Grant issued a proclamation encouraging a "stable wage for government workers," but the declaration had little effect on either public or private employees. By the early 1900s a minimum wage became a central tool advocated by reformers to fight poverty and economic inequality, but another decade would pass before any progress was made on state minimum wage laws, and it would take almost forty years before minimum wage legislation was enacted at the national level.

The policy of a living or minimum wage was first implemented outside the United States. Belgium enacted a minimum wage law in 1887 for laborers in public works. The first minimum wage law governing *private* employment originated in New Zealand in 1894. Under the Industrial Conciliation and Arbitration Act, employer lockouts and labor strikes were outlawed. District Conciliation Boards, tasked with the compulsory arbitration of labor disputes, had the authority to fix minimum wages in order to preserve industrial peace. The law was a response to employers blacklisting union members and cutting wages following the failure of the trans–Tasman Maritime Strike of 1890. The New Zealand system of compelled arbitration remained in place until 1973.

In 1896 the state of Victoria, Australia, established the first independent government agencies with the power to set minimum wages. Called Special Boards, the agencies were initially an experiment to deal with the problem of sweatshops that employed both men and women. The boards were composed of an equal number of employer and employee representatives and chaired by an outside person, nominated by both sides, who represented the public interest. The law did not specify cost-of-living criteria for determining wage rates; it was expected that the board would debate a reasonable wage. With labor in short supply, weak labor unions, and a more homogeneous culture, the process often resulted in wages that met or exceeded basic living requirements. Though rudimentary, the system was successful, and it was extended to more trades and adopted by other Australian states. When Australia became a nation in 1901, a minimum wage was the law of the land, and the Aussie experience influenced reformers in the United Kingdom and United States.

England embraced the Australian model in 1909 with a few tweaks that made the British system more conservative. Under the Trade Boards Act, the minimum wage provisions could be extended beyond the four specified trades only if the Board of Trade determined that wages in other trades were exceptionally low by comparison and that the financial status of the industry was sufficiently healthy. In other words, business considerations were given priority over humanitarian goals. The Board of Trade also had the power to suspend indefinitely any wage ruling that it felt was "premature or otherwise undesirable." One progressive feature of the law was that wage rulings applied universally to a trade and to any class of worker.

The Minimum Wage Movement in America

Various social and religious groups were at the forefront of the minimum wage movement in the United States during the Progressive Era. The National Consumers' League, formed in 1898, worked unsuccessfully for years to obtain a voluntary commitment from employers for a $6 a week minimum wage. By 1909, Florence Kelley and the NCL lobbied for legislative minimum wage laws. One vocal advocate within the organization was Mary Williams "Molly" Dewson. Often called "Minimum Wage" Dewson, she joined the minimum wage movement in 1911 and as executive secretary of the NCL Minimum Wage Investigative Committee attained national recognition for a report in Massachusetts that led to the nation's first-ever minimum wage law. Other groups pushing for minimum wages included the General Federation of Women's Clubs, the National Women's Trade Union League, and National Child Labor Committee. The Progressive Party in its 1912 platform also had a plank advocating statutory minimum wages for women and children.

Responding to Pope Leo XIII's 1891 encyclical *Rerum Novarum* (Of New Things), subtitled "On the Conditions of Labor," Catholic leaders began promoting labor legislation, especially minimum wage laws. Pope Leo tried to find a middle ground between laissez-faire capitalism and Marxist ideology. Rejecting the socialist call to destroy private property in response to the extremes of wealth and poverty caused by the Industrial Revolution, the Pope argued that workers and employers should be free to negotiate and agree to conditions of employment. Natural justice, however, must ensure that wages are sufficient to support a "frugal and well-behaved wage earner." Pope Leo's encyclical turned the doctrine of a living wage into an explicit component of Catholic ethics and social teaching. Prominent Catholic clerics, including Father John A. Ryan of Catholic University, Edwin V. O'Hara, Peter E. Dietz, and William Cardinal O'Connell, all argued that minimum wages for men and women were necessary for a living wage. In 1906, Father Ryan published *The Living Wage: Its Ethical and Economic Aspects*, which generated a lot of discussion. Father Ryan made the moral case for a living wage and criticized as ineffective efforts to encourage employers to voluntarily increase wages. He believed only a government-mandated minimum would work.

Protestant teaching on an ethical standard of wages, although more varied and less pronounced, also argued against the classical economic doctrine of unlimited wage bargaining. To exploit a vulnerable worker under the guise of freedom of contract violated principles of Christianity. Martin Luther, although he did not devote much time on the issue, believed that prices should be tied to costs and fairly compensate for labor, noting that the gospel says, "the laborer deserves his wages." John Calvin preached in 1555 that God wished "to correct the cruelty of the rich who employ poor people in their service and yet do not sufficiently compensate them for their labor." In his 1907 book *Christianity and the Social Crisis*, which influenced the social gospel movement, Protestant minister Walter Rauschenbusch supported labor organizing and a living wage. Middle-class Protestant reformers were some of the leading advocates for minimum wage laws and other fair labor standards.

Arguably one of the most important groups impacting fair labor standards was the American Association for Labor Legislation (AALL), which formed in 1906. The organization became a forum for the new school of institutional or welfare economists, including Richard T. Ely, John R. Commons, Richard Lester, and John B. Andrews. Institutional economists argued that wage rates in the real world were influenced not only by supply and demand but also by concerns over employee morale, loyalty to the firm, turnover and retraining costs, and relative bargaining power. The association studied labor conditions in the United States; drafted model bills on workmen's compensation, unemployment insurance, social security, and minimum wages; and lobbied for their passage. The organization created a women's committee and recruited female labor reformers to advocate for protectionist labor laws. The AALL achieved some success at the state level in these areas during the Progressive Era. Decades later, much of the work of the group influenced the labor and social welfare policies of the New Deal.

State Minimum Wage Laws

The minimum wage became a prominent policy issue between 1910 and 1915. A series of investigations and reports by reform groups and state labor bureaus revealed that millions of women and children were employed in factories, mills, retail establishments, service industries, and sweatshops at wage rates too low to sustain a basic living. A multivolume study conducted from 1907 to 1910 by the federal government, entitled *Woman and Child Wage Earners in the United States*, found that pay rates were shockingly low across many industries. More than half of working women earned less than $6 a week, or $300 annually. Just like the studies and exposés on child labor exploitation, the findings aroused public opinion. Many state legislatures introduced minimum wage bills over the next few years.

Organized labor long feared that a statutory minimum wage would become the maximum, and unions supported these minimum wage proposals only to the extent that they applied to the employment of women and children or covered public employees at all levels of government. "We want a minimum wage established," Samuel Gompers wrote in 1913, "but we want it established by the solidarity of the working men themselves through the economic forces of their trade unions rather than by any legal enactment." The American Federation of Labor continued to advocate this position on the minimum wage well into the 1930s.

At the urging of social reformers, Massachusetts enacted the first minimum wage law in the United States in 1912, with full implementation the following year. The statute requested that the governor appoint an investigating commission "to study the matter of wages of women and minors, and to report on the advisability of established . . . [wage] boards." The commission submitted a comprehensive report with a draft bill. The proposed law contained many features of the Australian and British systems, with certain limitations based on prevailing US constitutional law. First, the wage protections applied only to women and to minors under age eighteen. At the time, an estimated 350,000 women worked in textile mills, retail establishments, service industries, and other jobs. The commission discovered that a substantial percentage of female employees in these jobs were being paid less than $8 per week, an amount believed to be necessary to meet basic living expenses. In the cotton mills, for example, 67 percent earned less than $8 per week, and 38 percent earned less than $6.

The Massachusetts law only applied to women and minors because minimum wage laws for men were believed to be unconstitutional under the "liberty of contract" doctrine and *Lochner v. New York* precedent. In *Lochner*, the Supreme Court declared that "grown and intelligent" male bakers did not lack the capacity to "assert their rights and care for themselves without the protecting arm of the State." Although many women and children worked under employment contracts, their perceived physical limitations and lack of political power engendered paternalism and the need for labor protections under a police powers exception. The idea of a living wage and statutory minimums then was closely linked to the movement for women's rights in the early twentieth century.

In addition to limiting their reach to women and children, the proposed minimum wage legislation had to meet constitutional requirements for delegating power to administrative agencies. The separation of powers principle contends that legislatures make laws, executive officials enforce laws, and the courts interpret laws. Under a nondelegation doctrine applied by the courts, at least rhetorically, state legislatures and Congress should not transfer lawmaking power to executive officials. Any law that delegates such power had to specify the conditions and procedures for a wage board or commission to exercise lawmaking authority.

The Massachusetts draft bill provided for a permanent commission with the power to investigate wage conditions and, if necessary, establish a minimum wage that was obligatory on employers. Violations were misdemeanors punishable by fine and imprisonment. H. LaRue Brown, a Boston attorney who helped draft the legislation and chaired the first Massachusetts Minimum Wage Commission, recalled that when the bill was first introduced to the General Court (the state legislature), it was denounced as "socialistic . . . revolutionary . . . and subversive of the conservative traditions of the commonwealth." Opponents predicted that industries would flee the state for jurisdictions that were more welcoming to business. Regardless of the strong vocal opposition, the bill passed, with only one dissenting vote in both chambers.

That level of political consensus, however, was only achieved by compromises that weakened the protections of the law. The most critical provision on enforcement had been deleted. The "orders" of the commission had been changed to "recommendations," and the potential penalty of fine and imprisonment had been reduced to bad publicity. An employer paying substandard wages might have his name published in a newspaper, but even that minor punishment could be avoided if he demonstrated in court that the recommendations of the commission made it impossible "to conduct his business at a reasonable profit." Although the Massachusetts law had significant limitations, it was innovative and appears to have had some success in raising wages. The law drew attention to the problem, and potential public shaming encouraged employers to improve wages.

Fourteen more states enacted minimum wage laws for women and children (but not men) between 1913 and 1923. Following Massachusetts, eight states passed minimum wage laws in 1913: California, Colorado, Minnesota, Nebraska, Oregon, Utah, Washington, and Wisconsin. Five of these states had tougher laws than Massachusetts because they provided minimum wages based on a cost of living, made final orders binding on employers, and imposed fines or imprisonment for violations. California was unique, as voters approved a state constitutional amendment providing for a minimum wage against the opposition of organized labor. Three state laws had provisions that undermined their effectiveness. Like Massachusetts, Nebraska's law was enforced only by bad publicity. Colorado borrowed from the UK model in that it required consideration of the financial condition of the industry in setting wage rates. In Utah, the legislature set the minimum instead of delegating authority to an administrative board, and legislators fixed the rate so low that it did nothing to improve wages. Because of political opposition and uncertainty about the constitutionality of such laws, Colorado and Nebraska never established a minimum wage, and Nebraska repealed its law in 1919.

After the burst of legislation from 1912 to 1913, the state minimum wage movement lost momentum. The National Consumers' League and Women's Trade Union League continued to lobby for minimum wage legislation, but only Arkansas and Kansas passed laws in 1915, and Arizona added a minimum wage law in 1917. Congress also provided for minimum wage rates for women and minors in the District of Columbia in 1918. After World War I, North Dakota, Texas, and Puerto Rico passed laws in 1919, and South Dakota enacted a minimum wage law in 1923. Because most of the fifteen states with minimum wage laws were either primarily rural or less-densely populated western states, the impact on workers was limited.

Several factors contributed to the decline in the minimum wage reform movement. Business interests organized in opposition to wage bills, arguing that they were contrary to American individualism and led to socialism. Also, the start of World War I in Europe in 1914 focused public attention on other concerns, as did US entry into the war in 1917. By the end of the war in 1918, the coalition of groups supporting Progressive reforms began to unravel, as the interests of industrial workers and farmers diverged.

Challenges to Effective Minimum Wage Laws

Two major problems plagued the unprecedented experiment with state minimum wage laws: difficulties in determining wage rates and a spate of legal challenges. First, instead of delegating authority to a wage board, in several states the legislature imposed a fixed or flat-rate minimum wage that was not adjusted for inflation. Rapidly rising consumer prices during the war, however, soon made those rates too low to adequately provide for living expenses. This is the same problem with the minimum wage provision in the Fair Labor Standards Act. Unless the legislature enacts periodic increases to the minimum, the purchasing power declines.

Even in states that adopted a more flexible structure by having a wage board or commission establish a minimum rate, there were numerous disagreements over what factors to consider in translating a "living wage" into dollars and cents. The process was very subjective. Because the laws applied only to women and minors, any wage board or administrative body had to first decide who fit the description of the typical worker. For adult females, the standard became the "single self-supporting woman living away from home." Two methods were used in calculating the minimum cost of living. The first sampled a group of female wage earners and identified their actual weekly expenditures. Critics argued that this approach often resulted in wage rates that were too low because few respondents remembered all their weekly expenses. A second approach was more theoretical. It listed items deemed essential for a single working woman, added up their estimated cost, and arrived at a weekly wage rate. Many employers questioned the inclusion of expenses for laundry, a vacation, a dress, or a party hat. In practice then, wage boards exercised a lot of discretion in determining a "living wage."

A study by the Women's Bureau found that in states with minimum wage laws, the initial cost of living estimates made between 1913 and 1915, before US involvement in World War I, fell within a narrow range of $8.50 to $10.74 a week. Those rates appeared to be a close approximation of typical living expenses. But there was an unprecedented 100 percent increase in the cost-of-living index between 1913 and 1920. As prices rose during the war, there were attempts to adjust rates, but they were not increased fast enough or set high enough to keep pace with inflationary pressures. An analysis by Elizabeth Brandeis, daughter of Associate Justice Louis Brandeis and an economics professor at the University of Wisconsin, concluded that overall, only California, Arkansas, and the District of Columbia provided wage increases with legal minimum rates that substantially impacted worker earnings. Both California and DC set initial minimum rates high enough to make a difference. In states with lower mandatory minimum rates, only the poorest paid workers benefited from the laws.

Beyond the problems of measuring an appropriate wage rate, numerous lawsuits sought to have the courts declare minimum wage laws unconstitutional as a violation of the liberty of an employer to set wages for employees. Most state courts affirmed the laws under the doctrine of state police powers to promote the public health, safety, welfare, and morals. Like the state police power to fix maximum hours in dangerous industries, minimum wage laws were deemed important for worker health and morals. One 1924 study found that twenty-seven of twenty-nine judges in Oregon, Minnesota, Arkansas, and Washington considered such legislation constitutional. Even the US Supreme Court provided early, albeit weak, support.

Oregon was one of the states in the vanguard of minimum wage laws. In 1912 the Consumer's League of Oregon, a branch of the National Consumers' League, conducted a statewide survey of wages and working conditions of women and minors. A Catholic priest, Father E. V. O'Hara, led the investigation, and he helped draft a minimum wage bill with the assistance of the American Association of Labor Legislation. The Consumer's League report led to passage of a state minimum wage law on February 17, 1913. The bill had received unanimous support in the state Senate, and it passed the House with only three nay votes. The minimum wage law stated: "The State of Oregon requires that woman [*sic*] and minors should be protected from conditions of labor which have a pernicious effect on their health and morals."

Under the authority of the act, the Oregon Industrial Welfare Commission, which was first chaired by Father O'Hara, issued an order providing that no manufacturing establishment in the City of Portland shall employ "any experienced, adult woman worker, paid by time rates of payment . . . a weekly wage of less than $8.64, any lesser amount being hereby declared inadequate to supply the necessary cost of living to such woman [*sic*] factory workers, and to maintain them in health." The commission had determined that the minimum living budget of female workers in Portland was $9.62 per week, or $500 per year. The budget consisted of expenses for room and board, clothing, laundry, carfare, and doctor's bills. At the time, 48.1 percent of female workers in Portland were paid less than $8.00 per week, and 60.1 percent made less than $9.00 a week. Many female factory workers, therefore, were not earning enough to pay for basic living expenses. Although the proposed minimum wage of $8.64 a week was short of the estimated $9.62 needed for living expenses, the order improved the wages of almost half of all female factory workers.

Some employers and employees opposed the state's intervention in the workplace. Frank C. Stettler, a paper box manufacturer in Portland, and Elmira Simpson, an employee at the company, filed lawsuits against the Oregon Industrial Welfare Commission asserting that the commission illegally exercised legislative authority and that the order violated Simpson's "freedom of contract." At the time of the lawsuit, Simpson earned $8.00 weekly. She stood to make an extra sixty-four cents a week under the order, so it is not clear from the historical evidence why she chose to challenge the law. Perhaps she objected to a minimum wage on principle. Stettler claimed that he would lose his business if he had to pay his female employees $8.64 a week. The state supreme court, however, unanimously upheld the minimum wage law in both cases, and Stettler appealed.

In *Stettler v. O'Hara* (1917), the US Supreme Court addressed the constitutionality of state minimum wage laws for the first time. The case was initially argued on December 16 and 17, 1914. It was restored to the docket on June 1916 and reargued January 18 to 19, 1917. On April 9 the Court issued a *per curium* opinion that simply stated: "Judgments affirmed with costs by an equally divided court." Justice Louis Brandeis, because he was involved in defending the Oregon statute, did not participate. Brandeis and Josephine Goldmark of the NCL had prepared a "Brandeis brief" that rivaled the one submitted in *Muller v. Oregon*. When Brandeis left following his Supreme Court appointment, Felix Frankfurter, a Harvard law professor and future justice himself, finished litigating the case. The brief defending the Oregon law consisted of fifty-four pages of legal argument and over 780 pages identifying and summarizing national and state minimum wage laws and research publications on minimum wages!

The 4 to 4 vote meant that Oregon's law was upheld. Although the result in *Stettler* was not a clear statement by the Supreme Court on minimum wage laws, Justice Brandeis certainly would have provided the fifth vote to sustain such laws had he participated in the case. The decision in *Stettler* prompted other states to pass minimum wage legislation. But Brandeis's recusal had historical consequences. The Supreme Court did not grant review in another minimum wage case until the 1920s. By then, the political composition of the Court had become more conservative. Constitutional law scholar Clement E. Vose noted that the first four Supreme Court appointments of President Warren Harding included "two ardent conservatives of the old school—Sutherland and Butler—to serve along with two justices similarly committed who were already sitting—Van Devanter and McReynolds." By 1922 then, the bloc of four economic conservatives the media eventually dubbed the "Four Horsemen," in reference to the Four Horsemen of the Apocalypse, was in place, and they soon made their presence felt.

In *Adkins v. Children's Hospital* (1923), the Four Horsemen, joined by Justice Joseph McKenna, struck down minimum wage laws. The *Adkins* case began when Congress passed an act in 1918 to establish minimum wage pay rates for women and children in Washington, DC. The rates were to be at levels sufficient "to supply them [women and minors] with the necessary cost of living . . . to maintain them in good health and to protect their morals." In her 1919 study of the wages of industrial women, Emilie J. Hutchinson and other reformers worried that if women did not earn a subsistence wage, they might be tempted to engage in prostitution and other vices. The Minimum Wage Board created by the law ordered restaurants, hotels, and other establishments to pay women workers a set minimum wage. Children's Hospital refused to comply, asserting that the law violated the Due Process Clause of the Fifth Amendment, which, its lawyers argued, encompassed the liberty to enter into salary contracts with employees. The Fifth Amendment's Due Process Clause was used to challenge the wage order because the District of Columbia is under the jurisdiction of Congress.

By a vote of 5 to 3 (Brandeis did not participate in the case), the Court ruled in favor of Children's Hospital. Writing for the Court in *Adkins*, Justice Sutherland "conceded" that workers have an "ethical right . . . to a living wage," but he found the law problematic because it ignored "the moral requirement implicit in every contract of employment . . . that the amount to be paid and the service to be rendered shall bear to each other some relation of just equivalence." Here, Sutherland argued, the statute is simply and exclusively a price-fixing law. He identified several flaws: "The problem is that this act makes the employer pay an arbitrary amount determined by the board as to what living wages would be without consideration of concerns related to the job." "Indeed, the amount set aside has nothing to do with the services rendered and is completely related to circumstances apart from the employment. But a law that prescribes payment without regard to any of these things," Justice Sutherland warned, "is a naked, arbitrary exercise of power that cannot be allowed to stand."

Sutherland admitted that the liberty to do as one pleases is not absolute. It must sometimes yield to the common good. However, he emphasized there are limits to the power, and when the limits have been passed the courts have the duty to declare it so. Sutherland wrote: "Restraint on the right to contract is the exception and not the rule." He concluded that the "act here exceeds the limits allowed in the Constitution."

Justice Oliver Wendell Holmes dissented: "The power of Congress seems absolutely free from doubt." The end it seeks here is without question, and the means of achieving that end are legitimate. Due Process has become dogma for the right to liberty. The interference here, he argued, was no different than the interference we have upheld in other cases. Holmes questioned the constitutional basis of the liberty of contract doctrine. Noting that "pretty much all law consists in forbidding men to do some things that they want to do," Holmes pointed out that the Court had sustained many laws that limited contractual freedom. He argued that legislators might reasonably conclude that fixing minimum wages for female employees would improve their health and morals.

In the aftermath of the *Adkins* decision, the Manufacturers' and Merchants' Association of Oregon urged its members to voluntarily observe the minimum wage rates set by the Industrial Welfare Commission for the next seven years. It is unclear how many business owners complied with the recommendation. Ultimately, the Court would overturn the *Adkins* precedent in 1937, but the failure to generate a majority in 1917 placed state minimum wage laws on hold for twenty years.

Many women's organizations swiftly denounced the *Adkins* decision.

According to *Time* magazine, a "chorus of protest went up from women leaders" representing the National Women's Trade Union League, the National Congress of Mothers, the National League of Women Voters, the Woman's Christian Temperance Union, and the Women's Bureau in the Department of Labor. The decision was described as "the destruction at one blow of 20 years' work for the improvement of women." Another activist called the opinion "a calamity to the women workers of the country" and "slavery for women who earn their own living." Molly Dewson was so frustrated with the Court's decision that she viewed the cause of minimum wage laws as hopeless—and she resigned. She became president of the New York Consumers' League and advocated for a forty-eight-hour workweek for women and children.

The National Woman's Party was nearly alone in applauding the *Adkins* decision. The organization defended its position by stating: "An employer who has to choose between a woman with restricted legal limit in the hours she works and the wages she gets, and a man with no corresponding limitation, will naturally choose the man." The NWP opposed all sex discrimination in labor. Mrs. Alice Paul, vice president of the National Woman's Party, explained: "We do not disapprove of minimum wage legislation. We do disapprove of its being put on a sex basis." This goal, however, would not be realized for another forty years, when Congress passed the Equal Pay Act of 1963, which amended the FLSA to protect against wage discrimination in employment, and enacted Title VII of the Civil Rights Act of 1964, which prohibits sex discrimination in employment.

The *Adkins* decision was a striking expression of laissezfaire constitutionalism. The opinion demonstrated the Court's conviction that wage and price determinations were at the heart of the freemarket economy and must be secured against unwarranted legislative interference. During the 1920s and early 1930s, the Supreme Court frequently cited *Adkins* for a broad interpretation of the liberty of contract doctrine. In particular, the justices invoked *Adkins* to overturn state minimum wage laws in Arizona and Arkansas, and, following the doctrinal lead of the Supreme Court, state supreme courts overturned state laws as well. Accordingly, no legislative or judicial progress was made on minimum wage laws between 1923 and 1933.

By 1923 the US economy had improved, and the nation entered into a period of "Coolidge prosperity" based on business expansion and reckless stock market speculation. Although the real wages of some workers improved during the decade, millions of Americans lived paycheck to paycheck. In *A Living Wage for the Common Man*, George E. Paulsen notes that about 76 percent of workers had no savings or property holdings. Farmers in particular struggled because of high debt loads and decreased commodity prices following World War I.

Toward a Federal Minimum Wage

The stock market crash in October 1929 and resulting Great Depression set the stage for the eventual demise of the liberty of contract doctrine and laissez-faire constitutionalism. As economic conditions worsened, public opinion shifted in favor of government playing a more active role in creating jobs, regulating labor conditions, and promoting economic growth. Child labor restrictions and minimum wage laws at both the state and federal levels ultimately triumphed, but not without first experiencing some bumps in the road.

In a campaign radio address from Albany, New York, on April 7, 1932, now known as the "Forgotten Man" speech, Governor Franklin D. Roosevelt compared the military and economic challenges of World War I to the crisis of the Great Depression. In mobilizing the nation for war in 1917, Roosevelt explained, the military, industrial, and cultural resources of the nation were organized from the ground up. He argued that a similar plan was needed to meet the emergency of the Depression by placing "faith once more in the forgotten man at the bottom of the economic pyramid."

Roosevelt's use of the "forgotten man" phrase surprised some listeners and alarmed many members of his party, including Alfred E. Smith, former Democratic governor of New York and FDR's rival for the Democratic nomination for president. Smith seized upon the speech, calling FDR a demagogue. Not only did Roosevelt seem to be advocating a type of class warfare by championing the working poor, but also, he turned the historical meaning of the expression on its head. Prior to that time, the invocation was associated with William Graham Sumner, a Yale sociology professor and Social Darwinist who believed in an economic survival of the fittest. In an 1883 address entitled "The Forgotten Man," Sumner argued that the hard-working common man should be liberated from the social welfare demands of the weak, undeserving poor. But by the early 1930s, the common man was struggling to find work and put food on the table. Roosevelt's rhetorical inversion expressed an economic populism that was the core of his New Deal agenda. Rather than "walking back" his comments, as some politicians might do today, he expanded on his ideas to help the forgotten man. Roosevelt adamantly believed that the key to economic recovery was to improve the wages and purchasing power of urban workers and farmers.

That message clearly resonated with many voters who for several years had been trying to survive. In November 1932, Franklin D. Roosevelt won the presidential election, and the Democratic Party secured huge majorities in Congress. In the depths of the Great Depression, public opinion had suddenly shifted in favor of government efforts to regulate the economy. When Roosevelt took office in 1933, his New Deal programs harnessed the power of the federal government to increase employment, stabilize financial markets, regulate various industries, and promote economic growth. During the first three years of the Roosevelt administration, Congress passed landmark legislation creating new federal regulatory agencies in all sectors of the economy and significantly expanding the welfare state. Complex and hastily crafted, many of these laws faced constitutional challenges and Supreme Court review.

The National Industrial Recovery Act, enacted in June 1933 as part of the first hundred days of Franklin D. Roosevelt's New Deal, required companies to write industry-wide codes of fair competition that fixed prices and wages, set production quotas, and gave employees the right to organize and bargain collectively. In the two years that the law was in force, 585 codes of fair competition contained minimum wages ranging from a low of 12.5 cents in the needle trades in Puerto Rico, to a high of seventy cents in the construction industry. More than 55 percent of the codes provided for a minimum wage of forty cents an hour or higher—a level that would not be achieved under the Fair Labor Standards Act until 1945. As previously discussed, these federal minimum wages under the codes were overturned when the Supreme Court declared the NIRA unconstitutional in *Schechter Poultry Corporation v. United States* (1935).

FDR's New Deal suffered several other defeats during the 1935 to 1936 Court term. On May 18, 1936, the Supreme Court announced another decision impacting Congress's power to regulate commerce. When the NIRA was voided in 1935, Congress passed the Bituminous Coal Conservation Act to establish a new code for the industry. The law stated that the coal industry was "affected with a public interest" feature that was used to justify governmental price fixing. The goals of the law included the promotion of interstate commerce in coal and provision of the general welfare. The statute created a commission empowered to develop regulations regarding fair competition, production, wages, hours, and labor relations. The act also levied a 15 percent tax on coal sold at the time. Ninety percent of that tax was refunded to producers who accepted the code.

Stockholders of the Carter Coal Company, including James W. Carter, sued the company to test the validity of the law. The stockholders did not want the company to agree to the code. Carter argued that coal mining was not in interstate commerce. The decision in *Carter v. Carter Coal Company* (1936) was closely divided, with Justice Owen Roberts joining the Four Horseman for a 5 to 4 majority, but the outcome was the same for Roosevelt's New Deal policies as the Court invalidated several provisions of the law and rebuffed arguments concerning congressional power. The Court rejected the assertion that Congress has an inherent power, apart from the Constitution, to deal with problems that affect the nation as a whole. It also rejected the contention that Congress can pass laws to promote the general welfare, independent of its delegated powers.

Probably the biggest blow concerned the scope of congressional power under the Commerce Clause. The majority opinion, written by Justice Sutherland, held that matters leading up to the mining of coal, such as employment, wages, hours, and working conditions, are part of production, not commerce, and are local in nature. Production, including mining, manufacturing, and farming, is a purely local activity and not part of commerce. Wages and hours, it was argued, do not have a direct effect on interstate commerce. Justice Sutherland extended the *Schechter* precedent to cases where interstate commerce had not yet begun.

In what was to be the last defeat for the minimum wage, the Supreme Court struck down New York's wage law in *Morehead v. New York Ex Rel.*

Tipaldo (1936). Labor advocates saw an opening in Justice Sutherland's reasoning in the *Adkins* case. The National Consumers' League developed a new model bill that abandoned the health and morals standard as a measure for minimum wages and replaced it with a "fair value of the services rendered" standard. New York enacted a law in March 1933 based on the new standard. About a month after his inauguration, Roosevelt endorsed the new model minimum wage bill, and he asked the governors in thirteen industrial states to pass legislation similar to New York's law "for the protection of the public interest." The states included Pennsylvania, Illinois, Indiana, Ohio, Maryland, Alabama, and North Carolina. Roosevelt described the new minimum wage law as a "great forward step against the lowering of wages."

The National Consumers' League sent President Roosevelt a telegram expressing appreciation for his support of the minimum wage. FDR's appeal to the governors, the organization noted, "marks a new era in recognition of basic economic and social necessity for eliminating dangerous competition in lowering wages." However, Roosevelt also received a protest telegram from the National Woman's Party criticizing his appeal to the governors. The NWP urged the thirteen governors to "do nothing" on the minimum wage. The organization claimed that Roosevelt's recommendation was the first time that a president ever endorsed unequal laws for men and women. Consistent with its reaction to the *Adkins* decision, the NWP stood for equal pay for equal work, and its members opposed protective legislation for women.

The New York law prohibited any employer to employ any woman at an oppressive or unreasonable wage, which was defined by two elements: a wage that is "both less than the fair and reasonable value of the services rendered and less than sufficient to meet the minimum cost of living necessary for health." Joseph Tipaldo managed a Brooklyn laundry. He paid nine employees at his laundry $10 a week. When New York State's new minimum wage law increased this to $14.88, Tipaldo forced his workers to kick back the difference. He was jailed on forgery and conspiracy charges. Tipaldo challenged the law on due process grounds. The National Woman's Party supported Tipaldo's claim in an amicus curiae brief. New York appellate courts ruled that the law violated due process under the state and US Constitution.

Justice Pierce Butler wrote the majority opinion in *Morehead v. New*

York. The "Four Horsemen" in the majority were joined by Justice Owen Roberts. Butler argued that unless the *Adkins* precedent could be distinguished, the lower court decision must be affirmed. He saw no difference, however, between the congressional act overturned in *Adkins* and the New York law. Butler boldly declared that the *Adkins* decision and the reasoning upon which it was based "clearly show that the state is without power by any form of legislation to prohibit, change or nullify contracts between employers and adult women workers as to the amount of wages to be paid." The Supreme Court decision in *Morehead* had effectively slammed the door shut on any minimum wage laws.

Chief Justice Hughes and Stone, Brandeis, and Cardozo dissented. In response to Butler's assertion that a state was powerless to enact minimum wage legislation—even in the depths of the Great Depression—one of the dissenters, Justice Stone, who would author the *Darby Lumber* decision five years later, accused the majority of acting on the basis of their "personal economic predilections" and suggested that "there is grim irony in speaking of the freedom of contract of those who, because of their economic necessities, give their services for less than is needful to keep body and soul together." Justice Stone had a valid point. The majority opinion was not well received by the public, media, and many in the legal community. All but ten of the 344 newspaper editorials written in response to the *Morehead* decision attacked the majority opinion. Even the Republican Party platform of 1936, in addition to the Democratic Party, repudiated the decision, as would the Supreme Court in the following term.

In the national elections of 1936, Roosevelt was reelected in a landslide victory over his Republican opponent, Kansas governor Alf Landon, capturing 98 percent of the electoral votes (523 to 8). Democrats also won huge majorities in Congress, controlling about 80 percent of the seats in both the House and Senate. The election results were a clear endorsement of Roosevelt's New Deal policies.

At a press conference in late December, a reporter asked the president about a meeting with Sidney Hillman, president of the Amalgamated Clothing Workers of America. Hillman was one of organized labor's leading statesmen who fought for improved wages and elimination of the sweating system. The president responded that they discussed a lot of issues, including the "breakdown" of the maximum hour, minimum wage, and child labor provisions of the NIRA. He recalled an incident in Bedford, Massachusetts, during the reelection campaign. Thousands of people were jam-packed around his automobile. A young girl tried to make her way through the crowd to pass the president a note. When a police officer pushed her back, Roosevelt told an aide to retrieve the note.

The note pleaded with the president to do something to "help us girls" who were working in a garment factory. They had been making $11 a week, but their wages had been "cut down to $4 and $5 and $6 a week. You are the only man who can do something about it." The president said that there were many such examples during the campaign, and people believed that he had the power to restore things like minimum wages and eliminate child labor. Roosevelt admitted to the reporters that he did not have the power to enact those policies himself, but he believed "something has to be done about the elimination of child labor and long hours and starvation wages." One of his priorities during a second term would be a general wages and hours bill to replace the NIRA. But there was a major stumbling block—the Supreme Court.

Emboldened by his electoral majority and frustrated with Supreme Court decisions invalidating his New Deal programs, FDR announced his plan to reorganize the federal judiciary on February 5, 1937. Publicly, the president characterized the plan as administrative relief for an overworked and understaffed judiciary. The plan featured proposals to increase the number of lower federal court positions, streamline federal jurisdiction, and make it more flexible to move judges to jurisdictions with backlogs. To many observers, even within his own party, these reforms were a smokescreen for proposals impacting the Supreme Court. The president asked Congress to authorize the creation of one new seat on the Supreme Court for every justice who had attained the age of seventy but did not retire. The maximum number of these new positions would be six, bringing the potential size of the Court to fifteen. At the time of the proposal, six sitting justices were over seventy years old. If the plan was enacted, Roosevelt could appoint six New Deal justices, who would certainly pick up the support of two of the current liberal justices for a pro–New Deal majority. Critics dubbed the proposal the "Court-packing" plan. The plan never had the support of a majority in

Congress or in public opinion, but subsequent events made the proposal unnecessary.

The Constitutional Revolution of 1937

In 1937 the Supreme Court abandoned laissezfaire constitutionalism and permitted both federal and state governments to play a major role in directing economic life. The Court's new outlook was revealed in *West Coast Hotel Co. v. Parrish* (1937), in which the justices narrowly upheld a Washington minimum wage law for women and minors and overruled the *Adkins* precedent. The decision in *West Coast Hotel* marked the effective end of the liberty of contract doctrine as a constitutional norm. In what is widely known as the Constitutional Revolution of 1937, Justice Roberts switched to the liberal bloc, and with the support of Chief Justice Hughes, the Supreme Court in *West Coast Hotel Co. v. Parrish* and *National Labor Relations Board v. Jones and Laughlin Steel Corporation* abruptly shifted its view of economic regulation. *West Coast Hotel* dealt a major blow to substantive due process. In rejecting the freedom of contract challenge to a Washington State minimum wage law, Chief Justice Hughes stressed that the Constitution neither mentions liberty of contract nor recognizes "an absolute and uncontrollable liberty."

On the same day as the *West Coast Hotel* decision, known among liberals as White Monday, the high Court upheld three acts of Congress that expanded federal power, including the revised Frazier-Lemke Act. Writing for the Court in *Wright v. Vinton Branch of Mountain Trust Bank of Roanoke* (1937), Justice Brandeis sustained the new federal farm bankruptcy law because it limited state mortgage moratoriums to three years and gave secured creditors the opportunity to force a public sale, although the farmer could redeem the sale by paying the same amount.

Two weeks later, on April 12, the Court handed the Roosevelt administration a landmark victory in five consolidated cases involving the National Labor Relations Act. In *National Labor Relations Board v. Jones and Laughlin Steel Corporation*, Chief Justice Hughes argued, "Although activities may be intrastate in character when separately considered, if they have such a close and substantial relation to interstate commerce that their control is essential and appropriate to protect that commerce from burdens and obstructions, Congress cannot be denied the power to exercise that control." A month later, the Court sustained the Social Security Act in *Helvering v. Davis* (1937). In upholding Washington State's minimum wage, the National Labor Relations Act, the Social Security Act, and other New Deal programs in a span of a few months, the Court applied a new deferential stance to government regulation of economic activity. States now had significant authority to regulate intrastate commerce using their police powers, and Congress had broad powers under the Commerce Clause to regulate the market and enact social welfare programs, including fair labor standards.

The "Switch in Time That Saved Nine"

Why did Justice Roberts switch his votes in 1937 to affirm state and federal regulation of the market? The question has generated volumes of scholarly research and debate. A traditional interpretation, articulated by many observers in the 1930s and some historians thereafter, assumes that Roosevelt's plan to "pack" the Supreme Court with justices more receptive to the constitutionality of New Deal initiatives was the catalyst for Roberts's reversal. Traditionalists stress other external factors as well, such as public protests for economic relief and the Democrats' landslide victory in the 1936 elections.

Other constitutional scholars note that Roberts had voted in conference in December 1936 to sustain wage regulation in *West Coast Hotel*, over two months before the Court-packing plan was made public. Roosevelt administration officials also suspected that electoral politics played a role. But Roberts may have changed his mind even before the election. On October 10, 1936, weeks before the fall elections, the Court granted review of the *West Coast Hotel* case. Roberts joined the three liberals and Chief Justice Hughes in voting to consider the case. Eighteen years later, Roberts attributed his switch to a legal technicality in the *Morehead v. Tipaldo* minimum wage case, but few scholars find this explanation convincing. The truth is that we may never know for certain. Justice Roberts burned his personal and judicial papers because, as a friend explained, "he did not want them subject to interpretation which he would not approve or correct."

Regardless of the motivations for Justice Roberts's switch, the decision in *West Coast Hotel* had immediate consequences for minimum wage laws. Four states—Arizona, Nevada, Oklahoma, and Pennsylvania—passed new minimum wage laws, and Massachusetts and New York reenacted their moribund statutes. Colorado, Connecticut, Minnesota, and Wisconsin amended their laws and made them effective. Other states passed legislative mandates on wages in the years preceding the *Darby Lumber* decision.

In addition to the seismic shift in constitutional philosophy on state and federal regulation of wages and working conditions in 1937, several laws enacted in the years prior to congressional debate over the Fair Labor Standards Act required a minimum wage for federal contractors and public works projects. For example, the Davis-Bacon Act, as amended in 1935, contained a provision that all contracts for public works must include a clause for wages at rates the secretary of labor found prevailing. The US Housing Act of 1937 also included a section that all contracts "shall contain a provision requiring that the wages or fees prevailing in the locality, as determined, or adopted . . . by the Authority, shall be paid . . . / to all laborers and mechanics employed in the development or administration of low-rent housing or slum-clearance project involved."

Probably the most important precursor to the FLSA was the Walsh-Healey Act of 1936. The law applied to all large federal contracts for the purchase of commodities. As previously discussed, the law provided for an eight-hour day and forty-hour workweek, but it also delegated authority to the secretary of labor to fix wage rates at the prevailing minimum wages for persons employed in similar work in a locality. Exercising that authority, the secretary fixed a minimum rate of 32.5 cents an hour for the manufacture of men's underwear in certain areas of the South and 67.5 cents an hour in the men's hat industry. The rates exceeded the starting minimum rate of 25 cents an hour provided in the FLSA two years later. These examples illustrate that in the five years before passage of the Fair Labor Standards Act, minimum wage provisions were embodied in several federal laws.

As President Roosevelt started his second term in office, there was a burst of congressional and administrative activity in Washington, DC, on the problems of minimum wages, maximum hours, and child labor. Reformers, lawyers, and politicians immediately recognized the implications of the 1937 Supreme Court decisions. It was now possible that wages, hours, and oppressive child labor could be addressed without the Court-packing plan. All that was needed was for Congress to send the president a general wages and hours bill. Congress reacted, but it would spend the next thirteen months in a contentious debate over appropriate fair labor standards.

CHAPTER FOUR

"That Nice Unconstitutional Bill": Congress Passes the Fair Labor Standards Act

The most important advocate for fair labor standards during the New Deal period was Frances Perkins, the first woman to serve in a presidential cabinet. Perkins had years of experience advocating for workplace safety and fair labor standards. Early in her career she worked with Florence Kelley and the New York chapter of the Consumers' League. Former New York governor Al Smith appointed her to a vacant seat on the state Industrial Commission. She later served as an industrial commissioner of New York under Governor Franklin D. Roosevelt and in that capacity became the nation's leading expert on state labor issues.

In 1933 President Roosevelt asked Perkins to be his labor secretary. Perkins responded that she would accept only if she could advocate a wages and hours bill and to abolish abuses of child labor. According to a Department of Labor history, when Roosevelt enthusiastically agreed to the terms, Perkins asked him, "Have you considered that to launch such a program . . . might be considered unconstitutional?" The president retorted, "Well, we can work out something when the time comes." Two years later, as the National Recovery Act (NRA) codes were being challenged in the courts, and ultimately overturned in *Schechter Poultry*, Secretary Perkins asked lawyers at the Labor Department to draft both a wage-hour and child labor bill. When the legal staff completed the task, she informed Roosevelt that she had "something up [her] sleeve." She had two labor bills "locked in the lower left-hand of my desk against an emergency." The president responded, "You're pretty unconstitutional, aren't you?" The "emergency" was soon at the administration's doorstep.

One of the bills locked in Perkins's desk was dusted off and sent to Congress before the Constitutional Revolution of 1937. The bill was based on the purchasing power of the federal government. Jonathan Grossman, a former Labor Department historian, explained that under the bill, federal government contractors would have to pay the "prevailing wage" and meet other fair labor standards. The idea had its origins in World War I, when the Davis-Bacon Act required similar protections. Roosevelt and Perkins were appalled to learn that many federal contractors paid substandard wages for excessive hours because the government was required to award contracts to the lowest bidder. According to Grossman, in 1935 "approximately 40 percent of government contractors, employing 1.5 million workers, cut wages below and stretched hours above the standards developed under the National Recovery Act. After intense congressional debate and numerous amendments, the Roosevelt-Perkins proposal became the Walsh-Healey Public Contracts Act of 1936. Limited to government contractors, the Walsh-Healey Act did not replace the labor protections of the NRA, but it was viewed "as a token of good faith" that the administration was committed to a broader fair labor standards bill.

Following his unsuccessful attempt to pack the Supreme Court with justices supportive of his New Deal policies and after the "switch in time" in 1937 where the Court upheld state and federal regulation of wages, hours, and workplace conditions, President Roosevelt asked Frances Perkins what she had done with "that nice unconstitutional bill you had tucked away?" The bill that Perkins had locked away, which was the second bill in her desk, was a general fair labor standards act. Anticipating Supreme Court review, Labor Department lawyers based the bill on several constitutional principles, hoping that if one or two were rejected by the Court, the law would still stand. Perkins sent the bill to the president. White House lawyers Thomas G. Corcoran and Benjamin V. Cohen spent months revising the bill and adding more provisions. A late change at the urging of Grace Abbott, chief of the Children's Bureau, was a clause prohibiting goods produced with the labor of children under age sixteen in industries engaged in or affecting interstate commerce. "You are hoping that you have found a way around the Supreme Court," Abbott pleaded. "If you have, why not give the children the benefit by attaching a child labor clause to this bill?" Believing that a child labor provision would increase support for the legislation, Roosevelt readily agreed.

On May 24, 1937, the president sent the bill to Congress. In his remarks to legislators, he urged support for fair labor standards: "A self-supporting and self-respecting democracy can plead no justification for the existence of child labor, no economic reason for chiseling workers' wages or stretching workers' hours." He continued, "All but the hopelessly reactionary will agree that to conserve our primary resources of man power, Government must have some control over maximum hours, minimum wages, the evil of child labor, and the exploitation of unorganized labor." Multiple bills on labor conditions were introduced on the same day as the president's message to Congress.

Congress Debates a Wages and Hours Bill

The first bill under consideration was the administration plan, known as the Black-Connery bill, in honor of Senator Hugo Black of Alabama and Representative William Connery of Massachusetts, both of whom had worked tirelessly for years on wage and hour legislation. Black chaired the Senate Labor Committee, and Connery held a similar post in the House. Recall that Senator Black had been persuaded by the president to drop his plan for a thirty-hour workweek, which he had sponsored as early as 1932, in favor of the administration plan known as the National Industrial Recovery Act. When that legislation was struck down by the Supreme Court, the second-administration attempt to address labor issues eventually became the Fair Labor Standards Act (FLSA), popularly called the wages and hours bill. The road to the FLSA, however, was long and winding. Thirteen months and one day expired before the bill reached President Roosevelt's desk, and it was amended so many times during legislative negotiations that few features of the original bill remained intact.

A Joint Hearing of the Senate Committee on Education and Labor, chaired by Senator Black, and House Committee on Labor, chaired by Representative Connery, held hearings for over a month on the Black-Connery bill. When Congressman Connery died on June 15, leadership in the House on the bill passed to Representative Mary T. "Battling Mary" Norton of New Jersey, a reformer who fought for labor.

Like most southerners, Senator Black was inclined to support states' rights, but he came to believe that the country's economic problems could only be solved through national legislation. Black's biographer, Virginia Van Der Veer Hamilton, commented that Alabama's industrial leaders viewed Black's support for the wages and hours bill as "virtually treasonous." Lumber interests bitterly opposed the bill, although a few small mill owners from Alabama and Mississippi wrote to Senator Black complaining that "chiseling operators" who paid "starvation wages" could only be controlled by a federal minimum wage.

The original bill provided for the creation of a five-member regulatory agency called the Fair Labor Standards Board to enforce the provisions of the law. Although the bill did not specify a statutory minimum wage or maximum standard workweek, it was widely assumed by witnesses and others that the legislation would establish a minimum hourly rate of forty cents and a maximum standard workweek of forty hours. The board, after investigation and within limits, had the power to set wages higher. Fear over the scope of discretionary power wielded by the board became a major point of contention during congressional testimony.

The measure relied on the power of Congress to regulate commerce between the states. It banned the movement of goods produced under substandard labor conditions from entering interstate commerce. Firms producing for an intrastate market would fall under the provisions of the act if the "unfair" conditions of work in these establishments gave the owners a competitive advantage over those outside the state. This authority followed established precedent in the *Shreveport Rate* case, where the Supreme Court affirmed the power of Congress to regulate intrastate railroad rates if those rates negatively impact interstate commercial activity.

Flexibility was the hallmark of the bill. Unlike the NIRA, it did not regulate fair trade practices and marketing methods, nor did it specify work hours or a fixed minimum wage for all industries. Congress would give the proposed board the authority to fix minimum "fair" wages and a maximum "reasonable" workweek of not less than thirty and not more than forty hours. Child labor under the age of sixteen was prohibited, and the chief of the Children's Bureau was authorized to bar the labor of those under age eighteen in any occupation that was thought to be "particularly hazardous" or detrimental to their health or well-being.

Supporters and Opponents of the Bill

Assistant Attorney General Robert H. Jackson, who within a few years would serve as US attorney general, US solicitor general, associate justice of the US Supreme Court, and lead US prosecutor at the Nuremburg war crimes trials following World War II, testified on the constitutional foundations of the bill. Jackson stated that the proposed bill, except to the child labor case of *Hammer v. Dagenhart*, was "backed by long established precedents defining Federal power to regulate interstate commerce." He cited the *Shreveport Rate* cases, *National Labor Relations Board v. Jones and Laughlin Steel Corporation*, and *Kentucky Whip and Collar Co. v. Illinois Central Railroad Co.* (1937) as supporting a broad authority of Congress to regulate unfair competition within a state, competition in interstate commerce, the movement of goods across state lines in violation of national policy, products moved in interstate commerce in violation of state laws, and labor conditions that lead to conflicts that obstruct or burden interstate commerce.

The only exception was the child labor decision in *Hammer v. Dagenhart*, which, Jackson noted, affected only a portion of the bill. The assistant attorney general asserted that "the doctrine of the majority in the *Child Labor case* belongs to the same dark era of legal thought as the decision holding that the minimum-wage law was unconstitutional [referring to *Adkins v. Children's Hospital*, 1923].... We should give the courts a chance to remove this blemish from our judicial history." Aware of the Supreme Court's abrupt change in doctrine since 1937, Jackson concluded: "We may reasonably entertain the hope that *Hammer v. Dagenhart* will be laid to a tardy and unmourned repose beside the lifeless remains of *Adkins v. Children's Hospital.*"

Industry leaders were divided on the bill. The northern textile industry favored the legislation and opposed regional differentials in wage scales. Northern mill owners preferred a national scale as a means of protecting themselves against competition from southern mills with lower wages. Liberal-minded employers also spoke in favor of the bill. Robert Johnson, president of Johnson and Johnson, urged that the bill be approved out of self-interest and social awareness. He acknowledged that business succeeds when workers have adequate wages to purchase products, and that to enact the bill would be "a great thing for business and a great thing for millions of American employees." Jay C. Hormel, owner of the Hormel meat-packing company, also backed adequate wage and hour legislation. He believed that stable worker income and employment were good for his business. Another business leader, R. C. Kuldell, head of the Hughes Tool Company in Texas, an oil-well machinery and equipment firm with four thousand employees, told the Joint Committee that he was "fully in accord" with the purposes of the bill. Kuldell remarked, "If the Labor Standards Board administered the law as a doctor and not a policeman, it can be assured of the whole-hearted cooperation of industrial employers."

Powerful business groups, however, appeared before the Joint Committee against the bill. The US Chamber of Commerce, the National Association of Manufacturers, the National Publishers Association, the National Association of Wood Manufacturers, and most southern manufacturers opposed the bill, either in principle or because they demanded regional differentials in wages. George H. Davis, president of the Chamber of Commerce of the United States, worried about uncertainty in future labor costs if the bill passed. James A. Emery, general counsel of the National Association of Manufacturers and veteran of the campaign against the Child Labor Amendment, argued that "the bill used an unconstitutional view of the commerce power, and was also an invalid delegation of power." Southern mill owners and manufacturers demanded lower wage scales for the South because compared to the North, the cost of living was alleged to be lower in the South, employees were less skilled, and freight costs were higher. Other business leaders assailed the legislation as "a bad bill badly drawn" that would take the country down a path to "tyrannical industrial dictatorship." Industry representatives pointedly asked how could business "find any time left to provide jobs if we are to persist in loading upon it these everlastingly multiplying governmental mandates and delivering it to the mercies of multiplying and hampering Federal bureaucracy?"

Secretary Perkins testified on June 24, 1937. She described the wage and hour bill as a measure that would stabilize employment, income, and the market for goods. She said the bill would "limit economic fluctuations both ways, thus providing security to industry ... investors ... labor ... and the consumer public." Because she was commenting on an early version of the legislation, she spent a significant portion of her testimony on the proposed Labor Standards Board. She acknowledged that there had been considerable disagreement over the wage provisions of the bill. Given different conditions in industry, the secretary admitted that she wasn't convinced of the "wisdom of inserting a specific figure [minimum wage] in the bill at present. She preferred to leave that decision to the board under guidelines from Congress. Finally, she asserted that it was important to pass legislation to replace the overturned NIRA.

Organized labor supported the bill but disagreed over wage provisions and the authority of the board. William Green of the American Federation of Labor (AFL) and John L. Lewis of the Congress of Industrial Organizations (CIO) differed on various aspects of the bill. Lewis favored a thirty-five-hour workweek but suggested that the board should have the power to raise the number to forty hours or lower it to thirty hours. He strongly opposed giving the board discretionary power to raise wages above forty cents an hour, and he urged the abolition of Section 5. His rationale for this position seemed to be a fear that minimum "fair" wages and maximum "reasonable" hours would actually become the maximum wage and minimum hours. Moreover, employers would have a powerful propaganda tool if unions decided to strike against the "fair" wages and "maximum" hours set by the board.

William Green of the AFL wanted no overlapping between collective bargaining and government control over wages and hours. He even opposed letting the board raise standards reached by collective bargaining. Green favored a forty-hour workweek but would allow the board flexibility to lower it to thirty hours. Unlike Lewis, he backed giving the board discretion to increase wages up to eighty cents an hour. But both Lewis and Green "favored legislation which would limit labor standards to low-paid and essentially unorganized workers." They did not want the board undermining union power by interfering in areas they wanted reserved for labor-management negotiations. When the bill was later amended to exclude work covered by collective bargaining, the two labor leaders were satisfied.

Sidney Hillman, president of the Amalgamated Clothing Workers of America and one of the earliest proponents of fair labor standards, and David Dubinsky of the International Ladies' Garment Workers' Union, supported a strong bill that would give the proposed board the discretion to set up "fair" wages and "reasonable" hours higher than the basic standards set by Congress. Hillman explained that unlike John L. Lewis's CIO and the United Mine Workers of America, which collectively bargain on a national scale, collective bargaining cannot effectively cover industries such as textiles, garments, and shoes, and the only way to raise standards uniformly is to have them established by government.

Courtenay Dinwiddie, general secretary of the National Child Labor Committee, drew on thirty-three years of organizational experience in commenting on the child labor provisions of the bill. His organization "vigorously" supported a new federal law restricting child labor, but he also warned that such a law would not entirely solve the problem. Child labor in interstate commerce encompassed only about 25 percent of the children employed, excluding agriculture. That left 75 percent of working children outside federal regulation. "The only permanent solution for this large area of exploitation," Dinwiddie argued, "is through the Federal child-labor amendment," which would give Congress the power to deal with child labor in the service trades, such as hotels, restaurants, and laundries, which are local in nature.

Mr. Dinwiddie noted that unlike the maximum hours and minimum wage provisions of the Black-Connery bill, the child labor regulations could easily be implemented with the Children's Bureau working with state agencies. All that would be needed were uniform national standards. Dinwiddie criticized several sections of the bill that applied the method of prohibiting prison-made goods to the interstate transportation of child-made goods. As he had argued previously, applying the prison-made theory to child-made goods would not work. It would be an administrative nightmare. Also, Dinwiddie recommended that the legislation abolish industrial home work, "one of the most vicious and persistent practices for sweating labor ever devised." Finally, he urged that the law cover smaller and more scattered manufacturing establishments, such as "fly-by-night tie and shirt factories, so-called 'wild' shrimp and oyster canneries, 'grasshopper' sawmills, and small box and crate factories," that use destructive child labor practices.

Mrs. Larue Brown, representing the National League of Women Voters, an organization that had fought for effective child labor legislation since its formation in 1921, echoed many of the arguments made by Courtenay Dinwiddie on the child labor provisions. While supporting the age restrictions for various industries in the bill, she "strenuously objected" to adopting the prison-goods theory of regulation, pointing out that the only way the model could be effective was if every state passed identical laws and enforced them uniformly, which was virtually impossible to accomplish. Brown favored a law based on the "simple and direct" congressional power to regulate interstate commerce, and she insisted that the Children's Bureau be responsible for administering the child labor provisions in cooperation with state agencies.

Also testifying in June 1937 was John P. Davis, representing the National Negro Congress, a federation of some six hundred organizations. While Davis fully endorsed the principle of minimum wages and shorter hours, he objected to certain sections of the bill that he believed failed to guarantee that Black workers would benefit from the legislation. Davis noted that Black workers were the lowest-paid and least-organized workers in America. His experience with the industry codes under the National Recovery Act, which catered to representatives of southern industry and allowed numerous wage differentials and exemptions that hurt Black workers, informed his criticism of the proposed legislation. He argued that the Labor Standards Board created by the bill would have the power to fix minimum wages by occupations rather than industries based on the cost of living or services rendered. These standards opened the "floodgates" of discrimination comparable to the NRA days, when employers claimed that it cost Black workers less to live and that they were less efficient. Davis saw nothing in the proposed wages and hours bill that would "prevent the same type of ruthless exploitation of Negro workers" that was prevalent under the NRA codes.

When the hearings concluded, the Senate Education and Labor Committee made substantial changes to the bill that weakened the power of the proposed board and narrowed the child labor provisions. The board would not be permitted to fix wages above forty cents an hour or mandate a standard working week of less than forty hours. Agricultural exemptions were broadened to include farming, dairying, forestry, fishing, horticulture, and local retailing. The child labor provisions excluded children in agriculture and those employed by their parents. Children under age sixteen were permitted to work in jobs that would not injure their "health and well-being" nor interfere with their education as determined by the chief of the Children's Bureau. The proposed prison-goods theory of regulation was rejected. Finally, to calm the fears of some business leaders that higher wages and lower hours would lead to competition from cheap foreign imports, a provision was added that gave the Tariff Commission investigatory power to see if higher tariff rates were needed. The revised bill was unanimously reported to the Senate on July 8, 1937.

The Senate Votes

The bill arrived on the Senate floor on July 26. Senator Black's southern colleagues denounced the bill, resurrecting sectional arguments that northerners wanted to "crucify" southern industry in order to stifle competition and prevent the South from rising from the devastation of the Civil War. Senator Ellison Smith of South Carolina declared that the spirit behind the bill was nothing more than a "vote-getting proposition," and he "bitterly condemned it as hostile to the South." Many Republicans opposed the bill, as did some Democrats from outside the South. Known for his hyperbole, Republican senator Arthur Vandenberg of Michigan called the wages and hours bill "the essence of Fascism." Senator William H. King, a Utah Democrat, refused to back the bill. "Wages and hours," he asserted, "are a matter for the states to decide."

According to his biographer, Senator Black replied with one of the most dramatic performances of his Senate tenure. "We must face two tribunals with this law," Black said. "The first is Congress. The second is the Supreme Court." He first dealt with Congress. Waving mill vouchers that showed pay scales at eight cents an hour, Black angrily chastised his colleagues. "I subscribe to the gospel that a man who is born in Alabama and who can do as much work as a man born in any state in New England is entitled to the same pay if he does the same work." Black was prepared to address the constitutional issues surrounding the FLSA as well. He had served five years on the Senate Judiciary Committee, honing his knowledge of constitutional law, and he had spent most of six months in the Supreme Court library studying precedents and doctrine relevant to the law. With an eye to the Supreme Court, Black praised the minority opinion in the *Dagenhart* case for being more faithful to the "plain intent and purpose of the Commerce Clause" and for being "more consonant ...

with progress than the majority opinion." He embraced a living Constitution approach. The Constitution, he said, "has been interpreted from time to time to meet new situations and conditions that could not have been foreseen by the writers of that great document. . . . If change is needed to cure evils growing out of old practices, change must come."

After five days of debate, the bill passed the Senate on July 31, 1937, by a vote of 52 to 48. Despite their strong testimony against the prison-goods theory of regulation, child labor advocates were deeply disappointed to learn that the only major change on the floor of the Senate was the substitution of the Wheeler-Johnson child labor amendment, which was based on the prison-goods formula, in place of all of the child labor provisions in the original Senate Committee bill. Under the prison-goods formula, a state would be empowered to prohibit products made by children from entering a state. Child labor reformers strongly opposed this idea because it created no national standards, relied on the states for implementation, and was difficult to enforce.

As the legislative wrangling continued that summer, seventy-eight-year-old Associate Justice Willis Van Devanter (one of the Four Horsemen) announced his retirement from the Court on June 2. President Roosevelt nominated Senator Hugo Black to take his seat, although he failed to carefully vet the nominee's political background. While Senator Black guided the Black-Connery bill through the Senate, his past Ku Klux Klan affiliation embroiled the nomination in controversy. Hugo Black was eventually confirmed in mid-August by a Senate vote of 63 to 16, and he took his seat on October 4. With Black's task in the Senate on the FLSA practically finished, the Roosevelt administration gained a potential New Deal ally on the Court.

Meanwhile, the debate on the wages and hours bill shifted to the House of Representatives. On August 6, 1937, the House Committee on Labor issued a favorable report on the Senate bill, with amendments. Among the changes, the AFL received protections for collective bargaining agreements by denying the board jurisdiction over wages and hours in areas where collective bargaining procedures were adequate. The House bill also eliminated the Wheeler-Johnson child labor amendment and restored the provisions in the Senate Committee bill. All subsequent attempts to reinsert the Wheeler-Johnson amendment during House debate were unsuccessful. With labor now strongly in favor of the legislation, it appeared that the amended House bill had enough votes to secure passage if it could be brought to the floor. A coalition of four Republicans and five southern conservative Democrats on the House Rules Committee, however, refused to permit the bill to be brought to the floor and even denied Chairwoman Norton's request to testify. Congress adjourned without a House vote on fair labor standards. *Time* magazine wrote that the wages and hours bill "lay as dead as a roast chicken."

President Roosevelt Calls a Special Session

In an October 12 radio address, President Roosevelt issued a call for a special session of Congress to convene on November 15, 1937, with wages and hours legislation as one of the top items on the agenda. Recently returned from a tour of western states, the president believed that he had the support of the American people. In an address to Congress in early November, Roosevelt identified a legislative agenda for the session. In addition to a farm bill to stabilize crop prices and executive reorganization, labor issues were a priority. The president said: "I believe that the country as a whole recognizes the need for immediate congressional action if we are to maintain wage income and the purchasing power of the nation against recessive factors in the general industrial situation. The exploitation of child labor and the undercutting of wages and the stretching of the hours of the poorest paid workers in periods of business recession have a serious effect on buying power." Roosevelt urged legislation relating to goods moving in or competing with interstate commerce for two purposes: banning child labor and ending the practice of some communities that seek new industry by maintaining low wages and excessively long hours.

When the special session convened, however, members of the Rules Committee had not changed their position, and they refused to issue a rule permitting House consideration of the bill. On the second day of the session, Mary Norton, chair of the House Committee, started a petition to discharge the Rules Committee from further consideration and allowing the bill to come before the floor. Although it took a lot of negotiation, which opponents claimed involved political favors in exchange for signatures, Norton secured the 218 signatures necessary for a petition on December 2. As Democrats cheered and whistled, Representative Joseph Mansfield, a seventy-six-year-old wheelchair-bound Texas Democrat, provided the last signature. It appeared that the House would now have a chance to vote on the measure. But renewed opposition from William Green and the AFL complicated the legislative maneuvers. Labor leaders from the AFL opposed granting discretionary power to an administrative board, charging that the NLRB had favored industrial unionism and the CIO over craft unionism and the AFL. Resistance from organized labor delayed and threatened to defeat the wages and hours bill.

Administration opponents in Congress were also emboldened by President Roosevelt's loss of political capital following the defeat of the Court-packing plan. Influential senator Joe Robinson, majority leader and the administration's advocate for the court reorganization plan in the Senate, died on July 14, and the court plan followed him to the grave. The Senate voted to recommit the judicial reorganization bill on July 22, effectively defeating the legislation—at least the provisions regarding Supreme Court appointments. Moreover, by fall 1937, the economic recovery collapsed. Industrial production fell by 33 percent, national income dropped by 12 percent, and stock prices lost 50 percent of their value. Unemployment jumped from 14.3 percent in May 1937 to 19.0 percent in June 1938. The "Roosevelt recession" within the Depression that hit the country during the president's second term was largely due to the administration scaling back government spending and focusing on balancing the federal budget. The continuing labor problem made passage of the FLSA a priority.

In an attempt to mollify AFL opposition, the House Labor Committee offered a new bill that replaced the board with a single administrator within the Department of Labor appointed by the president. But the AFL's Green was not satisfied. He wrote to House members that "if a Board is dangerous . . . certainly the Administrator is even more dangerous and should be rejected." Congressmen John Dockweiler and Glenn Griswold then offered an AFL substitute bill. The bill provided for a strict forty cents an hour and forty hours a week standard for workers in nonunionized plants with no regional or industrial differentials and enforcement by the US attorney general. The bill was defeated 162 to 131. On December 13 the House, by a vote of 258 to 113, discharged the Rules

Committee from further consideration, and it appeared the bill had enough support. President Green of the AFL, however, now aggressively lobbied against the bill, and more than sixty amendments were offered over the next five days. Finally, shortly before the Christmas recess, the House unexpectedly voted 218 to 198 to send the bill back to the Labor Committee. When the final tally was announced by Speaker William Bankhead, a fervent cry of "Thank God" erupted from the Democratic side before a burst of applause and shouting filled the House chamber.

In her memoir, Frances Perkins wrote: "This was the first time that a major administration bill had been defeated on the floor of the House." According to Perkins, the press characterized the vote as the "death knell of wage-hour legislation as well as a decisive blow to the President's prestige." President Roosevelt, however, was undeterred. In his State of the Nation address on January 3, the president reiterated his call for wages and hours legislation. "We are seeking only, of course, to end starvation wages and intolerable hours. More desirable wages are, and should continue to be, the product of collective bargaining." The following day, the *New York Times* published editorial excerpts from twenty-five major newspapers throughout the country. Many of the editorials noted that the president's remarks were more conciliatory and reasonable toward business, but a majority of them were critical of New Deal policies in light of the economic downturn.

FDR may have had a better grasp of the pulse of the average citizen than many of his critics. Several events improved the prospects for passage of fair labor standards during the regular session. The day after the president's address to Congress, Representative Lister Hill, an ardent Roosevelt supporter, won an Alabama election primary for Senator Black's vacated seat by an almost 2 to 1 margin over J. Thomas Heflin, an aging anti–New Deal former senator. Heflin was backed by the so-called Big Mules of Alabama business and agriculture that strongly opposed the Black-Connery bill. Hill's decisive victory was significant because much of the opposition to the wages and hours bill came from southern members of Congress. In February 1938, a national poll conducted by George Gallup's Institute of Public Opinion reported that 67 percent of the population favored the wages and hours bill, with even the South showing a substantial plurality of support for higher standards.

President Roosevelt privately told Secretary Perkins that he thought the wages and hours bill encountered so much opposition because of its length and complexity. Although miniscule compared to modern legislation, the president asked if the forty-page bill could be "boiled down to two pages." Perkins reminded him that the bill had been written more with an eye toward Supreme Court review than for the average layman. The Labor Department solicitor, Gerard Reilly, attempted but failed to meet the president's two-page goal, but he did cut the bill down to ten pages. Reilly and Perkins brought the revised bill to Roosevelt in late January. He accepted the revisions, and the bill was submitted to Congress.

The president and Perkins geared up for the legislative battle that was sure to come. Roosevelt arm-twisted Democratic members of Congress who had ridden his coattails to victory in 1936 but who then fought New Deal legislation. Secretary Perkins hired a young lawyer, Rufus Poole, a former assistant solicitor in the Interior Department, who was assigned to do nothing else but track the daily progress of the bill, identify difficulties, and forestall objections. Perkins recalled that Poole became so good at this task that he "could predict with reasonable accuracy the vote for or against any amendment."

Representative Norton appointed a subcommittee of the House Labor Committee, with Representative Robert Ramspeck as chair, to bridge the gap between various proposals and amendments. The subcommittee produced the Ramspeck compromise, which made some modifications to the truncated bill that the president had approved. The compromise provided for a five-member wage board less powerful than under the original Black-Connery bill, but with authority to gradually impose the forty-cent minimum wage and forty-hour maximum workweek. Perkins believed that the compromise "contained the bare essentials the administration could support."

In a case of politics creating strange bedfellows, both the American Federation of Labor and the National Association of Manufacturers opposed the Ramspeck compromise. The CIO favored the bill, but a canvass of the House indicated that there were not enough votes to carry the compromise. The House Labor Committee voted down the compromise 10 to 8, but Norton offered an alternative bill based on a proposal backed by the AFL. The bill provided for a "floor" of twenty-five cents an hour and a "ceiling" of forty-four hours per week, with the minimum wage to increase five cents a year until forty cents an hour was reached.

The maximum-hour workweek was to decrease two hours over two successive years until it reached forty hours. There were no regional or industry differentials. With this gradual scale, the idea of a wage board was eliminated and the secretary of labor was given investigatory and enforcement powers, including the authority to declare which industries operated in interstate commerce. The rationale behind the AFL-backed plan was to reduce or eliminate administrative discretion on wages and hours. This version contained the basic features of what would become the FLSA. The bill was reported favorably to the House on April 21.

As before, the Rules Committee refused to report a resolution allowing the House to consider the measure. President Roosevelt called Representative John J. O'Conner of New York, chair of the Rules Committee, an "obstructionist" who "pickled" New Deal programs. At that point, Roosevelt felt that a little pressure was needed. For the sixth time in his presidency, he communicated with Congress over the need for fair labor standards through a letter sent to Representative Norton. In his message, he did not comment on the specifics of the bill but emphasized the national importance of the legislation and urged the House to allow full consideration of the bill. The president hoped "that the democratic processes of legislation will continue." For this to happen, the House needed another discharge petition.

Several days after the president's message to Congress, a primary election shifted the landscape of debate over the bill. Senator Claude Pepper, who campaigned in Florida to retain his seat, won a resounding victory over Representative J. Mark Wilcox, an anti–New Dealer. Pepper was an ally of President Roosevelt and leader of the left-liberal coalition in the Senate, and he had campaigned in support of the New Deal and wages and hours bill. Wilcox had made New Deal programs his central issue and labeled his opponent "Roosevelt's rubber stamp." The more than 2-to-1 margin of victory sent a strong message to southern members of Congress regarding how their constituents felt about fair labor standards. On May 6 at noon, a petition to discharge the wages and hours bill from the Rules Committee was placed on the desk of the Speaker of the House. Unlike the special session, when it took several weeks to round up the necessary signatures, 218 members signed the petition in just two hours and twenty minutes, with more "waiting in the aisles" ready to sign. The bill then moved to the House floor for debate.

All but the most conservative members of the southern delegation abandoned their opposition. Labor standards in the South were the most divisive issue. Northern representatives shared "horror stories" of labor exploitation in the region. One Indiana congressman claimed that women in Georgia were working ten hours a day in canning factories for $4.50 a week, or the equivalent of nine cents an hour based on a five-day workweek. Southern congressmen accused their northern colleagues of "sentencing Southern industry to death," and they told the Labor Department that businesses could not survive with a twenty-five-cent minimum wage. Senator "Cotton Ed" Smith of South Carolina claimed that it "took only fifty cents a day to live reasonably and comfortably in his state." As a concession to these southern concerns, a requirement was added that wage administrators would consider lower costs of living and higher transportation costs in the region before recommending wages above the minimum. Exemptions were also made for the fishing industry and for some agricultural commodities. On May 24, 1938, the House passed the bill 314 to 97.

The Fair Labor Standards Act Becomes Law

Because there were significant differences between the Senate and House versions of the bill, a conference committee had to work out a compromise. A major point of contention, as it had been throughout the whole debate on the bill, was whether to provide regional differentials for minimum wages. Ultimately, southern members of Congress yielded on this point, and the conferees agreed on a national minimum wage of twenty-five cents an hour with increases to forty cents over a period of seven years. Concessions were also made to critics who claimed that immediately imposing a forty-hour workweek would be devastating to business. The conference agreed to set maximum hours at forty-four with a gradual reduction to forty hours over three years.

Labor leaders appeared satisfied with the compromise language. William Green sent a telegram commenting that although the conference report did not comply fully with the agenda of the AFL, he did not oppose its passage. John L. Lewis of the CIO was also on board. The House passed the conference committee report on June 13, 1938, by a vote of 291 to 89. The following day, the Senate approved the bill without a recorded vote. Congress then sent the Fair Labor Standards Act to the president.

In a "fireside chat" the night before he signed the law, FDR warned: "Do not let any calamity-howling executive with an income of $1,000 a day ... tell you ... that a wage of $11 a week is going to have a disastrous effect on all American industry." The president explained that the FL-SA's objective was the "elimination of labor conditions detrimental to the maintenance of the minimum standards of living necessary for health, efficiency, and well-being of workers." He described the law as "the most far-reaching, far-sighted program for the benefit of workers ever adopted in this or any other country." After more than a year of presidential speeches, three sessions of congressional debate, ten versions of the bill, and more than seventy proposed amendments, President Franklin D. Roosevelt signed the Fair Labor Standards Act on June 25, 1938. "That's that," he sighed as he put his signature to the bill. And it was that in more ways than one. Not only had the long fight over wage and hours legislation come to an end, but also the FLSA was the last piece of New Deal legislation passed during the Roosevelt presidency. On October 24, 1938, the minimum wage, maximum hours, and child labor provisions of the FLSA went into effect.

The Fair Labor Standards Act was historic legislation, but the original law had its limitations. Representative Herbert S. Bigelow (D-OH) was not far off when he described the FLSA as "merely the promise of a hope to come." It was estimated that the law initially applied to industries whose combined employment was one-fifth of the labor force, or roughly eleven million workers. The FLSA stipulated that all employers engaged in interstate commerce must pay their employees a minimum wage of twenty-five cents an hour and not permit them to work longer than forty hours per week without paying them time-and-a-half overtime pay. With exemptions for various business sectors, an estimated 750,000 workers benefited from the twenty-five-cent minimum wage provision, and the law reduced the hours of 1.5 million Americans who had been working more than the forty-four-hour weekly maximum. Employees of federal, state, and local government were not covered by the law.

The overtime provisions of Section 7, which require employers to pay time and a half for any work over the (ultimately) forty-hour week, were not originally viewed as a bonus to workers, but a "tax" on employers and a disincentive to have employees work excessive hours. For example, prior to the law, an employer might work a single employee sixty hours at regular pay. With overtime, that same employer must pay a premium wage rate for hours forty-one through sixty. To save on labor costs, an employer could have two workers employed for thirty hours. Consequently, the unemployment rate would decrease because more workers would be hired.

The twenty-five-cent federal minimum wage was certainly not a living wage. In 1938 the average annual subsistence cost of living was $1,250 for a family of four. At the initial forty-four-hour maximum, the twenty-five-cent minimum provided $11 per week, or $572 a year. The federal minimum was an improvement over no wage guarantee, but it was set so low that it was not sufficient to meet the needs of a one-wage-earner family. Because women occupied many of the lower paying positions, they were expected to disproportionately benefit from the FLSA provisions. Some female workers did see an improvement in their paychecks, but when enacted, the FLSA covered only 14 percent of working women, compared to 39 percent of adult male workers.

The child labor provisions of the FLSA received far less attention from the press and public than the wage and hour provisions, so it is worthwhile to examine them in detail. Like other provisions in the FLSA, the child labor sections had their limitations and exemptions. The law defined "oppressive child labor" as employment of a minor under the age of sixteen years, unless the employer was the child's parent or guardian. Even a parent or guardian, however, could not employ the child in manufacturing or mining operations. For children under age sixteen, employment in manufacturing and mining was banned in all circumstances. Children of age fourteen or fifteen who were not employed in those occupations were not deemed to be engaged in oppressive child labor if the chief of the Children's Bureau determined that such work did not interfere with a child's education or health and well-being. If minors between the ages of sixteen and eighteen were working in industries that the chief of the Children's Bureau determined to be hazardous, that was oppressive child labor.

Under the FSLA, "no producer, manufacturer, or dealer" was permitted to send into interstate commerce "any goods produced in an establishment in the United States in or about which within thirty days prior to the removal of such goods any oppressive child labor had been employed." Several general exemptions, however, weakened the protections of the law. Other than exempting children working for a parent or guardian, the law exempted children working in agriculture "while not legally required to attend school," and children employed as actors in movies or theatrical productions. Additionally, the law did nothing to protect child laborers in occupations that did not produce goods in interstate commerce. For example, girls working as domestic servants or boys and girls employed in local service trades at laundries, hotels, restaurants, and beauty parlors were not protected by the provisions. One early analysis of the FLSA concluded that the act did not begin to deal with the general problem of child labor. An estimated thirty thousand to fifty thousand minors under age sixteen were withdrawn from the workforce, out of a total of 850,000 children ages fifteen years and under who were working. The law only covered about 6 percent of working kids.

The biggest problem was the agricultural exemption, where an estimated 70 percent of all child laborers were employed. Half a million or more children were working in agriculture either as laborers on the family farm or in commercialized agriculture. Migrant labor and children working in tobacco or cotton fields, where some of the worst exploitation existed, received little protection under the law. Agriculture was defined so broadly that children who worked in turpentine camps were not covered. In a review of the law one year after enactment, Courtenay Dinwiddie noted that the child labor ban in agriculture only applied if a child worked in violation of compulsory school attendance laws, but in many states "school laws expressly permit children to be absent for farm work."

Even with the limitations and potential problems regarding the maximum hours, wages, and child labor provisions, the Fair Labor Standards Act had the potential to improve the living standards of millions of Americans. The task now was to implement the unprecedented law and defend the legislation against numerous expected court challenges.

CHAPTER FIVE

Implementation and Legal Challenges to the FLSA

Upon its enactment, some business groups and their supporters in Congress attempted to repeal or amend the Fair Labor Standards Act. The US Chamber of Commerce, which was fundamentally opposed to federal mandates on wages and hours, preferring instead state regulation of labor standards, continued to call for repeal of the FLSA as late as 1940—almost two years after the law had become effective. The chamber believed that "compensation for employment cannot be equitably apportioned, nor can enduring increases in employment be secured, through centralized Federal regulation of wages and hours." The organization also opposed delegating broad discretionary power to administrative agencies to issue rules and regulations and investigate businesses. The National Association of Manufacturers believed that the law would fail. Noel Sargent, a NAM economist, criticized the "purchasing power recovery theory" embodied in the law and warned that it would lead to government planning in other areas of the economy.

Although the FLSA exempted agricultural workers and "persons employed in the area of production to handle or prepare or can agricultural or horticultural commodities for market or to make dairy products," the National Grange opposed any legislation that resulted in "either the immediate or eventual regimentation of the farmer" or any "concentration of authority or infringement on States' rights." At the national conference held one month after the law was implemented, the organization urged that careful study be given to the impact of the FLSA on agriculture. Both the National Grange and the National Farm Bureau Federation regularly lobbied to exempt certain food packing and canning industries from the provisions of the wages and hours law.

Textile mill owners staunchly opposed the FLSA as well. The Cotton

Textile Institute described the legal foundations of the law as "not indigenous to America." David Clark, who was still editing the *Southern Textile Bulletin*, condemned the law as strongly as he opposed the Child Labor Amendment. He called the wages and hours law "an illegal usurpation of power by the Congress." He warned that the law marked the end of states' rights and America's form of government and would lead to a dictatorship. Perhaps too advanced in years to take up the cause himself, Clark urged a legal challenge to the act. Although efforts to repeal the law failed, the enforcement of the FLSA resulted in several lawsuits, and the Supreme Court would ultimately decide the fate of the law.

As might be expected from an unparalleled federal law that regulated labor standards and impacted over eleven million workers in diverse environments, numerous questions surrounded the initial implementation of the act. In fact, officials at the new Wage and Hour Division of the Labor Department received over a thousand inquiries each day from anxious employers about various provisions of the FLSA. *Time* magazine identified a Detroit hotel that feared elevator boys who served traveling salesmen were engaged in interstate commerce, and a turkey farmer in Texas who wondered whether the employees who gathered turkey eggs must be paid 25 cents an hour. Administrators conceded that they had neither the time nor the money to answer all the questions before the law became effective. Congress had appropriated only $400,000 for the initial implementation of the act, with $50,000 of that amount allocated to the Children's Bureau, and those funds were rapidly expended in hiring staff and issuing administrative rulings regarding the law.

Policymakers, interest groups, and scholars were mostly concerned with how the law would affect the economy: To what extent would the FLSA impact employers and cause disruptions in various industries? How many businesses, if any, would close down rather than pay the national minimum wage? Would the maximum hours provisions divide jobs and result in lower pay for some workers? Would the law increase the purchasing power of American workers and help the economy recover from the Depression? Answers to these questions were often colored by one's views of the New Deal and the role of government in market regulation.

Other questions addressed problems with enforcement: What was "production" for interstate commerce? Which industries and employees are covered by the law? Which are exempt? When must employers pay time and a half for overtime? Which groups should be invited to serve on the industry committees? It would take years and numerous administrative rulings and court decisions to adequately answer many of these questions. For example, under Section 13(a)(1) of the FLSA, persons employed "in a bona fide executive, administrative, or professional capacity" (known as EAP employees), are not protected by the act's wage and hour provisions. Attempts to define these three employment categories and determine which employees fell into them continued well into the first decade of the twenty-first century.

The Fair Labor Standards Act became effective on October 24, 1938. In a radio address broadcast throughout the country, Elmer F. Andrews, the first administrator of the Wage and Hour Division, celebrated the event as a memorable one for the United States. He described the FLSA as "one of the pillars of a sound economic system" and said the law was part of the administration's program to infuse "purchasing power into our channels of trade." Andrews, a soft-spoken civil engineer who brought to his job five years of experience as the industrial commissioner of New York and four years as the deputy commissioner (under Frances Perkins), explained to his audience that continued unemployment, with millions of workers competing for a limited number of jobs, was a major factor in congressional action in passing the law. "This situation," he expounded, "gave cutthroat employers an opportunity to operate on the basis of sweatshop wages and working conditions." The government was forced to act to protect wage earners, fair employers, and the purchasing power of the American consumer.

Enforcing the FLSA: A Difficult Task

When he assumed his new administrative position, Elmer Andrews expected active cooperation from many industries. As a practical matter, he needed that support because there were not enough staff at the Wage and Hour Division to effectively enforce the law. In the first year of implementation, only 109 inspectors were available to regulate a quarter of a million establishments covered by the law. Because of the heavy reliance on employer compliance, critics charged that the division was too business-friendly in the early months of implementation. Most of the congressional opposition to the FLSA came from southern legislators, but Andrews did not anticipate much difficulty in the South. He claimed that he had received numerous offers of cooperation from chambers of commerce and businesses in the region. Ten governors, including some from southern states such as Alabama, Georgia, Mississippi, and Texas, backed the FLSA and pledged their assistance in enforcing the law. The American Federation of Labor and Committee for Industrial Organizations also promised aid in implementing the law. William Green, president of the AFL, said that his organization had set up wage and hour committees in more than 520 cities to monitor implementation and receive complaints from workers.

As enforcement of the Fair Labor Standards Act began, a headline in the *New York Times* declared, "Pay Law Accepted Calmly by the Nation." Rosa Schneiderman, New York State's secretary of labor, anticipated few problems in states that already had minimum wage laws, and because the twenty-five-cent minimum was set so low that trade unions were not that interested in the wages part of the bill. Willis H. Hall, head of industrial relations for the Detroit Board of Commerce, also predicted few disruptions and no closures. He suggested that "employers are still pretty much confused by the law and are awaiting rulings to clear up borderline cases." In Massachusetts, wages were high in the textile mills compared to the South, but Massachusetts manufacturers were mostly concerned about the hours provision of the law. In seasonal industries like preserves or ice cream making, female employees worked long hours. Some employers doubted they could pay time and a half for overtime, but no closings were announced in the Bay State.

California, it was reported, largely welcomed the FLSA. Industry and agriculture would not be affected much because state laws already provided for a minimum wage, a ceiling over hours, and restrictions on child labor. If anything, employers stood to gain from the law because it "improved their competitive position." Officials in Washington State expressed similar views. E. Pat Kelly, director of the State Department of Labor and Industry, remarked that employers were complying and desired to cooperate. The state minimum wage scale for women was $13.20 a week, which was higher than the $11 a week mandated by the FLSA. Garment, women's clothes, and glove factories were "jubilant over the Federal act" because they would not suffer in competition with Eastern goods manufacturers. In Kansas City, for the first time in three decades, red caps (baggage handlers) employed by the Terminal Railway Company were now guaranteed a weekly salary rather than relying on tips for income. Overall, many employers complied with the wages and hours law, especially if it was perceived to reduce unfair competition and because the federal minimum wage rate was often lower than that required by states.

Although he did not specify which companies were involved, administrator Andrews revealed that in December many employer representatives sought the appointment of committees for their industries and higher minimum wage rates for their employees. "They wish to avoid delay in reaching the 40-40 goal [40-cent minimum/40-hour workweek]," Andrews stated, and they wanted full enforcement to ensure a level playing field. Andrews admitted that procedural requirements slowed committee formation. If an industry committee was defined too narrowly, he explained, "competitors might find themselves operating under different wage orders." Conversely, a committee defined too broadly might mandate minimum wages in industries that did not compete with one another. The interest that companies had in hastening the move toward the 40-40 goal reflects the fact that some industries were already working a forty-hour workweek and paying their employees more than the twenty-five-cent minimum.

Westinghouse Electric and Manufacturing Company, preferring not to wait for committee formation, announced one of the most progressive positions on the federal requirements. George H. Bucher, president of the company, declared that Westinghouse would "put the full requirements of the act in force at once, making overtime payments on the forty-hour basis immediately" for all nonexempt employees. This was three years in advance of the provisions of the law. The company even made the higher pay rate retroactive to the start of the FLSA. An estimated twelve thousand workers benefited from the plan.

Some industries, however, threatened to shut down plants, claiming that they could not afford to pay workers the basic twenty-five cents an hour. Fred C. Perkins, owner of a battery company in York, Pennsylvania, expressed outright defiance. "I cannot afford to abide by it," Perkins asserted. The business owner had been convicted and jailed in 1933 for violating the NIRA before the law was struck down by the Supreme Court. Perkins warned that if "they attempt to crush me I will do my level best to put their impractical notions to the acid test of public opinion in every hamlet in America." A calendar company in Detroit fired forty "girls" because it could not afford to pay them twenty-five cents an hour. Machinery was installed to replace the workers. Pecan-shelling businesses in the South reportedly shut down because of the minimum wage requirements. Some lumber, textile, and tobacco firms also closed, impacting an estimated eighty thousand workers. In San Antonio, Texas, an estimated 2,500 to 3,000 workers who were paid by the piece were dismissed by garment manufacturers who refused to pay the minimum wage.

Describing companies that closed down as "delinquents" that were either "unwilling or incapable of contributing to the common good," Elmer Andrews hoped that these shutdowns would be temporary, but he stated that most industries "were complying whole-heartedly with the law." In his first general report to President Roosevelt on the impact of the law one month into implementation, Andrews noted that earlier news stories considerably exaggerated the difficulties experienced under the new law. The number of workers affected by plant layoffs was no more than 30,000 to 50,000, and most of the layoffs were concentrated in the South. He estimated that 90 percent of the layoffs were in "pecan shelling, tobacco stemming, lumber, and bagging" positions.

There were doubts about the constitutionality of the FLSA, but most trade associations and business magazines recommended that firms comply with the provisions rather than face prosecution and the possibility of stiff fines. R. S. Smethurst, counsel for the National Hardwood Lumber Association, told lumbermen not to expect early administrative rulings on the more obscure sections of the law. "Comply with the law the best you can according to your understanding of what it means," he suggested. "If you do make a mistake while doing this sincerely, you will be absolved from criminal prosecution, although not from restitution of double the amount of wages involved." Smethurst concluded that most of the uncertainties of the act would have to be addressed by the courts. The American Bar Association recommended that the act be given a fair chance but also cited the need for clarifying amendments.

Two months after the FLSA became law, the Wage and Hour Division received numerous letters from banks, insurance companies, utilities, accounting firms, advertising agencies, stockbrokers, and a host of other companies seeking an exemption from the wage and hour requirements under the "retail and service" exemption. Each business claimed that it provided a service. The division, however, issued an interpretive bulletin stating that these types of companies were not service organizations. In defining typical service establishments that were similar to retail, the bulletin cited restaurants, hotels, barbershops, beauty parlors, and auto repair garages. The bulletin may have clarified some questions surrounding coverage of the FLSA, but the exercise illustrates how the interpretation of a single word could expand or restrict the protections of the law.

In December 1938 a Gallup Poll asked Americans the following question: Are you in favor of the new wage and hours law? The survey found that 71 percent of respondents favored the law and 29 percent were against it. By region, the highest support was found in New England, with 79 percent saying that they backed the law; the lowest approval was in the South, with 59 percent favoring the law and 41 percent opposed. Respondents who identified as Democrats supported the FLSA by 80 percent while only 51 percent of Republicans approved. No other political parties were mentioned in the poll, and there was no option for unaffiliated respondents. Even with some of the methodological issues surrounding polling in the 1930s, the results indicated broad public support for the wages and hours law.

Several months after the Fair Labor Standards Act became law, Elmer Andrews traveled eight thousand miles across the country on an inspection trip, asking both employers and employees how well the law was being implemented. Based on his interactions, Andrews concluded that there was widespread compliance with the new labor standards. He found that when employees complained of wage or hour violations and investigations confirmed that the company was noncompliant, employers admitted that "mistakes" were made, and they quickly corrected the situation. Andrews did not find any outright defiance of the law that required a referral to the Justice Department. Still, there were many questions surrounding the FLSA, and many were no doubt from employers who not only were evading the law but also desired to see the labor protections overturned by the courts.

The Children's Bureau, which was given responsibility for enforcing the child labor provisions of the Fair Labor Standards Act, picked up where it left off when the first federal child labor law, the Keating-Owen Act, went into effect September 1, 1917. The Keating-Owen Act was implemented for about a year before the Supreme Court struck it down. The Children's Bureau could draw upon that experience and the expertise gained in the subsequent twenty years dealing with child labor issues. The agency designated an expanded Industrial Division to oversee implementation of the act. Beatrice McConnell, who worked on programs for women and children in the Pennsylvania Department of Labor and Industry, was named the Industrial Division's director. The bureau hoped to work cooperatively with state agencies to avoid duplication of efforts. States themselves had improved their child labor and compulsory school attendance laws since 1917. Many had established labor departments and special inspectors to enforce child labor laws. The administrative machinery was now in place to implement the law and significantly reduce child labor exploitation.

Priority was given to the issuance of temporary certificates of age for all working children. The certificate system served as a preventive measure and protected employers who honestly attempted to comply with the law. The first child labor regulation issued by Katherine Lenroot, head of the Children's Bureau, announced that the certificates of age issued by thirty-one states would have the same effect as federal certificates for a six-month period. During that time federal and state officials would develop a more permanent plan. Within a year, state employment certificates were accepted in forty-three states and the District of Columbia. The first regulation also described the information that must be contained in a certificate, acceptable evidence of age, and rules governing approval, suspension, and revocation of certificates. Any employer of children holding a valid state or federal certificate would not be deemed as engaging in oppressive child labor.

Measuring compliance with the law was based on inspections carried out in cooperation with the Wage and Hour Division of the Labor Department. The Children's Bureau focused on canneries, packing plants, and local industries notorious for child labor. Inspections uncovered numerous violations of the law. During the first ten months under the FLSA, "nearly 500 children under sixteen years of age had been found working illegally in establishments producing goods in interstate commerce," with some as young as age eight or nine found at work. When violations were found, most employers dismissed the underage worker or sought to obtain a certificate of age. Court action was necessary in only three cases, with two resulting in a permanent injunction against the shipment of goods, and one ending in a criminal prosecution. Two years into implementation of the law, the Children's Bureau reported seven criminal and nineteen civil suits for flagrant child labor violations, none of which were contested by the employer. In assessing the impact of the law, the bureau cited "definite gains" in reducing child labor in interstate commerce, improved administration of state child labor laws, new state child labor legislation, and "greater realization on the part of the public and of employers of the value of good child labor standards." Many businesses voluntarily stopped employing children.

Despite some signs of progress on the child labor front, opposition to the FLSA persisted, and implementation prompted several lawsuits. A few of these, like *Darby Lumber*, challenged the constitutionality of the FLSA while others sought clarification on the scope of the provisions. In late December 1938, in what is considered the first formal test of the child labor restrictions, a state circuit court judge in Michigan ruled that newsboys operating under carrier contracts were not subjects covered by the law. Mac Myers, a thirteen-year old boy, had his carrier contract canceled after enactment of the act. Young Mac delivered papers in his hometown of Ithaca, Michigan, which was miles from where the paper was published, and had them delivered to him by truck.

The Children's Bureau did not intervene in the case because the solicitor of the Labor Department ruled that the boy's employment was not "in or about" the newspaper company's establishment and therefore did not fall under the child labor provisions. A ruling by the Children's Bureau a few months later concurred with that position. The administrative opinion held that minors under sixteen years of age fell under the reach of the act only if their work "required them to come in or about the establishment in which the newspapers are produced." Critics of the ruling pointed out that it would be easy for newspapers to deal with the "little merchant" by designating a delivery spot for the papers outside the place of business, thus making all carriers "independent contractors" outside the provisions of the law.

And that is exactly how the case of Mac Myers was decided. Judge Kelly S. Searl doubted the constitutionality of the FLSA, but he did not formally address that issue. Rather, his ruling established the concept of newspaper boys as "independent contractors" not protected by the act. The judge admitted that his ruling ran counter to decisions of the National Labor Relations Board. His opinion included a rambling diatribe against child labor reformers. He surmised that the FLSA was probably enacted in response to the lobbying of child welfare activists, but, "if the utterly fallacious and unsound theories of these well-meaning reformers, many of whom have never brought up a child to maturity, which find expression in this act and also in the so-called Child Labor Amendment, are adopted, except as applied to child labor detrimental to the health or dangerous to life and limb . . . it will result in the filling, by the coming generations, of the reformatory institutions and prisons beyond their capacity." As a young boy, Judge Searl delivered newspapers, and he attributed his success in life to being compelled to work as a child.

Newspaper companies themselves sued, claiming that the FLSA violated their free speech and press rights. When a lawyer for the Philadelphia office of the Wage and Hour Division issued a subpoena directing two Pennsylvania newspapers to produce employment records to show compliance with the law, the papers objected. Elisha Hanson, counsel for the American Newspaper Publishers Association argued in federal court that the Wage and Hour Division could not subdelegate subpoena power to regional administrators because only Congress has that authority. Moreover, he asserted, Congress had no power to control newspapers. "If it is held that Congress can regulate newspapers," Hanson said, "it is possible for it [Congress] to say who can or who can't engage in the publication of newspapers and magazines. It could limit the extent of the activities of newspapers [and] say when and where newspapers could be circulated." In response, Vernon Stoneman, attorney for the Wage and Hour Division, told the court that the agency was not seeking to censor newspapers but was only "interested in seeing whether newspapers are complying with the law."

The Department of Labor and federal courts eventually ruled that there is no across-the-board exemption for journalists and reporters. Newspaper and other media employees are exempt only if they earn a certain salary level or if they are in a narrowly defined category of "creative professionals." Reporters and journalists who only collect, organize, and record information that is routine or already public, or do not interpret or analyze the news, would not be exempt. Also, reporters for small community newspapers, who mostly report on local events from widely available information, are not exempt from the provisions of the law.

Some Businesses Game the System

Employers used a variety of tactics to evade enforcement of the wage, hour, and overtime requirements. Companies that tried to avoid compliance were often described by officials as "chiselers." Inadequate or falsified records were a major problem, especially with smaller companies. In response to minimum wage mandates, some businesses used a ploy where they paid the higher minimum wage but then required employees to return the difference between the mandatory minimum and their previous hourly pay, effectively nullifying any wage increase. The kickback scheme had been used for years by employers to circumvent state minimum wage laws, and a similar arrangement would become a central issue in the *Darby Lumber* case.

To avoid paying time and a half for overtime in a forty-four-hour workweek, some employers averaged a worker's hours over a two-week period. For example, if an employee worked forty hours one week and forty-eight hours the following week, the employee should be paid four hours of overtime for the second week. By calculating pay on a two-week basis, however, that same employee received no overtime pay because the two-week total was eighty-eight hours. In November 1938 the Wage and Hour Division, interpreting Section 7(a) of the act, ruled that a workweek was a separate entity, thus making this payroll practice illegal under the FLSA.

Another popular scheme converted employees to "independent contractors," therefore removing them from the payroll and obligations of the law. In *Southern Lumberman,* the leading voice of the southern lumber industry, which had strongly opposed the FLSA, an article suggested that lumberyard owners could avoid taxes and labor requirements by using independent contractors rather than employees. The article cited "many cases in which truck drivers have . . . hauled as independent contractors for their former employers." In some situations, owners would "sell" trucks to the former employees and have them make regular payments. However, investigations revealed that no title for the truck was transferred and no payments were ever made. This practice was used not only in the lumber and timber products industry but also in petroleum, chemicals, life insurance, dairy, radio, janitorial, and many homework industries.

One of the earliest and largest cases to use the contractor scheme involved eleven employers in New Jersey, New York, and Pennsylvania who organized as the Hand Knitcraft Institute. The institute "sold" yarn to its ten thousand employees and then "purchased" the processed knitted items from the employees, whose earnings as "independent contractors" were not only far below what was required by the FLSA but also lacked Social Security benefits and workmen's compensation. A federal judge enjoined the manufacturers from further violations and prohibited "any scheme or device involving so-called purchase and sale arrangements with any home workers or other employers." These schemes undermined compliance and denied workers the protections of the law.

While enforcement efforts continued, Congress debated amendments to the Fair Labor Standards Act. At least forty-three bills were introduced in 1939, many of which sought exemptions for occupations or from the wage and hour provisions. John L. Lewis, president of the United Mine Workers and Congress of Industrial Organizations, testified in July 1939 before the House Labor Committee. He "vehemently" opposed all efforts to exempt groups of employers from paying the minimum wage of "25 lousy cents an hour" established by the law. In comparison, his mineworkers earned $6 for a seven-hour day (about eighty-six cents an hour). Lewis "angrily denounced" a congressional conservative group of Republicans and "renegade Democrats" that he accused of conducting "a war dance around the bounden, prostrate, form of labor." Lewis had harsh words for the man he perceived as the leader of this group—Vice President John Nance Garner. Known as "Cactus Jack," Garner was a conservative Southern Democrat from Texas and former House Speaker. Lewis described Garner as "a labor-baiting, poker-playing, whisky-drinking, evil old man." Garner, who was seventy-one at the time, was widely expected to seek and perhaps secure the

Democratic presidential nomination in 1940 before FDR decided to run for an unprecedented third term.

John Lewis failed in his attempt to halt efforts to amend the wage and hour law. The day after Lewis testified, four bills were reported on the House floor that in various ways sought exemptions from the minimum wage and work hours requirements. One of the bills was sponsored by Representative Mary Norton, chair of the Labor Committee and the person responsible for successfully navigating the Fair Labor Standards Act through the House of Representatives. Considered to be the least radical in scope, the administration-backed Norton bill exempted certain telephone operators and white-collar workers as well as industries in Puerto Rico and the Virgin Islands where the wage and hour requirements were causing problems. Elmer Andrews had recommended many of the changes in the Norton bill, although he reversed his position on exempting white-collar workers making more than $200 a month after pressure from labor unions and employees at Westinghouse. Andrews explained that "organized labor had done such a fine job of fighting my battle for me . . . it would be very unethical for me to press that amendment if they are opposed to it." Opponents of the FLSA used the abrupt switch on the exemption to accuse Andrews of favoring certain groups in his rulings.

Representative Graham A. Barden (D-NC) introduced the most radical of the four bills. His legislation proposed to exempt dairies, cotton gins, processors of nuts and perishable fruits, and many other businesses connected with agriculture. The bill would also exempt all workers receiving a guaranteed $150 a month salary, potentially depriving hundreds of thousands of clerical workers overtime pay. President Roosevelt assailed the Barden bill, arguing that it would in effect be "sanctioning consciously low wages" for more than two million of the poorest paid workers. Administrator Andrews criticized the Barden bill's supporters as "dime-an-hour" advocates and opposed all the changes. In particular, he argued that the Barden bill would "emasculate" the employee lawsuit provision by "requiring suits within six months of a violation, irrespective of when the violation is discovered." All four proposed bills to amend the FLSA failed to win approval during the first session of the Seventy-Sixth Congress, and no amendments passed during the second session.

The Honeymoon Is Over: Prosecuting Violators

In March 1939 the federal government won the first criminal prosecution of a company alleged to have violated the wages and hours law. Brown Contract Stitching, Inc. of Lawrence, Massachusetts, a shoe company employing about three hundred workers, and Nathan Brown, its treasurer and general manager, were indicted for failing to pay the minimum wage, falsifying records, failing to keep records as required by the law, and moving goods in interstate commerce. Guilty pleas were entered, and Judge Elisha H. Brewster imposed $1,500 in fines. Joseph E. Brill, chief of the Wage and Hour Unit of the Justice Department, warned that other manufacturers in the area would be held accountable. "The government wants manufacturers to know the act is being enforced," he said, "and that it is unprofitable to violate it."

Elmer Andrews echoed this tougher enforcement policy in a speech before the Philadelphia Council for Social Progress. He noted that the efficacy of the FLSA in raising wages and improving the life of the American worker depended on rigorous enforcement. Andrews bluntly stated that the "honeymoon period" of the law's administration was over. He suggested that during the early months of implementation, the government had been lenient and flexible in working with companies to comply with the law. Now, however, any business owners who "monkey with the buzz saw" of enforcement would find the teeth "big and sharp."

The threatening rhetoric on criminal prosecutions resulted from a growing awareness that some companies were simply ignoring the law or finding ways around compliance. Even the *Southern Lumberman* candidly admitted that there was a "developing drift in the direction of non-observance of the law which should be checked immediately before it gathers too much momentum to be stopped." Responsible operators of large sawmills were making an honest effort to comply, but according to the publication, many small mill owners "are proceeding under the conviction that the law does not apply to them and are disregarding its provisions." These small operators tried to hide behind the clause exempting farm labor or claimed that they sold their products only to intrastate customers.

The Wage and Hour Division, however, had issued an interpretive bulletin clearly declaring that it is "immaterial that the producer passes title to the purchaser within the state of production." The division even provided an example: "If a lumber manufacturer sells his lumber locally to a furniture manufacturer who sells furniture in interstate commerce, the employees of the lumber manufacturer would likewise come within the scope of the Act." Whether the small mill operators were receiving bad legal advice or simply looking for loopholes in the law, the *Southern Lumberman* warned that there was "rapidly developing an intolerable condition" within the industry of uneven compliance, and it urged the Department of Labor to enforce the law strictly and impartially.

Andrews spoke at the annual meeting of the Southern Pine Association in April 1939. He tried to reassure mill owners that the law was being enforced in an aggressive but fair manner. "We are primarily less interested in putting people in jail—as much as we know some should be there—than in winning for the workers of the country the benefits to which they are entitled under the law." He acknowledged that most southern businessmen strongly opposed the FLSA but were now patriotically complying with the law. He argued that it was in their financial interest to abide by the provisions of the law. Andrews cited a "Report to the President on Economic Conditions in the South," prepared by southern economists and policymakers, that described terrible housing conditions in the region. The South had an average annual income of just $314. In nineteen southern cities, "dwellings rented for less than $15 a month or are valued at less than $1,500." Homes in rural areas needed significant repairs and had the lowest value of any farmhouses in the country. If workers were paid a minimum wage and time and a half for overtime, Andrews reasoned, there would be money available for repairs and the construction of new houses. The lumber industry would be a direct beneficiary of increased wages for employees. He shared the story of a Chattanooga, Tennessee, lumber company vice president who originally opposed the FLSA but now understood that uniformly higher wages across the South would improve the market for lumber.

There was, however, a "fly in the ointment." There were claims that noncompliance was rampant in the lumber industry, and if backwoods sawmills were not made to comply immediately, mills now following the law might "join the rebellion." Andrews conceded that there were challenges with enforcement in the South. In eleven southern states there were more than five thousand widely scattered lumber and sawmill operations employing over 178,000 workers. In comparison, California, Oregon, and Washington had fifteen hundred establishments and half as many workers. Andrews reported that since February, the Wage and Hour Division had been concentrating its investigations in the lumber industry. There were 139 ongoing investigations, and reports of noncompliance in forty-two additional cases. The administrator forewarned "studied and intentional violators" that they would not escape the reach of the law.

But Andrews would not be around much longer to oversee the new period of aggressive implementation. Elmer Andrews announced his departure as administrator of the Wage and Hour Division effective October 16, 1939, and President Roosevelt accepted his resignation. Press reports indicated that the resignation had been anticipated for some time, although the correspondence between Andrews and the president gave no hint of the reasons for the administrative change. During Andrews's fifteen-month tenure, the Wage and Hour Division had come under increasing criticism for its slow pace of industrial committee formation. One year after the law was in force, wage and hour standards had been fixed in only the textile and apparel industries. Southern senators and representatives also objected to an early ruling by Andrews that there would be no differential wages for workers in the textile industry in the North and the South. The ruling was consistent with congressional intent, but President Roosevelt had made concessions to southern officials on regional wage variations. In accepting the resignation, Roosevelt thanked Andrews for his "pioneering" work in "the new field of responsibility authorized under the Fair Labor Standards Act." The president appointed Colonel Philip B. Fleming, district engineer for St. Paul, Minnesota, of the Army Engineering Corps, as the new Wage and Hour Division administrator.

In a memo to the president on August 18, Secretary Perkins had recommended Fleming for the position. She noted that many potential job candidates had politely declined when approached, unsure how long the job would last and fearful of leaving good positions for what many viewed as a demanding and stressful job. Perkins liked Fleming because he was a military man with administrative and executive experience who had a history of working well with civilians. Perkins described Fleming as someone "accustomed to getting things done the quickest and cheapest way." He was neither vain nor possessing of a domineering personality. In short, he was the best person to handle the problems with the Wage and Hour Division and "quickly squelch the jealously that exists there." Finally, because Fleming was a military officer, Perkins told the president that he could simply order him to take the position.

Around this time Secretary Perkins announced that during the first year of the FLSA's operation, wages and employment increased. Women were the leading beneficiaries of the wage and hour gains. Women's pay rose faster than men's, but both sexes enjoyed wage increases of 10 percent or more in factories producing radios and phonographs, electrical machinery, hardware, cotton goods, auto tires, and glass products, among others. With the minimum wage set to increase to thirty cents in October and the maximum weekly hours reduced to forty-two, an additional 250,000 workers were due to receive pay increases, and over 400,000 were to work fewer hours per week.

Several months after he resigned his position, Elmer Andrews reflected on the challenges faced in implementing the wages and hours law during the first year. He acknowledged that the Wage and Hour Division may have proceeded from the start with a policy of "business appeasement," but early interpretations of the act that expanded coverage to thousands of workers generated enough criticism from employers to assure the division that it was not "unduly pro-industry." Congress also required that employees for the division be drawn from the civil service pool, which prioritized administrative experience but also slowed staff hiring. For the first two weeks, Andrews was the only person on the payroll of the division. Because of a shortage of funds and personnel, the division had to rely on labor unions, trade associations, chambers of commerce, and other federal agencies to print and distribute more than five million informational booklets for workers.

Andrews also admitted that industry committee formation was slow and difficult. Priority was given to those industries, like textiles, with the largest number of low-paid workers. There were conflicts over geographical balance for industry representation, labor unions fought over the number of seats on each committee, and identifying spokespersons for nonunionized workers "was a poser." Finally, Andrews conceded that the attempt to amend the FLSA in 1939 was premature and a mistake. Some of the reforms of the Norton bill were needed, but the process gave congressional opponents an opening to severely weaken the protections of the law with the Barden bill. There was so much political wrangling over the Barden bill, however, that all efforts to amend the law were unsuccessful.

The picture of general compliance with the FLSA drawn by former administrator Andrews one year earlier was now about as complex as any abstract painting by Jackson Pollock. Wage complaints skyrocketed in 1939, coming in at a rate of a thousand a week by December, and the Wage and Hour Division found itself overwhelmed with a backlog of 15,547 complaints to investigate. By late December the division had received 32,087 complaints and had analyzed 31,000 of them. Of the roughly 24,400 complaints that had been classified according to various provisions, almost 85 percent indicated the probable existence of violations.

The division admitted that it confronted a task "far beyond" its resources, but in its first report to Congress, it appeared confident that the implementation of the law was going well. The division planned to increase the number of inspectors from 290 to seven hundred and even suggested that it might implement regular inspections of the estimated 250,000 businesses that fell under the requirements of the law. Even with a "desired goal" of one inspection every four days, which totaled sixty-five a year (per inspector) based on an average workweek, it was not clear how the administrators would achieve the herculean task of regular business inspections. At least fifteen hundred inspectors were needed for effective enforcement, and the division was nowhere near that total.

Federal Lawsuits Challenging the FLSA

The Wage and Hour Division report noted that almost half of the complaints involved the payment of time and a half for hours beyond the maximum workweek. There appeared to be some confusion or ignorance about the provisions of the law. A *New York Times* article revealed that many employers believed the FLSA was just a federal twenty-five-cent minimum wage law. They failed to realize that the law also required time and a half for overtime for employees "no matter how highly skilled or how well paid if they worked more than the [initial] forty-four hours a week."

The division's report also stated that the FLSA had been held constitutional in separate cases by four federal judges. In 139 legal actions initiated by the division and the Department of Justice, only three were defeats for the government. In thirty-seven cases, the Justice Department had a perfect record of obtaining criminal convictions. Most defendants pled guilty and paid the fines. Over $247,000 in fines had been imposed, but payment of $132,350 of that total was suspended on the condition that the employer provide full compensation of the wages illegally withheld. Investigations and litigation produced agreements for restitution for wages in excess of $1 million. Finally, with the minimum wage increasing to thirty cents and the workweek reduced to forty-two hours in 1939, the report concluded that there were no significant dislocations of employment.

As the report indicated, several federal cases involving the FLSA had been decided or were pending at the time. One involved a challenge by the Opp Cotton Mills, fifteen other southern textile mills, and the Southern Cotton Manufacturers Association. As provided for in the wages and hours law, Industry Committee No. 1, the Textile Committee, consisting of twenty-one members (seven each representing the public, employers, and employees), devoted more than three months to the study of wage conditions in the textile industry. The committee voted 13 to 6 to recommend a uniform minimum wage of 32½ cents for the entire textile industry. The administrator of the Wage and Hour Division then published a notice of a hearing. More than a hundred witnesses testified at the hearing, amounting to three thousand pages of testimony. After the hearing, the administrator issued a wage order on September 29, 1939, providing that by October 24, 1939—in less than a month's time—wages at a rate of 32½ cents an hour were to be paid to all employees in the textile industry. This amount was 2½ cents more than the thirty-cents minimum for 1939. The wage rate applied to an estimated 175,000 workers. Opp Cotton Mills, a small cotton mill in Opp, Alabama, contended that the FLSA was unconstitutional and that fixing a uniform minimum wage of 32½ cents for the textile industry was illegal.

However, in *Opp Cotton Mills, Inc. v. Administrator Wage and Hour Division*, the Fifth Circuit Court of Appeals ruled on April 2, 1940, that the FLSA was a valid exercise of congressional power under the Commerce Clause. The three-judge panel said that "any doubts that may have existed heretofore as to the constitutionality of such legislation have been dispelled by recent decisions of the Supreme Court." The court cited the precedents of *NLRB v. Jones and Laughlin Steel Corporation, Kentucky Whip & Collar Co. v. Illinois Central Railroad Co.*, and other cases decided since the Constitutional Revolution of 1937. The court also concluded that the wage determination met the due process requirements of the Constitution. The parties received proper notice and a fair opportunity to be heard. In appealing the ruling, Opp Cotton obtained an injunction from a federal court in New Orleans restraining the Wage and Hour Division from enforcing the new minimum wage of 32½ cents an hour for the textile industry while the case was appealed to the Supreme Court.

A federal grand jury also brought indictments against a couple of southern Georgia lumber companies in November 1939. The Waynesboro Veneer Company, Arvil W. Welborn, and Oscar Welborn were charged in a twenty-count indictment with failure to pay the minimum wage, failure to pay overtime, falsification of the company's records, and shipping goods in interstate commerce without meeting the wage-hour provisions of the FLSA. The indictment alleged that the company instructed, permitted, and caused employees to punch their time cards after eight working hours but required them to return to work without credit or compensation for additional hours.

Fred Darby and His Lumber Mill

A second case involved the Darby Lumber Company, a mill owned by Fred W. Darby in Statesboro, Georgia. Established in 1919 on seven acres of land adjacent to a railroad line, the lumber mill had more than fifty employees. The company thrived during the 1920s and had even managed to do well during the Depression. It was the largest lumber business in Statesboro, and it shipped products in interstate commerce. A recent expansion of facilities and payroll had made the company more efficient. In 1938 Darby paid his employees from 12½ cents to seventeen cents an hour, well below the federal minimum. An article in the *Statesboro News* described Fred Darby as "one of the livest wires in the lumber business." Darby's company, however, was indicted on multiple counts for not adhering to the minimum wage requirements of twenty-five cents per hour, working his employees more than forty-four hours a week without paying them one and a half times their normal pay, and failing to keep employment records as required by law. Darby contested the indictments. Few participants probably realized it at the time, but the litigation became the most important case challenging the FLSA.

US District Court Judge William H. Barrett presided over the case *U.S. v. F. W. Darby Lumber Company*. Barrett received a bachelor of philosophy degree from the University of Georgia in 1885 and read law to enter the bar two years later. He served as city attorney of Augusta, Georgia, from 1898 to 1904, and in 1916 he and James Meriwether Hull established a local law firm. Barrett was appointed to the federal bench by President Warren G. Harding and confirmed by the Senate on June 22, 1922. He was among a group of "old school" federal judges who clung to the laissez-faire legal doctrines of the pre-1937 period. On April 29, 1940, Judge Barrett quashed the indictments against Darby Lumber in a strongly worded opinion that ignored the Fifth Circuit decision in the *Opp Cotton* case and six other federal district judges who had by then upheld the FLSA.

Using the distinction between manufacturing and commerce, which had been largely discredited in *NLRB v. Jones and Laughlin Steel Corporation*, Judge Barrett criticized the FLSA as it applied to both the production of goods for interstate commerce and the prohibition of shipment of articles in interstate commerce produced under substandard labor conditions. Grounding his decision in *Hammer v. Dagenhart*, Barrett argued that the alleged violations involved primarily intrastate activities, rather than interstate commerce. The judge asserted that Darby Lumber did not have fair notice that it was violating the law because the lumber company was unaware that production of goods within intrastate commerce would be connected with interstate commerce to the extent that Congress could regulate with criminal penalties.

In quashing the indictments, Judge Barrett commented on the constitutionality of the Fair Labor Standards Act. He warned that if the law was upheld, government regulation of labor could extend not only to the "man who cut the timber or hauled it to the mill, but also to the man who planted and cultivated the trees." Such a view of federal power, he contended, was dangerous. If the interstate commerce clause embodies the power to create a centralized government against "an in-destructible union, composed of indestructible States," then the sooner that is revealed, the better. While the judge believed that Congress had not extended federal power to that level, if it had, he claimed that the FLSA would be unconstitutional. Within days, Judge Barrett signed a petition allowing the federal government to appeal directly to the Supreme Court.

Oral Arguments before the Supreme Court

Both the *Darby Lumber* and *Opp Cotton Mills* cases were granted review by the Supreme Court on October 14, 1940. The two cases involved several major constitutional issues: (1) the scope of congressional commerce clause power over labor standards, (2) the authority of Congress to require employment records, (3) the meaning of due process of law under the Fifth Amendment, (4) congressional delegation of lawmaking power to the executive branch, (5) administrative procedures used by industry committees, and (6) the administrative power to investigate. Although there was some intersection, the *Darby Lumber* case addressed the first three issues while the *Opp Cotton* litigation concerned the last three questions. Parties on both sides now submitted briefs on the merits.

Darby Lumber was represented by Archibald Battle Lovett, a former judge of the Superior Courts of Georgia who was now in private practice in Savannah, Georgia. Using *Hammer v. Dagenhart* as precedent and other pre-1937 cases that made a distinction between manufacturing and commerce, Fred Darby argued that the FLSA violated the Tenth Amendment because it was an unconstitutional attempt to regulate conditions in production of goods and commodities. Darby's lawyers distinguished *NLRB v. Jones and Laughlin Steel Corporation* by arguing that federal control over manufacture and production is justified only when the relation to interstate commerce is "close and substantial." No precedents, they claimed, allowed the national government to directly regulate production that was primarily local.

Similar arguments were being made by conservatives at the time. In a speech reported in the *American Bar Association Journal*, Arthur A. Ballantine, former undersecretary for the Treasury Department in the Hoover administration, argued that there were clear differences between the precedents that upheld the National Labor Relations Board and the provisions of the wages and hours law. In *Jones and Laughlin*, Ballantine stated, the steel company was sufficiently large, with more than twenty-two thousand employees and offices in twenty cities, so that a work stoppage by a strike might impact interstate commerce. But the provisions of the FLSA applied to all employees engaged in the production of goods for interstate commerce, "even in plants so small that a strike in them would produce an infinitesimal effect upon the flow of goods."

In sum, the Darby Lumber Company was not Jones and Laughlin Steel Corporation. The lumber company's failure to comply with the FLSA, Darby's lawyers asserted, did not affect interstate commerce, constitute unfair competition, or lead to labor disputes. Additionally, the FLSA deprived Darby of liberty and due process in violation of the Fifth Amendment. The act was arbitrary and capricious because Congress did not adequately define persons subject to its penal provisions. Finally, Darby claimed that the government was wrong to seek unrestricted power beyond its enumerated powers and to legislate for the general welfare.

Lawyers for Opp Cotton Mills argued in their brief on the merits that if the 32½ cents an hour wage was upheld by the Court, it would mean "the undoing of many small Southern cotton mills." The brief criticized the "theory and practical effect" of the wage order, warning that "the far-reaching effects of this experiment are hard to comprehend." The broad scope of federal power under the Commerce Clause underlying the Fair Labor Standards Act, it was argued, made it inevitable that "business would cease to be a local thing." "It is not charged," the brief claimed, "that the South has been party to any 'sweat-shop' conditions or is 'chiseling' in any degree." The region was compared to a baby that had not "yet outgrown its industrial swaddling clothes." Finally, the cotton-mill owners contended that there should have been wage differentials between the North and South and between rural and urban mills. Production and transportation costs and living expenses varied, they argued, making a uniform wage rate unworkable.

In its brief defending the wages and hours law, the US government made several constitutional and pragmatic arguments. When the Commerce Clause was drafted, the meaning of the phrase *interstate commerce* included production, manufacturing, and all aspects of commercial activity. Supreme Court decisions, from the earliest days of the Union, recognized that Congress has the power to confront the economic problems of the country. The government cited Chief Justice John Marshall's famous opinion in *Gibbons v. Ogden*, which held that Congress has power over "that commerce which concerns more states than one," including "those internal concerns which affect the states generally." The US government contended that no state alone could require standards higher than those of other states where competition exists. As had been the practice for decades, employers with weak labor standards would have an unfair advantage in interstate competition. Markets had become national rather than local, and only the federal government can impose uniform wage and hour standards.

The government's brief also argued that *Hammer v. Dagenhart* was now a constitutional artifact wholly inconsistent with subsequent decisions that have "repudiated or abandoned each premise upon which the opinion rests." Because the Fair Labor Standards Act is a valid exercise of congressional power under the Commerce Clause, the law does not violate the Tenth Amendment, which merely reserves to states those powers not delegated to the United States. The origins of the Tenth Amendment confirm that its purpose was merely declaratory. Last, the government argued that the FLSA does not violate due process and a liberty of contract under the Fifth Amendment. The Court had already upheld legislation fixing maximum hours for men and women and minimum wages for women generally and for men in some situations. Therefore, the Due Process Clause "imposes no greater restriction upon federal legislation in the field of interstate commerce than upon state regulation regulating intrastate activities."

While the Court considered these arguments, enforcement of the Fair Labor Standards Act progressed. On October 24, 1940, the forty-hour workweek became the law of the land. At the prevailing minimum wage of thirty cents, a worker covered by the law grossed $12.00 a week. With the reduction from forty-two hours to forty hours, employees stood to lose sixty cents a week if an employer decided not to work them beyond the maximum forty hours. Labor economists, however, predicted that the hourly reduction would have little effect on job conditions. Most workers were already on a forty-hour week, and the average for the manufacturing sector was 37.3 hours. Administrator Fleming reminded everyone that the minimum wage was not scheduled to increase to forty cents until 1945. In addition to textiles, ten other industry committees proposed minimums higher than thirty cents, including hosiery, shoes, woolens, leather, pulp, and paper. In many industries, wage rates seemed to be outpacing the federal minimum. Economic conditions in Puerto Rico and the Virgin Islands were unique from the mainland, and a special industry committee was established to permit rates below those set for the rest of the United States.

Oral arguments in the two FLSA cases were scheduled for December 19 to 20, 1940. Solicitor General Francis B. Biddle represented the federal government in defending the law. Archibald B. Lovett argued on behalf of the Darby Lumber Company, the appellees in the case. Unfortunately, a full transcript of the oral argument is not available, but there were several media reports of the proceedings. Solicitor General Biddle opened the argument by telling the Court that the "effect of low wages on interstate commerce supplied a sound constitutional basis for the authority granted the government in the Fair Labor Standards Act." He claimed that state efforts to solve the problem of low wages and long hours had been "futile." Biddle commented that the lumber industry was typical of any industry covered by the FLSA. He noted that wages paid in the "Georgia lumber industry in 1932 were at an average of 13.4 cents an hour, the lowest for that industry throughout the country." With the worst years of the Depression hitting from 1933 to 1934, wages had not improved much since then. In 1937 the average annual wage for all employees in the Georgia lumber industry was still only $388.91. Biddle argued that it did not matter whether the regulated industry deemed itself interstate or intrastate. The only thing that mattered was whether the wage rate affected interstate commerce. The solicitor general spoke for only a few minutes, and then the Court adjourned for the afternoon.

Continuing with the government's case the following morning, Biddle urged the Court to overturn the *Hammer v. Dagenhart* and *Bailey v. Drexel Furniture Company* precedents and the decision in *Carter v. Carter Coal Company* (1936). He pointed out that the Court had already sustained legislation fixing maximum hours for both men and women, fixing minimum wages for women generally, and fixing minimum wages for men under certain circumstances. Biddle insisted that the Fair Labor

Standards Act was necessary to keep employers who pay low wages and require long hours from gaining an "unfair advantage" in the market. Low wages affected interstate commerce, Biddle contended, and were a "vital and fundamental cause of labor unrest." "The health and welfare of both the worker and the nation," he added, "depend upon the elimination of sub-standard wage and hour conditions." Only national legislation, the government asserted, could solve the problem.

In representing the lumber company, Archibald Lovett described the Commerce Clause as "wise and useful" but argued that it should not be employed to interfere with the "autonomy of the States" in their internal affairs. Lovett said that the FLSA "goes much farther into the realm of state domain than any act thus far construed by this court." He warned that if the actions of a small southern sawmill can be regulated by Congress, then the "federal government can control agricultural labor." If the broad powers claimed by the government through the interstate commerce clause had been recognized long ago, Lovett asserted, then "slavery could have been abolished by an act of Congress." The FLSA, he concluded, "regulates production boldly, badly, and undisguised."

In the second case, *Opp Cotton Mills, Inc. v. Administrator Wage and Hour Division*, the cotton mills were represented by Ben F. Cameron of Meridian, Mississippi. Cameron focused his arguments on attacking the procedures used by the Wage and Hour Division administrator and the textile industry committee that had recommended a 32½ cents hourly minimum wage for the industry. Cameron asserted, contrary to the provisions of the FLSA, that wages should have been different in northern and southern sections of the country. By raising the minimum wage more than the twenty-five cents established under the law, Cameron claimed that the administrator "thwarted the will of Congress that existing wage differentials should not be suddenly disturbed." He also suggested that improper evidence was used as a basis for fixing the minimum wage. When Chief Justice Hughes asked if the Opp and other mills had ever met with the textile industry committee, Cameron's reply amused the justices: "No, we didn't get to the committee. Either properly or improperly, we missed the bus." And that moment of levity concluded oral arguments in the two cases.

CHAPTER SIX

The Supreme Court Decides *Darby Lumber*: Killing Laissez-Faire Constitutionalism

Following oral arguments in *U.S. v. Darby Lumber*, the nine justices met in conference on December 21, 1940, to discuss the case and take a vote on the merits. By the 1940 to 1941 term, the composition of the Supreme Court had changed significantly from the group that issued the landmark 5 to 4 decisions of the Constitutional Revolution of 1937. Between August 1937 and June 1941, President Roosevelt appointed six new justices. Chief Justice Charles Evans Hughes still presided over the Court, and Justices Harlan Fiske Stone and Owen Roberts continued their tenures. Three of the Four Horsemen, however, were gone, and the fourth, Justice James McReynolds, was about to retire. Both McReynolds and Chief Justice Hughes were seventy-eight years old at the start of the term.

Court vacancies were filled by dependable New Dealers Hugo Black, Stanley Reed, Felix Frankfurter, William O. Douglas, and Frank Murphy. Black had replaced Justice Willis Van Devanter in August 1937. As a senator, he had pushed for a thirty-hour workweek and defended a national uniform minimum wage. Stanley F. Reed filled the seat of Justice George Sutherland on January 31, 1938. President Hoover had appointed Reed counsel to the Federal Farm Board and later promoted him to general counsel of the Reconstruction Finance Corporation. In 1935 President Roosevelt tapped Reed to serve as special assistant to the attorney general. Within a year Roosevelt chose him to be solicitor general of the United States because he thought Reed would be effective in defending New Deal programs before the Supreme Court. Felix Frankfurter replaced Justice Benjamin Cardozo almost one year later, on January 30, 1939. During his tenure as a Harvard law professor Frankfurter supported the efforts of the NCLC to end child labor, and he defended Oregon's maximum hour and minimum wage laws. William Douglas was selected to fill the seat of Justice Louis Brandeis. The former chair of the Securities and Exchange Commission, Douglas supported the New Deal, especially on labor issues and market regulation. He would serve on the Court for thirty-six years. Frank Murphy, who had been governor general of the Philippines in 1933, governor of Michigan for two years, and attorney general of the United States in 1939, replaced Justice Pierce Butler on February 5, 1940.

Through deaths and retirements, President Roosevelt was able to reshape the Supreme Court and its jurisprudence without his Court-packing plan. Justice McReynolds, the last of the Four Horsemen, heard oral arguments in *Darby Lumber* and was present for the conference, but he retired from the bench on January 31, 1941, just days before the decision was announced. Roosevelt did not nominate his successor, James F. Byrnes, until June 12, so McReynolds's seat was vacant when the Court announced the opinion in *U.S. v. Darby Lumber* on February 3, 1941. Overall, the Court appeared more receptive to New Deal regulatory and social welfare policies, and that would prove to be true.

For decades, the docket books of the justices for the important 1937 to 1940 terms were held by the Office of the Curator of the Supreme Court, and access to the records was tightly restricted. New guidelines established in 2014 increased the availability of the material. Barry Cushman was the first to review the voting records, and his analysis sheds new light on the internal discussion of the *Darby Lumber* case. In the initial vote on the merits following conference discussion, seven justices voted to reverse the district court decision: Murphy, Douglas, Frankfurter, Reed, Black, Roberts, and Stone. Chief Justice Hughes and Justice McReynolds voted to pass. As mentioned earlier, McReynolds, the Court's most conservative opponent of the New Deal, did not participate in the decision.

Conference on the Merits

Conference notes taken by Justice Douglas reveal that the two biggest issues were the definition of "production for commerce" and whether the statute provided adequate notice for a criminal prosecution. Both issues had been raised by Judge Barrett in his trial court opinion. In the conference discussion and circulation of the draft opinion, Chief Justice

Hughes was troubled by the lack of clear definitions under the law and the potential scope of congressional power under the Commerce Clause. The notes indicate that Hughes was unconcerned about the transportation counts in the indictment. If lumber was shipped in interstate commerce without paying the wages required by the law, then that was a clear violation of the FLSA. The historical precedent of *Gibbons v. Ogden* was cited as holding that "the interstate commerce power knows no limitations."

But the production counts were different because they seemed to be based on an employer's intent to engage in interstate commerce. Court precedents had established that local acts may be within the reach of Congress if there is a "close and substantial" relationship to commerce. During the discussion, Hughes pointed out that Congress usually had stipulated wording for resolving the issue, but the act provided "no machinery for determining" whether that relationship exists in a particular case. Justice Douglas's notes mention a Labor Committee report that explained the provisions were intended to govern "every act no matter how trivial which has a relationship to commerce." Someone commented—apparently Hughes—that if congressional power was extended to "remote relationships our dual system [of federalism] would be at an end."

By custom, the senior associate justice speaks after the chief. Normally, that would be Justice McReynolds, but he seems to have played no active role in the discussion. Justice Stone, the second-most senior associate justice, took the lead defending the FLSA during conference deliberations. Justice Stone argued that the transportation provisions were valid. As to the other phrase, he stated that "low wages do have [a] profound effect on commerce." Once you acknowledge that a "substandard wage operates to disrupt commerce, then you do not need [a] finding in [a] particular case." Justices Roberts and Black agreed with Stone on the commerce issue. Because the chief justice voted to pass, he did not exercise his prerogative of writing the opinion of the Court, and that responsibility fell to Stone, who within a few months would be appointed the next chief justice of the United States.

Stone circulated a first draft of the opinion in early January 1941. In the last substantive paragraph, he addressed the Fifth Amendment due process issue in the case. Citing *West Coast Hotel Co. v. Parrish*, Stone wrote that "it is no longer open to question that the fixing of a minimum wage is within the legislative power and that the bare fact of its exercise is not a denial of due process under the Fifth more than under the Fourteenth Amendment." But Stone did not stop there. He commented on whether the minimum wage was fair or just: "There is no contention that the wage rate fixed by the present statute is unfair or oppressive, nor could there well be in view of the fact that the minimum standard wage applicable here for a full year of labor is less than $600. A minimum so low not thus assailed with respect to its application in any place cannot be objected to because it is given a nationwide application." Stone's point about the minimum wage was valid but probably unnecessary.

Justices Black and Douglas expressed concern about this language. Black sent Stone a handwritten note on January 25 urging that the two sentences be deleted. "The inference is left that had we found the wage rate 'unfair or oppressive' we would hold the law offended the due process clause. I would not agree to such a conclusion," warned Justice Black. He did not believe that the Due Process Clause of the Fifth Amendment could be used to challenge a law that had been properly enacted under the commerce power of Congress. Justice Douglas made a similar comment on page 14 of the draft opinion. Both sentences were removed in the final draft.

Memos exchanged between Chief Justice Hughes and Justice Stone on January 27 reveal that Hughes still had his doubts about the FLSA. "Of course, there is much that could be said with respect to the indefiniteness of the present statute, because of the failure of Congress to define the phrase 'production for commerce.' Congress gives a sweeping definition of 'production' and of 'goods' but not of production *for* commerce." Hughes made several suggestions to clarify the meaning of the phrase. "Even with the best possible test," he concluded, "the statute is a highly unsatisfactory one, but as it is a border line case I should prefer not to write." Justice Stone responded by saying that the phrase "for commerce" was no more vague than the criminal conspiracy provisions of the Sherman Antitrust Act, which had been sustained by the Court in *Nash v. United States* (1913). Stone was worried about overelaboration: "But I should not like to have the phrases you propose taken to mean that one who normally had no interstate commerce but who manufactured goods to fill a single order requiring shipment in interstate commerce was not within the Act." He invited Hughes to suggest something that will solve the problem.

The chief justice replied that he was still struggling with the intent to ship goods in interstate commerce: "It seems to me that it is necessary to couple the expressions with some limitation either with respect to a usual or normal course of business or actual transactions. It ought not to be left to what is simply in a man's mind." The chief, however, appreciated the difficulty and conceded that "it would be wise to avoid overelaboration." Despite his concerns with the law, Hughes ultimately joined Justice Stone's opinion. When the final draft was circulated, Hughes surrendered his objections and tersely commented, "I will go along with this."

A Landmark Decision in *U.S. v. Darby Lumber*

On February 3, 1941, the Supreme Court upheld the Fair Labor Standards Act by a vote of 8 to 0 in *U.S. v. Darby Lumber Co.* Writing for the Court, Justice Stone used many of the arguments in Justice Holmes's dissenting opinion in *Hammer v. Dagenhart* in defense of congressional powers. Stone stated that the motive and purpose of this regulation of interstate commerce are "to make effective the congressional conception of public policy that interstate commerce should not be made the instrument of competition in the distribution of goods produced under substandard labor conditions." These matters are for the legislature, upon which the Constitution places no restrictions, and over which the courts are given no control. Justice Stone wrote: "The power of Congress over interstate commerce is not confined to the regulation of commerce among the states. It extends to those activities intrastate which so affect interstate commerce or the exercise of the power of Congress over it as to make regulation of them appropriate means to the attainment of a legitimate end, the exercise of the granted power of Congress to regulate interstate commerce." Moreover, the value or amount of shipments in commerce or of production for commerce does not matter because even a small part may affect national commercial activity. Thus, regulations of commerce that do not infringe on some other constitutional prohibition are within congressional power.

Most importantly for the child labor provisions of the FLSA, the Court declared that *Hammer v. Dagenhart* is overruled. The Court characterized the precedent as an artifact of a bygone age. The distinction on which the opinion was based limited congressional power "to articles which in themselves have some harmful or deleterious property—a distinction which was novel when made and unsupported by any provision in the Constitution—has long since been abandoned." "The conclusion is inescapable," Stone argued, "that *Hammer v. Dagenhart*, was a departure from the principles which have prevailed in the interpretation of the Commerce Clause both before and since the decision, and that such vitality, as a precedent, as it then had, has long since been exhausted."

Accepting the argument made by the US government, the Court concluded that the decision is unaffected by the Tenth Amendment. Justice Stone wrote:

> The amendment states only a truism that all is retained which has not been surrendered. There is nothing in the history of its adoption to suggest that it was more than declaratory of the relationship between the national and state governments as it had been established by the Constitution before the amendment or that its purpose was other than to allay fears that the new national government might seek to exercise powers not granted, and that the states might not be able to exercise fully their reserved powers.

Stone explained that the amendment gives the government the authority "to resort to all means for the exercise of a granted power which are appropriate and plainly adapted to the permitted end." Precedents upholding the Sherman Antitrust Act and National Labor Relations Act, the opinion stated, affirm the broad powers of Congress.

The remaining issues, the record-keeping requirement and Fifth Amendment due process claim, were addressed in the last paragraphs of Stone's opinion. As a means of enforcing a valid law, Congress can require records "even of the intrastate transaction." Stone dispensed with the due process issue by citing *West Coast Hotel Co. v. Parrish, Holden v. Hardy*, and *Muller v. Oregon* as establishing that state legislatures and Congress have the power to fix minimum wages and maximum hours. Those precedents involved state wage and hours legislation enacted under police powers rather than federal law, but Stone made no distinctions with regard to the exercise of commerce clause powers: "The authority of the Federal government over interstate commerce does not differ in extent or character from that retained by the states over intrastate commerce." The FLSA, Stone concluded, is "sufficiently definite to meet constitutional demands" for due process. Employers who violate the wage and hour provisions have received fair warning of potential criminal prosecution. That is all that is required by the Constitution.

In *Opp Cotton Mills, Inc. v. Administrator Wage and Hour Division*, decided the same day as *Darby Lumber*, a unanimous Court, minus Justice McReynolds, specifically upheld the wage and hour requirement and industry committee procedure for raising wages. The Court reached several conclusions. First, the Fair Labor Standards Act, to the extent that it authorized the administrator and the industry committees appointed by him to classify industries and fix minimum wages, was not an unconstitutional delegation of legislative power. Congress had established standards, procedures, and record-keeping requirements such that Congress, the courts, and the public can ascertain whether the administrative actions are consistent with the legislative power. Also, the administrative proceedings met the standards for constitutional due process. The orders of the administrator were made based on fact-finding committees. He was not required, Stone argued, to make "mathematical geographical apportionment" of industry committee membership or conduct quasi-judicial hearings. The opinion was an important statement on federal administrative procedure five years before Congress passed the Administrative Procedure Act of 1946—the most comprehensive and significant law governing federal administrative agencies.

Newspaper headlines and stories recognized the importance of the *Darby Lumber* decision. The *Los Angeles Times* declared that the New Deal "won a sweeping victory" for its social agenda. The *Arizona Republic* also called it a "sweeping decision that upheld the constitutionality of the wage-hour law in all its phases." Some papers highlighted the child labor provisions. "Pay-Hour Law Ruling Curbs Child Labor" was the headline in the *New York Herald Tribune*. "The change that has been effected," the *Washington Post* commented, "is scarcely less significant than it would have been if accomplished through a constitutional amendment," adding that the federal government "emerged as a government of almost unlimited powers in the economic and social field." The *Wall Street Journal* also admitted that the decision gave the federal government sweeping powers "over local conditions of employment and the maintenance of national wage levels to which low-wage areas would have to adjust themselves." In the Tarheel state, editors bitterly acknowledged that states' rights were as dead as "the gallant boys from North Carolina who fell on the scarred slopes of Gettysburg" and that the states "have no real rights which the Federal government is bound to respect."

An editorial in *Southern Lumberman* noted that the *Darby Lumber* decision was "received calmly—probably because the Court's decision had already been foreseen and discounted." Fred Darby and his lawyers were praised for their courage and legal arguments, but because of "Justice Black and his associates," the outcome was inevitable. The authors were upset that the original intent of the framers on the separation of powers and checks and balances was "entirely thwarted by the existence of a dominant executive, operating in conjunction with a rubber-stamp legislative group, and a hand-picked bench." The editors still believed that the wages and hours law was "unwise and impracticable" and hoped for its eventual repeal or amendment. For now, the FLSA was acknowledged as the law of the land, and it was the duty of lumbermen to obey its provisions.

Colonel Philip Fleming, administrator of the Wage and Hour Division, hailed the *Darby Lumber* decision and noted that the *Opp Cotton Mills* opinion upheld an additional $35 million in wage increases imposed by the industry committee procedures. Alex Elson, regional attorney for the Wage and Hour Division, identified three immediate effects of the *Darby Lumber* decision. First, it removed any doubt about the constitutionality of the FLSA. Combined with the decision in *National Labor Relations Board v. Jones and Laughlin Steel Corporation*, Congress now had broad authority to regulate labor, wages, and working conditions under the Commerce Clause. According to the division, the decision sustained wage increases amounting to $100 million. Second, the decision gave legal standing to the fourteen interpretive bulletins issued by the administrator of the division in implementing the law. One of those bulletins defined "production for commerce" as production of goods "where the employer, according to the normal course of his business, intends or expects to move in interstate commerce." Stone's opinion uses that language almost verbatim. Finally, the opinion made it clear that the

FLSA applies regardless of the volume of goods shipped in interstate commerce.

For constitutional law, the *Darby Lumber* decision is significant because it upheld broad congressional power to regulate wages and hours. And even though the case had nothing to do with child labor, the opinion erased the *Hammer v. Dagenhart* precedent—a decision that had frustrated the efforts of child labor reformers for more than twenty years—and for the first time affirmed federal power to regulate oppressive child labor. Finally, the landmark *Darby Lumber* decision impacted our federal system by holding that the Tenth Amendment does not limit the delegated or implied powers of Congress under the Commerce Clause. One historian commented: "It is not much to say that *United States v. Darby* is one of the half-dozen most important cases in the whole . . . history of American constitutional law." Justice Stone's biographer, Alpheus T. Mason, suggests that the justice had waited five years for a chance to exorcise from constitutional jurisprudence laissez-faire principles and the belief that "dual federalism under the Tenth Amendment limited federal power." The *Darby Lumber* decision was Stone's magnum opus on the issue.

But Alpheus Mason also noted that the sweeping nature of the decision "dampened Stone's own pleasure in his achievement." In a letter to Columbia law professor Milton Handler just weeks after the opinion, Stone felt "that not everyone will like the Wages and Hours decision. . . . It seems to be the fate of the judge that he can never please more than fifty percent of his customers, and sometimes not even that." Stone also personally opposed a national minimum wage, preferring instead the values of hard work and thrift. He even commented, with specific reference to the FLSA, that truthfully, he felt "obliged to uphold some laws which make me gag." In the end, it was Stone's constitutional jurisprudence, rather than his personal policy views, that triumphed in the *Darby Lumber* case.

Regardless of how Justice Stone perceived his work, his colleagues praised the opinion. Justice Frankfurter said: "But I especially rejoice over the way you buried *Hammer v. Dagenhart* and your definitive exposure of the empty hobgoblin of the Tenth Amendment." Justice Douglas wrote: "I heartily agree. This has the master's real touch!" Justice Black wrote a brief note congratulating Justice Stone "on obtaining unanimous approval of the wage and hour cases." Justice Reed opined: "It has been a long journey, but the end is here. We should have overturned *Hammer* years ago." In a letter to Noel T. Dowling, a member of the NCLC board, Stone explained that the *Darby* decision was designed to "make two things clear, namely (1) that the commerce power of Congress is not restricted to intrinsically harmful commodities, and (2) that the motive of Congress in passing commerce clause laws is none of the Court's business."

The National Child Labor Committee, which had lobbied for federal child labor legislation for nearly three decades, described the decision as "most gratifying." The editor of the *Social Service Review*, the leading professional journal of social workers, was more critical of the Supreme Court. Describing the Court as a "sinner who finally repenteth," the editor bitterly suggested that the decision was poor compensation for the damage done to children in *Dagenhart*. "But what of the army of children who have come and gone from the mills and factories and lumber yards, the millions of weary days of work, and the lost vision of an education to do a proper share of the world's work? These children now living as unemployed workers should indict the Supreme Court of these United States for their stunted minds and broken lives." For many reformers who had devoted much of their lives to abolishing child labor, it was a bittersweet victory.

The Trial of Fred Darby and His Lumber Company

The Court's decision in *Darby Lumber* had another major consequence: Fred W. Darby and his lumber company were to be tried in Savannah on nineteen counts for violating the Fair Labor Standards Act. On May 1, 1941, District Judge William Barrett died, and Darby's counsel, Judge Archibald Lovett, was appointed by President Roosevelt to replace him. Because of a conflict of interest, Lovett was disqualified from the case. Darby was then tried before District Judge Bascom S. Deaver for the Middle District of Georgia. Deaver had experience as a federal prosecutor. He earned his law degree from Mercer University School of Law in 1910 and worked in private practice for twelve years, then served as assistant US attorney for the Southern District of Georgia from 1922 to 1926. After working as US attorney for the Middle District of Georgia,

1926 to 1928, Deaver was appointed by President Calvin Coolidge to the federal bench in March 1928.

The trial commenced on December 15, 1941, in Savannah. George A. Downing, regional attorney for the Wage and Hour Division of the US Department of Labor, and Julian Hartridge, assistant district attorney, served as counsel for the United States. Fred Darby and the lumber company were represented by Robert M. Hitch Jr., Shelby Myrick, and Fred T. Lanier of the firm Hitch, Morris, and Harrison. The first witness called by the government was F. C. Temples, an agent for the Georgia and Florida Railroad. He produced copies of bills detailing shipments from the Darby Lumber Company. It was stipulated by counsel for the government and defendant that the shipments in counts thirteen through nineteen were made as alleged in the indictment; that is, they were out-of-state shipments. Those facts were not contested.

Robert K. Miller, an inspector for the Wage and Hour Division, testified next. He had inspected the payroll books and shipping records of Darby Lumber from September 14 to 19, 1939. He estimated that about 75 percent of the business of Darby Lumber was interstate. He learned that Fred Darby owned another lumber company in Jacksonville, Florida, and the Statesboro mill supplied the Jacksonville business. Darby had lived in Jacksonville since 1938, and that was his residence at the time of the trial. Employees at the Statesboro mill were paid on a bi-weekly basis on Saturdays. When Downing asked if Miller could state the number of instances when employees were paid less than twenty-five cents an hour, Miller replied that he couldn't because "there were too many of that general nature." He also testified that there were many such instances of failing to pay time and a half for overtime. When asked by counsel to give an estimate, Miller responded that there were about fifty employees and at least that many violations every week from October 1938 to September 1939.

Miller also revealed that the company maintained two sets of payroll records—one for "wholesale" and the other for "retail"—and that employees were sometimes on both payrolls during the same week. Workers on wholesale were paid twenty-five cents an hour while those on retail earned fifteen cents an hour. When Miller asked E. S. Lane, the bookkeeper, and Fred Darby the meaning of the two categories, he was told that retail was for work done on goods shipped locally and wholesale was for goods transported across state lines. When Miller informed Darby that it was a violation of the FLSA to pay employees at two separate rates during the same week, Darby denied that it was a violation. Miller then testified that Darby asked what the division planned to do about the issue. Miller replied that in some cases they permitted the employer to make restitution for past violations. The witness said that Darby refused to even consider such payments.

On cross-examination, Shelby Myrick pointed out to Robert Miller that the law does not say anything about the commingling of wholesale and retail hours of work and that it took an interpretive ruling to make that clear. Based on a Prentice-Hall publication, Myrick suggested that it was not until June 1941 that the administrator of the Wage and Hour Division made that interpretation. Miller, however, insisted that the ruling was issued in March or April 1939 because he did not audit the lumber company until September of that year, and he told Fred Darby at the time that the practice was forbidden.

According to press reports and court documents, trial arguments hinged on an alleged agreement between Fred Darby and his employees that had been entered into before the Fair Labor Standards Act had become effective on October 24, 1938. Six weeks prior to that date, testimony showed that Darby had agreed to pay his employees at half their current rate. When the law went into effect, they would receive the twenty-five-cent minimum. Half of that amount, however, was considered actual wages, and the remainder a "loan" to be repaid by employees after the FLSA was enforced. Under the terms of the agreement then, employees had the loan amount deducted from their paychecks and were effectively earning well below the twenty-five-cent minimum wage required by the federal law. The plan was typical of kickback schemes used by employers to shirk minimum wage requirements.

Fred Darby later testified that this arrangement was necessary to avoid sudden increases in pay that he could not afford. He had entered into a contract with a firm in South Carolina to provide lumber at a price that was so low that it was impossible for him to compensate his workers at the rate required by the law. He told his men that he might have to close the mill. They could either quit or agree to work under the plan. Given a choice between no job and continued employment at half their normal pay rate, though much less than the required minimum wage, all the men agreed to the arrangement. Darby mentioned several times that none of his men complained about this plan or filed a lawsuit against him.

One employee, Roger Stone, who operated a skidder at the mill—a machine that picks up logs and unloads trucks—testified on the proposed pay plan. Stone said that Darby told employees that "things were kinder tight, but that he was going to try to operate if he could. If you all help me, I will help you." Darby explained: "I will cut your wages in half; it will be cut but it won't be; you will get your checks straight, and when they start paying the 25¢ an hour I will deduct it back." Roger Stone testified that after the law was in force, $2.00, or $1.00 a week, would be deducted from his check and altogether took out $39.30. He was making seventeen cents an hour and $10.10 a week. After the law and loan deductions, his pay was cut in half.

A witness for the government named Daniel B. Gay, a timber contractor who furnished the Darby firm with logs, testified that he told Fred Darby that he could not comply with the Fair Labor Standards Act and accept a reduced price for timber, which Darby had allegedly demanded. Gay said that he paid his men "as cheap as I could hire them, from $1.25 to $2.00 a day," and they worked twelve hours or more each day. Under questioning from Downing, Gay recalled that Darby had explained to him a way to "get by" under the law. Darby said that if you pay a man $2.50 a day, to pay him that but to charge back half the amount; in other words, make him pay back half of his paycheck. Daniel Gay admitted that he did not use the plan, nor did he pay his employees the minimum required by the law.

The government then called Lynn Haydell, a supervising inspector for the Wage and Hour Division, who made a visit to the Darby Lumber Company to inspect the books and talk to Fred Darby. He testified that Darby explained the deductions from paychecks as "bills that employees owed" for various business expenses in Statesboro. Haydell then asked Darby to produce invoices for the deductions, but he was unable to provide satisfactory records to reconcile the accounts. On cross-examination, Myrick asked Haydell about the plan. Myrick suggested that Haydell criticized the plan because Darby could not produce vouchers for all of the deductions. But Haydell responded that the employees told him that the deductions were for money loaned to them, and that they had not borrowed any money.

After testimony by Temples, Miller, Stone, Gay, and Haydell, cross-examination by the defense, and redirect questioning by Downing, the government rested its case. Myrick then called Jewell Watson, Darby's sister-in-law, to the stand. A graduate of Statesboro High School, Watson had attended Statesboro College for two years and worked at the mill for nine years, doing payroll until January 1, 1939. She then left for a couple of months but returned to the job. On direct examination, she testified that Fred Darby told her to "be sure to comply with all the laws." She also said that he had made frequent trips to meetings to learn about the act (FLSA) and returned and told her what had to be done. Despite these instructions, she admitted to several errors in calculating overtime.

Further testimony revealed payroll practices that were violations of the Fair Labor Standards Act. On cross-examination, Downing was able to get Watson to admit that there were numerous errors in paying overtime. Instead of calculating overtime based on a forty-four-hour week, it appeared that she lumped the two weeks together and often paid no time and a half. For example, if a man worked fifty-two hours one week, and thirty-six the next, he earned eight hours of overtime for the first week and should have been paid 37½ cents an hour for those hours. However, Jewell Watson added fifty-two and thirty-six to total eighty-eight hours. Because the maximum was forty-four hours a week at the minimum wage, no overtime was paid. This was a clear violation of the law. Whether the payroll practice was intentional was something the jury would determine. Pay stubs and accounting records indicated that nearly every employee was shorted overtime pay. Downing tried to get Watson to admit that she was told to calculate the pay this way, but she stated that Darby "had nothing to do with the records and he never checked them."

Another witness for the defense, E. S. Lane, was the superintendent of the Darby Lumber Company. He was responsible for keeping the time cards and the payroll books for the two months that Jewell Watson was absent. Under direct examination from defense counsel, he admitted to making errors in calculating payroll for about a dozen employees during the two-month period. He attributed the mistakes to "haste or oversight" or "clerical error." On cross-examination by Downing, Lane testified that Darby "frequently gave him instructions about complying with the act; he had done that before the act became effective." Downing, however, was able to get Lane to admit that the retail versus wholesale categories were ambiguous and that accurate records were not maintained on how long each employee worked each day and in what capacity. Like Watson, Lane simply combined two weeks together rather than paying a worker overtime past forty-four hours per week. For example, one employee named Williams worked forty hours one week and fifty-six the next (ninety-six total). He should have received twelve hours at time and a half for the second week but was paid overtime for only eight hours beyond the eighty-eight for two weeks.

When the defense called Fred Darby to the stand, Myrick asked him to whose benefit did he make the contract or plan? Darby responded: "It was entirely for the employees; I would have had no loss to shut down. No sir, I did not enter into that plan to avoid or evade the law; I tried to comply with the law." When Myrick asked him if he paid his employees twenty-five cents an hour when the law became effective, Darby said, "I intended to and presumed we did." He also stated that he was unaware that it was illegal under the law to classify employees as retail or wholesale during the same week and pay a wage less than the minimum.

Counsel for the defense tried to argue that Fred Darby never had a chance to comply with the law and that he was treated unfairly. Government investigators and the defendant offered conflicting testimony. Darby argued that investigators told him there were minor discrepancies in his payroll practices, while Miller and other government witnesses testified that they informed Darby that there were obvious violations of law. Darby testified that after Robert Miller inspected the books in September 1939, Miller and H. Douglas Weaver, a special assistant to the attorney general, returned on October 26 and seized his payroll books. Within days, a man arrived at the mill to serve subpoenas. Downing objected to the line of questions. The Court pointed out to defense counsel that the indictments were for actions taken after the law went into effect and how Darby was treated "would not have anything to do with whether he had actually violated the law." Upon further questioning, Darby denied that he told Daniel Gay that he had a plan to evade the law and stated that he "positively did not know" that Gay was not in compliance with the law.

In its closing argument, the prosecution contended that lumber executives at Darby Lumber knew that the timber supplied by Daniel Gay was not produced under the provisions of the law, and therefore they knowingly and willfully violated the law. Downing suggested that Fred Darby was trying to deflect blame for his failure to comply with the federal wage requirements. He also demonstrated that Darby was not hurting financially. When asked if he made money in 1938, Darby responded that he thought he earned $230 that year. Downing then produced a copy of Darby's income tax return from 1938 showing that he made in excess of $9,500. Darby admitted that he had earned that amount based on his tax returns from his four businesses. Downing declared that the guilt of the lumber firm was confirmed by the defendant's own records and the testimony of Daniel Gay.

In his closing argument for the defense, Shelby Myrick first attacked the Fair Labor Standards Act, claiming that it was "the first law in history to make a criminal offense of a civil matter." He criticized federal investigators "who sit up in Washington" and tell citizens what to do. Those contentions, of course, carried little weight because the Supreme Court had already upheld the law in its entirety. Myrick also played the victim card. He argued that the government was trying to make an example of the Darby case, and he questioned why Daniel Gay, who had testified that he did not pay his workers the minimum wage, was not prosecuted as well. With the United States now engaged in World War II, Myrick suggested that it was not "the proper time to take up a . . . man and convict him when no harm has been done." As they had argued during the appellate litigation challenging the law, the defense claimed the agreement had been negotiated in good faith by the lumber company, that no employees objected, and that there was no attempt to conceal it from federal investigators. Defense counsel also argued that Fred Darby's record showed no criminal intent, and that any errors in record keeping were accidental with no intention to defraud.

The defense motioned to exclude any evidence about the contract or plan that Darby had discussed with his employees before the law became effective. Judge Deaver, however, denied the motion and said he would tell the jury that the evidence can be used to determine whether Darby had a plan to evade the law and used that as a scheme or device to accomplish that objective. The defense also asked for a directed verdict of not guilty, but that was overruled by Deaver. The case would go to the jury.

In his charge to the jury, Judge Deaver addressed the constitutionality of the FLSA because both the government and defense counsel had commented on the issue. He told them that even though an act of Congress may be of doubtful constitutionality, "a man cannot assume that it is unconstitutional and then proceed to violate it and then be excused on the ground that it might have been unconstitutional." The defense had claimed that none of the employees complained about how they were treated, and therefore everyone should be satisfied. The judge noted, however, that whether the employees complained or not was entirely irrelevant and not for the jury's consideration.

Judge Deaver also emphasized the importance of determining the intent of the defendant. According to the statute, the "willful violation of the terms of the FLSA constitute a crime." The judge went into great detail about the plan or agreement between Darby and his employees. He explained that it was up to the jury to decide whether employees of Fred Darby, in calculating overtime, paying the minimum wage, and keeping records, made honest mistakes, done without his knowledge, or, as the government contended, engaged in willful schemes to evade the law. Shelby Myrick was not satisfied with the jury instructions on the "willful intent" issue, so Judge Deaver had to recharge the jury.

The jury deliberated for only two hours. Darby Lumber was acquitted on eight counts and convicted and sentenced on eleven. Fred Darby was found guilty on eight counts of violating the overtime provisions of the FLSA, one count of failure to keep adequate records as required by the law, and two counts of "shipment in interstate commerce of lumber produced in violation of the FLSA." Judge Deaver fined Darby $2,500 for the convictions: $500 on count four of the indictment, which involved employing workers beyond the maximum forty-four hours and not paying overtime, and $200 each on the remaining ten counts. Adjusted for inflation, the $2,500 fine would equal $49,168 in 2024. For a small regional company, that was a significant penalty.

Darby appealed the convictions to the Court of Appeals for the Fifth Circuit. The appellant continued to be represented by Robert Hitch Jr. and Shelby Myrick. Darby specified that several errors were made during the trial: "the overruling of his motion for a directed verdict of acquittal, the admission of oral evidence as to his work records, the refusal to rule out evidence of an arrangement with his employees made before the Act became effective, and the refusal to give two written requests to charge the jury." However, the three-judge panel unanimously affirmed the convictions and fine in *Darby v. United States* on January 15, 1943. Circuit Judge Samuel H. Sibley argued that Judge Deaver had properly instructed the jury and that evidence of the agreement with the employees was properly retained because it tended to show Darby's willingness to evade, in part, the wage provisions of the act. The decision brought an end to the nearly four-year litigation involving the Darby Lumber Company. The company continued to operate and serve the local Statesboro community until it closed in 1978. Fred W. Darby died on March 14, 1972, and is buried in the Eastside Cemetery in Bulloch County, Georgia. In 2011 the Bulloch County Historical Society erected a historical marker on the former site of the Darby Lumber Company.

The FLSA and World War II

Six months after the Supreme Court decision in *Darby Lumber*, the Japanese attack on Pearl Harbor thrust the United States into World War II. As the economy geared up for war production, there were renewed calls to repeal or at least suspend parts of the FLSA. Thomas J. McCormick, liaison officer for the Wage and Hour Division, announced in mid-December that there were no plans to change the wage or hour provisions. McCormick believed that the forty-hour workweek would be retained "because industrial experience has shown that the short work week is more efficient than a longer week." He claimed that the excessively long hours that Germans must work, with some reports of eighty-hour workweeks, seriously reduced their output, and that if those hours continued, the Nazis will soon "crack up" to the advantage of the Allies.

But some members of Congress pressed for changes. In February 1942, Representative Howard W. Smith (D-VA) proposed to suspend for the duration of the war federal maximum hour and overtime pay laws. He was joined by Senator Clyde L. Herring (D-IA). Herring said that he planned to move in the Senate to discharge the Education and Labor Committee from consideration of broad labor policy, which had been languishing there, if the committee did not act soon. Representative

Smith noted that there were seventeen different federal laws, including the FLSA, fixing a limitation or penalty on work beyond eight hours a day. His amendment to a second War Powers bill would suspend all those laws. He explained: "Obviously we cannot compete with the labor of dictator countries if we stubbornly persist in operating our war effort on a basis of maintaining during the crisis all of our so-called labor social gains." House labor forces geared up to defeat the amendment.

A series of labor strikes in war industries alarmed some representatives and increased support for the Smith amendment. It appeared that the votes were there to rebuke organized labor. Overnight, however, cooler heads prevailed, and opposition to the amendment came from an unlikely source. Representative Frank B. Keefe (R-WI), a strong critic of the Roosevelt administration, announced his intent to vote against the Smith amendment. "The amendment does not clear up the situation. It serves only to muddy the waters," he said. "Merely permitting a lengthening of the 40-hour week and eliminating time and a half for overtime does not approach the problem at all." Other speakers noted that the law would hurt the lowest-paid workers, who, unlike union members, had no labor contract to protect them.

President Roosevelt also made it clear that he opposed any suspension of labor protections, especially proposals targeting the forty-hour workweek. The president believed that the media had exaggerated the impact of "petty strikes," with one involving just fifteen men, and that there was no major strike problem in the nation. He warned that the Smith amendment would diminish the pay of millions of workers at the lower end of the pay scale because they have no contracts with overtime provisions. Before the vote, a copy of a statement by William Green, president of the AFL, emphasized this point about union contracts. Those agreements called for time and a half for overtime and double time on Sundays and holidays. The Smith amendment suffered a crushing defeat in the House, 226 to 62, but the result did not end attempts to weaken employment laws for the duration of the war.

One month after the vote on the Smith amendment, Representative Smith co-sponsored a bill with Carl Vinson (D-GA), chair of the House Naval Committee. The Smith-Vinson bill included provisions to limit profits on war contracts to 6 percent of costs, suspend the forty-hour workweek, eliminate overtime pay, and outlaw the closed shop, where employers agree to hire and retain only union members, in war industries. Ostensibly, their action was in response to floor reports that about twenty House members had received thousands of letters from constituents demanding that Congress do something on the labor issue.

A frustrated and critical President Roosevelt told reporters in March he thought that part of the campaign against the forty-hour workweek was organized and part of it was not. He suggested that the organized part had subversive consequences. He explained that "writing and conversation, along with rumor, cocktail parties, and tea fights, were implements used by the sixth column in spreading Fifth Column poison." When asked by a reporter if the president could provide evidence that a "sixth column" was behind the campaign to eliminate the forty-hour week, Roosevelt said that he did not know enough about the effort but suggested that many of the reporters in the room were responsible for helping distribute propaganda. Both War Production Board chief Donald M. Nelson and Secretary of Labor Frances Perkins testified before the House Naval Committee against the Smith-Vinson bill. Secretary Perkins said the measure would hinder, not help, war production. Workers in war industries were working beyond forty hours. "Suspension of overtime after 40 hours," she said, "will mean only a reduction in the men's pay envelopes."

Opponents of the forty-hour workweek and overtime pay persisted. They claimed that the wages and hours law was more appropriate for a depression economy, where work was scarce, because limiting the workweek made more jobs available. The law, they argued, was inefficient for wartime production. While large corporations with wartime contracts can afford to make their employees work beyond forty hours a week and pay overtime because the government is footing the bill, thousands of employers, they contended, engaged in the production of civilian goods have profit margins so low that they cannot afford a workweek of more than forty hours. An editorial in the *Wall Street Journal* asserted the "40-hour rule produces a waste of manpower resources" and adds to the "forces making for scarcity of consumer goods."

Eddie Rickenbacker, the World War I ace and owner of Eastern Air Lines, was a vocal critic of not only the forty-hour workweek but also every labor policy of the New Deal and organized labor. He favored a "piecework rate" to increase production. That practice, however, was associated with the sweating system and opposed by many. Ricken-backer spoke before the War Labor Board. "It seems incredible to me," he argued, "that we should be working under this depression theory of spreading work (through the 40-hour week)." He continued: "Industry should be given an opportunity to minimize government interference and to eliminate racketeering elements in labor." For all his anti-labor rhetoric, Rickenbacker did make one accurate statement. He predicted that the country was in for "a long, hard war that will not end before the spring of 1945, if then."

In May 1943 a labor relations consultant released the results of a survey of three hundred companies of all sizes, from fewer than fifty workers to one firm with more than thirty-five thousand employees. Three out of five companies opposed repeal of the wages and hours law. Larger companies favored retention of the law by a 2-to-1 margin, while most of the opposition came from smaller firms. There were strong and conflicting opinions on both sides of the issue. Employers in favor of the FLSA said that it provided an incentive for regular attendance and discouraged absenteeism because of the overtime provision. Supporters also argued that repeal "would upset economic stability, cause no end of trouble with labor, and have a bad effect on the morale of the public." Those against the law argued that it encouraged absenteeism because of the high wages and that it was no longer necessary to spread jobs around. Opponents claimed that the law hurt small start-up businesses that needed to pay lower wages to survive.

Wartime Pressure to Weaken Child Labor Laws

World War II also threatened to undermine the child labor provisions of the FLSA. With millions of adult males going off to war, numerous jobs became available for school-age children. In the two decades prior to 1940, child labor had been steadily declining. The number of employed minors fourteen through seventeen years of age dropped from 2.5 million in 1920 to one million in 1940. All of these gains in reducing child labor were lost during the war years. The National Education Association's Commission for the Defense of Democracy noted that youth work permits had increased 400 percent since 1940, creating what the commission called "a real threat to the future of this country." The appeal of high wages, state compulsory attendance laws that exempted fourteen- and fifteen-year-olds if they were employed, and the gaps in child labor restrictions under the Fair Labor Standards Act combined to produce an increase in child labor during the war years.

By 1944 almost three million boys and girls under eighteen years of age either quit school for work or tried to balance their studies and work obligations. Of this number, about nine hundred thousand were fourteen to fifteen years old, with many working illegally. A report written by L. Metcalfe Walling, director of the Wage and Hour Division of the Labor Department, identified 1,722 establishments employing 4,567 minors in violation of child labor laws during 1942 and 1943. The number was a 200 percent increase from 1941. In just the first six months of 1943, a total of 3,658 children were found working illegally in various industries. Those figures only covered businesses engaged in interstate commerce. The numbers may have been worse because Congress cut appropriations for the Children's Bureau in 1943, making inspection and enforcement of child labor laws difficult.

Schools that initially encouraged part-time work as a patriotic contribution soon noticed a high drop-out rate because a decent paycheck was more appealing than sitting in the classroom. Across the country, schools reported many empty seats in the classroom. In Starbuck, Washington, 20 percent of the students under age sixteen left school for full-time jobs. In Oakland, California, where 15 percent of the children under age sixteen quit school for employment, officials complained that child labor and school attendance laws could not be enforced. Other school districts warned that child labor laws were being ignored. In East St. Louis, Illinois, high school enrollment dropped 20 percent. Often, the child workers were earning higher wages than their teachers. In Cherryvale, Kansas, a senior classman was earning more money than his teachers even though he was working only part-time. In Gary, Indiana, high school boys were paid more money working part-time in the steel mills than their teachers. As more children left school for factory jobs or worked late hours after school, some "broke down physically under the combined strain of study and excessive work." In Cleveland, Ohio, forty children in a single school fell asleep in class one morning because all of them had been setting up pins in a bowling alley the previous night.

Most educators agreed that the best contribution students could make to the war effort was to stay in school until they graduated and were called into service.

A sharp increase in delinquency, particularly by girls, was reported in many areas of the country. Alarmed by reports of young girls roaming the streets and boys hanging out in taverns, First Lady Eleanor Roosevelt hosted a forum at the White House attended by more than a hundred social workers, educators, and government administrators in the field of child labor. Mrs. Roosevelt blamed the increasing delinquency rates on the appeal of high wages for young workers, the lack of recreational facilities for youth, and the loss of parental supervision because fathers and mothers were preoccupied with war duties. To solve the problem, Charlotte Carr, head of Chicago's Hull House, suggested "vocational counseling to steer youth into the right kind of employment." Others recommended closer cooperation between social agencies and families with children, more emphasis on "responsibility" in school curriculums, and "enlightening" the proper officials who have the resources to address the problem.

Employers and some officials in the Defense Department, however, sought to relax, if not repeal, child labor laws. Governors, anxious to demonstrate their patriotism, also backed legislation to repeal state labor laws with the support of some army and navy officials. According to Frances Perkins, "Army-Navy procurement offices were harassed by contractors who constantly complained of their inability to operate with speed and efficiency under state and federal labor laws." In some situations, federal defense agencies themselves were to blame for employing children in wartime industries. A report from Somerville, Massachusetts, found navy yards and arsenals where fourteen- and fifteen-year-old boys were employed operating machines in violation of the sixteen-year-old minimum.

The National Child Labor Committee, the National Education Association, the Children's Bureau, Secretary Perkins, and President Roosevelt resisted these efforts to weaken or abolish child labor protections. The issue was not so much prohibiting all work, because children could contribute to the war effort, but making sure that child welfare was protected. In January 1942 the National Child Labor Committee issued a policy statement: "The chief contribution a child can make to his country in the present crisis is to remain in school and prepare himself for future work and for the future responsibilities of citizenship." The NCLC board recognized that child labor restrictions imposed in peacetime might have to be modified to meet national emergencies and wartime necessities, but the welfare of children must be safeguarded.

Facing constant pressure to relax definitions and regulations under the FLSA, the Children's Bureau established a fifty-six-member Commission on Children in Wartime "to consider urgent steps for the protection and welfare of children in emergency situations resulting from the war." Toward this goal, the commission organized a forum on delinquency held at the White House in 1943. While Allied troops invaded the beaches of Normandy in June 1944, the Commission on Children in Wartime announced specific recommendations to protect children and youth during demobilization: (1) extend health service and medical care for all mothers and children, (2) regulate child labor and plan for young workers during the demobilization period, (3) develop community recreation and leisure activities for young people to keep them out of trouble, and (4) safeguard family life in wartime and during the post-war period.

Even though the Children's Bureau, the NCLC, and other organizations tried to hold the line against weakening child labor protections, many states revised their laws to allow for more young workers. Two years into the war, more than three-fourths of the states had considered modifications to their child labor laws, and twenty-seven changes had been made either to the statutes themselves or granting executive authority to alter or suspend the laws. Most of the changes involved allowing sixteen- and seventeen-year-old minors to work longer hours. Laws allowing the employment of children in bowling alleys as pin setters were relaxed in nine states. Also, age limits were reduced from eighteen or twenty-one years to fourteen or sixteen years for girls doing messenger work and jobs in restaurants, hotels, theaters, and drugstores. Eleven states relaxed their laws to enable employment of school-age children in agriculture by permitting alterations in the school day and calendar.

When President Roosevelt was informed of the continued attacks on state and federal labor laws, he agreed that the laws must be defended. "The eight-hour day," he argued, "is the most efficient productive day for the worker." He believed that three eight-hour shifts were the most effective way to maintain wartime production. The president asserted: "Protection of workers against accidents, illness, and fatigue are vital for efficiency. Children under sixteen, certainly under fourteen, are not productive workers." The only concession that he made to wartime manpower needs was part-time or vacation employment of older high school students to help harvest crops or work in nonhazardous war industries. Although there were some modifications, Secretary Perkins credited the president's position with blocking efforts to repeal labor legislation and making it through the war with fundamental labor protections intact.

In January 1943, the War Manpower Commission issued a statement on the employment of minors. While acknowledging that many young people under age eighteen would be needed in the workforce, it emphasized the importance of safeguarding their physical and intellectual development. The statement pointed out that in most cases, the best thing that youth under age eighteen could do for the war effort was to stay in school, and when their services were needed, work during vacations or part-time. The War Manpower Commission announced a "basic National policy" consisting of ten items. These items included a declaration that existing school attendance and child labor standards should be preserved and enforced, a prohibition on either full or part-time employment for children under fourteen years of age, and a recommendation that children ages fourteen or fifteen should only be employed if adult workers are unavailable and never in manufacturing or mining operations. The policy also suggested that youth should not be employed during school hours except when a temporary emergency might require such activity, and that the combined hours for school and work should not exceed eight a day for children under sixteen years of age.

Working with the War Manpower Commission and federal procurement agencies, the Children's Bureau adopted a flexible policy to meet wartime needs for labor. A few exemptions were granted to employers, but none that exposed child workers to serious risk to their health. For example, fourteen- and fifteen-year-old children were permitted to work until 10:00 p.m. rather than 7:00 p.m. in fruit and vegetable packing plants, but only outside of school hours and not more than forty hours a week or eight weeks a season. Some industries were exempted from the eighteen-year minimum age in hazardous occupations. There were abuses of child labor, but those primarily happened outside the legal regime established by the FLSA and state regulations. The FLSA stood as a bulwark against such exploitation, and any exemptions made during the conflict were revoked following the war.

By the time the Supreme Court validated federal power to regulate child labor in *U.S. v. Darby Lumber*, the most egregious forms of the practice had ended. But there were still several areas ripe for reform. The NCLC noted that legislation was urgently needed to protect four large groups of children not covered by the FLSA: children under sixteen years old working in commercialized agriculture, in street trades, and in intrastate industrial employment; and sixteen- and seventeen-year-olds laboring in hazardous jobs in intrastate industries. Those battles would continue for decades.

Post–*Darby Lumber* Decisions on the FLSA

Over the next five years, the Supreme Court clarified some of the ambiguities in the general coverage provisions of the FLSA. In *A. B. Kirschbaum v. Walling* (1942), the Court decided whether custodians, elevator operators, and various maintenance personnel of a building owned by a New York firm but leased to a company producing textiles for shipment in interstate commerce fell under the provisions of the law. The building owners claimed that they were detached from any production for interstate commerce. The Wage and Hour Division argued that the workers were involved in a "process or occupation" that was necessary to the production of goods shipped in interstate commerce.

Writing for an 8 to 1 majority, with only Justice Owen Roberts dissenting, Justice Felix Frankfurter applied the *Darby Lumber* reasoning that Congress has broad power to regulate interstate commerce, and he asserted that Congress had not even reached the outer limits of its authority. Frankfurter concluded that it was the activity of the worker, rather than the nature of the employer, that was the appropriate test, and the building personnel fell under the provisions. "Without light and heat and power the tenants could not engage, as they do," Frankfurter wrote, "in the production of goods for interstate commerce." The "activity of the worker" interpretation expanded the reach of the FLSA to thousands of employees.

In another victory for child labor reformers, homework was prohibited in several industries where it was most predominant. Industrial homework involved workers and their children toiling long hours at poverty wages, often in unsanitary conditions that threatened not only their own health but also had the potential to spread disease to anyone who purchased the products. States attempted to regulate homework, but enforcement was difficult. Under the FLSA, the administrator of the Wage and Hour Division was empowered to issue regulations to protect the minimum wage and prevent the circumvention or evasion of wage orders. The administrator convened a committee for the embroideries industry. The committee recommended a minimum wage rate of forty cents an hour. The administrator accepted the recommendation and promulgated a regulation banning all homework in the industry on the grounds that it was necessary to enforce the wage order. An estimated 40 percent of all workers engaged in the industry—some 8,500 to 12,000 individuals—performed their work at home. Several home workers and employers who used home workers sued to challenge the regulation.

Two important Supreme Court decisions in early 1945 held that piece workers and industrial homework were covered by the provisions of the Fair Labor Standards Act. In *U.S. v. Rosenwasser*, Justice Frank Murphy, writing for an 8 to 1 majority, argued that Congress did not intend to exclude piece-rate employees from the wage and hour standards. "Neither the policy of the Act nor the legislative history," Murphy wrote, "gives any real basis for excluding piece workers from the benefits of the statute." The intent of the FLSA, Justice Murphy explained, was to "raise substandard wages and give added money for overtime work to such employees." Only Justice Roberts dissented, but without comment. The decision impacted thousands of workers. Government officials said that 80 percent of shoe and boot workers were paid by a piece-rate basis, as were 81 percent in the glove trade.

In *Gemsco, Inc. v. Walling* (1945), the Supreme Court held 7 to 2 that under Section 8(f) of the Fair Labor Standards Act, the administrator has the authority, if necessary to make effective a minimum wage order for the embroideries industry, to prohibit industrial homework. Writing for the Court, Justice Wiley Rutledge noted that the statute itself provides the answers in two ways: by its explicit terms, and by the necessity to avoid self-nullification. In his findings, the administrator construed "necessary" not as helpful or convenient, but as meaning that "the prohibition is absolutely essential to achieve those purposes." If the prohibition on homework did not exist, it would be impossible to secure a floor of minimum wages. Because Section 8(f) commands the administrator to include in the order "such terms and conditions" as he "finds necessary to carry out" its purposes, the administrator has the authority to prohibit industrial homework. Secretary of Labor Perkins described the Court's opinion as a "major advance in the control of homework which has baffled State labor departments for over half a century."

By the end of World War II, all the provisions of the FLSA were in force. The Supreme Court had issued more than thirty opinions on various sections of the law. This chapter has highlighted several of the most important court decisions. Fourteen cases concerned the general coverage provisions, deciding who is covered and who is exempt. For example, in *Warren-Bradshaw Drilling Co. v. Hall* (1942) the Court held that members of a crew digging wells to produce oil are covered by the FLSA. Over a dozen other cases involved the problem of defining the "regular rate of pay" for overtime purposes and sorting out diverse contract schemes used by employers to avoid paying overtime. Throughout the war, the forty-hour workweek was in place, and the federal minimum wage was forty cents an hour. For the average worker, the maximum hour and minimum wage provisions grossed $16 per week, or $830 per year, well below the subsistence standard for a family of four. Federal child labor provisions established a national floor of protections for minors that no state could fall below.

Of course, states were free to implement labor protections that were higher than FLSA standards, and eventually, most did. Many private employers also could and did pay their workers more than the federal minimum wage. L. Metcalfe Walling, the third administrator of the Wage and Hour Division, declared that the wage and hour provisions of the FLSA had become part of a "broad humanitarian program" and a long-term fact of the nation's economic life. By establishing a ceiling on hours, a floor on wages, and child labor restrictions, the Fair Labor Standards Act contributed to the growth of the middle class and propelled a post–World War II America economic boom.

CHAPTER SEVEN

The Modern FLSA: Amendments and New Labor Conflicts

The Fair Labor Standards Act of 1938 has been amended more than twenty times, although most of the changes involved Congress raising the federal minimum wage. Following World War II, reformers sought major changes in two of the act's child labor provisions. First, they wanted to directly prohibit child labor, as found in state laws, rather than prohibit the shipment of goods that had used child employment within thirty days prior to shipment as a standard. Some companies tried to avoid the restrictions by simply holding back shipments for more than a month. Second, reformers wanted to prohibit the employment of children "in commerce" as well as goods produced in interstate commerce. The text of the original child labor provisions did not cover children employed as telegraph messengers or working on boats or railroads. As part of the Pepper-Hook bill, the Senate enacted the changes in April 1946, but the House did not follow.

By midcentury, the power of labor unions had ebbed. The percentage of wage and salary workers who are members of unions (called union density) declined significantly starting in the 1950s. Union membership peaked at about 35 percent in 1954, and the total number of unionized workers reached its apex at twenty-one million in 1979. In 1983 the union membership rate was 20.1 percent; in 2023, the membership rate was 10 percent. Unions gained 139,000 members in 2023, but the number of non-union jobs in the economy increased, so union density declined. The rate of public-sector unionized workers (32.5 percent) is more than five times higher than private-sector workers (6 percent).

A host of factors contributed to the decline of union density and power. Backed by Republicans and Southern Democrats, Congress passed the Taft-Hartley Act in 1947, over President Truman's veto. The law gutted many of the hard-earned labor protections guaranteed by the Wagner Act. Employers were guaranteed free speech rights, and they could hold mandatory meetings to warn employees of welcoming a union into the workplace. The amendments also imposed on unions the same obligation to bargain in good faith that the Wagner Act placed on employers. They prohibited industry-wide strikes and secondary boycotts, making it unlawful for a union that has a primary dispute with one employer to pressure a neutral employer to stop doing business with the first employer. Union officers were required to sign an affidavit confirming they were not Communist Party members. Taft-Hartley also allowed states to pass "right to work" laws, which gave workers, even in a union shop, the right to refuse to pay fair-share fees, basically allowing those employees to become free-riders to union negotiated wages and benefits. Ten states, mostly in the South, passed right-to-work laws immediately after Taft-Hartley became law in 1947. According to the National Conference of State Legislatures, twenty-six states and Guam now have such laws.

The movement from an industrial, blue-collar based economy to a high-tech service economy also contributed to the decline in union density. As wages, hours, and benefits improved for American workers, corporations relocated manufacturing facilities overseas to countries with weak labor standards. Globalism challenged the ability of unions to meet the demands of members without reducing labor protections. With organized labor losing ground in the years following World War II, the provisions of the FLSA became more important as a source of employment protections for the average worker.

The 1947 Portal-to-Portal Act provided the first substantial changes to wages and hours under the FLSA. The law, which became effective on May 14, 1947, clarifies the kind of work time for which an employee should be paid. Judicial interpretation of the FLSA raised the possibility of employers being responsible for back wages for activities that were not traditionally considered work. The law was designed to relieve employers and the government from potential liability. Commuting time or preliminary work are not compensable, but employees deserve pay regardless of where the work is done if the activity is designed to benefit the employer. The law also establishes a two-year statute of limitations for violations of the FLSA and a three-year limitation for willful violations. In signing the legislation, President Truman urged Congress to consider raising the minimum wage during its next session.

The 1949 Amendments

After four years of hearings and approximately twelve thousand pages of testimony, Congress amended the Fair Labor Standards Act on October 19, 1949. President Truman signed the legislation one week later, and the changes took effect on January 25, 1950. Certain employees previously covered were removed from the scope of the act on the notion that their involvement with interstate commerce was not sufficient to justify coverage. The original standard of "engaging . . . in any occupation necessary to production of goods for commerce" was restricted to include only employees engaged in operations "closely related" and "directly essential" to the production of such goods. This change was prompted by members of Congress who believed that the law permitted too much federal authority over local commerce.

Other revisions in 1949 included a higher minimum wage: seventy-five cents an hour. Opponents of increasing the minimum were backed by a broad coalition of agricultural and manufacturing groups. They argued that raising the minimum wage would force employers to cut payrolls, and such a large increase would ruin small businesses. The debates were contentious, but there was a moment of levity when Representative Helen Gahagan Douglas (D-CA), a strong supporter of the New Deal, rose to defend telephone operators who might be exempt from FLSA protections. In a passionate defense of her amendment, Douglas said, "Unless you adopt this amendment, 10,000 women will be uncovered." In response to her comment, the House erupted in raucous laughter for two minutes. When decorum was restored, her amendment passed.

A Labor Department report to Congress summarized other changes to the FLSA. The 1949 amendments eliminated industry committees except in Puerto Rico and the Virgin Islands. A specific section was added granting the Wage and Hour administrator in the US Department of Labor authorization to control the incidence of exploitative industrial homework. To strengthen enforcement of the act, Congress empowered the department to force payment of back wages.

In addition to almost doubling the minimum wage, the 1949 amendments broadened the child labor provisions to prohibit the employment of children in commerce or the production of goods in commerce. Also, the definition of "oppressive child labor" was changed to include "parental employment of a child under sixteen years of age in an occupation found by the Secretary of Labor to be hazardous for children between the ages of sixteen and eighteen." The amendment closed a loophole because the original law prohibited parents from employing a child between sixteen and eighteen years of age in a hazardous occupation but allowed the employment if the child was fifteen and younger. The 1949 amendments also tightened the agricultural provisions. Children could be employed on farms only outside school hours in the district in which they lived. Other changes specified an exemption for newsboys (and girls) and extended exemptions for performers and actors to radio and television.

There were constant attempts in the 1950s to weaken child labor laws by lowering standards and protections. Opponents continued the old argument that child labor regulations resulted in idleness and contributed to delinquency. They proposed that fourteen- and fifteen-year-olds who are "incorrigible" or bored in school should be permitted to work. The National Child Labor Committee, however, responded to those claims in its fiftieth-anniversary report, asserting that there was no general relationship between employment and juvenile delinquency. "Delinquency," the report stated, "is the result of the interplay of many forces, internal and external." For some youth, work was a steadying influence; for others, the wrong job may push a teen toward antisocial conduct. No significant changes were made to the child labor provisions in the 1950s. In 1955 the minimum wage was increased to $1.00 per hour.

Expanding Coverage: The Enterprise Amendments and Public Employees

In 1961 Congress expanded by several million persons the coverage of the FLSA, introducing the "enterprise" concept by which all employees in a business producing anything in commerce or affecting commerce were brought within the protection of the minimum wage–maximum hours standards. Prior to 1961, an individual employee was subject to coverage strictly on the basis of his or her personal relationship with interstate commerce. The effect of the "enterprise amendments" was to bring within the terms of the act all employees of any "enterprise" having at least one employee so involved in interstate commerce with sales exceeding $1 million annually (now at least $500,000). In the retail industry alone, the changes extended the FLSA protections from an estimated 250,000 to 2.2 million workers. The 1961 amendments also increased the federal minimum wage to $1.25 an hour by September 1965.

The Fair Labor Standards Act was amended again when Congress passed the Equal Pay Act and President John F. Kennedy signed it into law on June 10, 1963. The law prohibits discrimination on account of sex in the payment of wages by an employer engaged in interstate commerce. It covers all forms of compensation, including salary, overtime, bonuses, vacation pay, and other benefits. The statute reads: "If there is an inequality in wages between people of different sexes who perform substantially equal jobs, employers must raise wages to equalize pay but may not reduce the wages of other individuals." Enforcement of the Equal Pay Act transferred to the Equal Employment Opportunity Commission in 1979. Although the law helped to end some pay discrimination, there is still room for improvement. In 1963 full-time female workers earned fifty-nine cents for every dollar a male worker received. A White House statement on the sixtieth anniversary of the Equal Pay Act in 2023 noted that "challenges remain in ensuring equal pay for equal work." In 2022, among full-time wage and salary workers, "a woman made just 83 cents for every dollar paid to a man."

The Fair Labor Standards Act of 1938 expressly exempted all states and their political divisions from the federal minimum wage and overtime provisions. In 1966 Congress extended federal minimum wages and overtime pay to employees of public hospitals and nursing homes, schools, and institutions of higher learning. The state of Maryland, joined by twenty-seven other states, sued to enjoin enforcement of the amendments. Two years later in *Maryland v. Wirtz*, the Supreme Court upheld (6 to 2) both the enterprise concept and the public employee amendments as rationally based, determining that Congress had properly considered the effect on interstate commerce and the promotion of peaceful labor relations. According to the majority opinion by Justice John Harlan, the act did "not interfere with states' sovereignty; rather, it subjected a state that employs people to the same restrictions on private employers whose activities affect commerce."

The 1966 amendments gradually increased the minimum wage to $1.60 an hour. Other changes extended minimum wage protections to workers employed on large farms that use the equivalent of seven full-time workers per year. The 1966 amendments also narrowed or repealed exemptions for an estimated three hundred thousand employees of hotels; five hundred thousand employees of restaurants, laundries, and drycleaners; and four hundred thousand agricultural and food service employees. All other farmworkers, however, continued to be exempt from overtime pay. Because the service and agricultural jobs were disproportionately represented by women and Black workers, the amendments extended badly needed protections. However, the 1966 amendments also allowed employers to credit a portion of employee tips toward workers' minimum wages, permitting employers to reduce wage obligations to tipped staff. For example, a tipped worker might be paid only $1 an hour when the minimum wage is $1.60, provided a portion of the tips combined to meet the minimum wage threshold. Many of these types of workers were women and workers of color.

In 1974 Congress again amended the FLSA to include *all* public employees previously not covered. The substantial expansion of coverage to employees in any government agency at the state and local levels reignited a debate over federalism that resulted in a series of important Supreme Court decisions. The National League of Cities and the National Governors' Association contested the changes, arguing that it represented a collision between federal power and states' rights in violation of the Tenth Amendment. The government argued that the Tenth Amendment was inapplicable because Congress had passed the 1974 amendments under its power to regulate commerce and because under the *Darby Lumber* precedent, the Tenth Amendment does not limit congressional power.

A Major Blow to Congressional Power

After thirty-five years of decisions deferential to congressional power under the FLSA, in *National League of Cities v. Usery* (1976), the Supreme

Court ruled 5 to 4 in favor of state and local governments. The majority opinion, written by Justice William Rehnquist and joined by Chief Justice Warren Earl Burger, and Justices Potter Stewart, Harry Blackmun, and Lewis F. Powell Jr., held that Congress may clearly regulate businesses within states, but it cannot regulate states as states. "One undoubted attribute of state sovereignty," Justice Rehnquist wrote, "is the power to determine wages to be paid to its public employees." Quoting from *Lane County v. Oregon* (1868), Rehnquist noted that the question the Court must resolve is whether these determinations are "functions essential to separate and independent existence" so that Congress may not infringe on the states' authority to make them. The FLSA standards, Rehnquist claimed, place substantial costs upon the states that will have a significant impact on the functioning of the governmental bodies involved. They displace state policies in the manner in which they will provide the delivery of governmental services to citizens.

Justice Rehnquist focused on the nature of our federal system and the impact of the FLSA amendments. He claimed the act impermissibly interferes with the governmental functions of local bodies. Rehnquist asserted that if Congress removes these decisions from states, there will be little left of the states' separate and independent existence. The key is that Congress has used the Commerce Clause to prescribe wage restrictions. In doing so, it impairs the states' ability to function effectively in a federal system. Rehnquist concluded: "Insofar as the challenged amendments operate to directly displace the States' freedom to structure integral operations of traditional governmental functions, they are not within the authority granted to Congress in Article I, Section 8, Clause 3." He said that the decision reaffirms "that States as States stand on different footing as individuals or corporations." Thus, the Court overruled the *Maryland v. Wirtz* precedent.

Justice William Brennan, joined by Thurgood Marshall and Byron White, authored a dissenting opinion, and Justice John Paul Stevens wrote a separate dissent. The four dissenters made several arguments. Justice Brennan expressed surprise and disappointment that the majority opinion chose the bicentennial of American independence to restrict a long-governing principle of congressional power under the Commerce Clause. Citing Chief Justice John Marshall's opinion in *Gibbons v. Ogden* (1824), Brennan asserted that Congress has broad and exclusive power to regulate commerce among the several states. Restraints on that power must come from "political, rather than judicial processes." Brennan quoted Justice Stone's famous statement from *Darby Lumber* that "the Tenth Amendment is but a truism." In short, it means nothing and gives no power to the states. Brennan accused the majority of using the Tenth Amendment as a transparent cover for invalidating a congressional judgment with which they disagree. He emphasized that judicial restraint in this area is quite important. It recognizes that the political branches of our government are structured to protect the interests of the states as well as the nation as a whole. Finally, Brennan said the Court's cavalier treatment of *Wirtz* was obvious. In the end, this case was a "body blow" to the power of Congress to regulate commerce.

In a separate dissenting opinion, Justice Stevens criticized the majority for holding that the federal government may not interfere with a sovereign state's right to pay a substandard wage to the janitor at the state capitol. He questioned the principle upon which the holding was based: "The Federal government may, I believe, require the state to act impartially when it hires or fires the janitor, to withhold taxes from his paycheck, to observe safety regulations while on the job, from dumping untreated refuse in an adjacent waterway, or from driving either the truck or the governor's limousine over 55 miles per hour. Even though these and other activities of the janitor are activities of the state as state, I have no doubt they are subject to federal regulation."

For the first time in four decades, the Court invalidated a statute passed by Congress pursuant to the Commerce Clause. Ultimately, Justice Rehnquist's distinction between traditional and nontraditional governmental functions could not be applied with confidence or consistency in either lower courts or in subsequent cases before the Supreme Court. The Court did not define these functions but did say that they were "essential to the separate and independent existence of the states." Examples of traditional state functions include fire and police protection, sanitation, public health, and parks and recreation. In his concurring opinion in *National League*, Justice Blackmun suggested that the Court was adopting a balancing approach to federal-state regulations.

Many Court observers did not view the opinion that way. Some saw the decision as an attempt to resurrect a pre–*Darby Lumber* doctrine of dual federalism, while others focused on the problems of defining functions that are "essential to the separate and independent existence of the states." Numerous policy issues are shared by the federal government and the states. For example, states are primarily responsible for public education, but public schools operate within federal regulations, and they receive financial support from the US government. Subsequent decisions over the next few years severely weakened the holding in *National League*.

National League Precedent Overruled

The decision in *Garcia v. San Antonio Metropolitan Transit Authority* (1985) returned to a cooperative federalism approach to government relations. This case was virtually a carbon copy of *National League of Cities*. It focused on an amendment to the FLSA that required states to pay virtually all public employees minimum wages and overtime. In 1959 San Antonio, Texas, created a mass transit system (SAMTA) that was ultimately subsidized by federal grants. In 1979 the Department of Labor issued an opinion that SAMTA must abide by the FLSA. Joe G. Garcia and other employees filed a suit for overtime pay from SAMTA.

In a narrow 5 to 4 decision the Court ruled in favor of Garcia. Justice Blackmun, who had concurred in *National League*, authored the majority opinion in *Garcia v. SAMTA*, so he eventually concluded that the traditional governmental function framework created in *National League* was unworkable and inconsistent with ideas of federalism. As such, *National League of Cities* was overruled. Blackmun said that to be faithful to the principles of the Constitution, we must look for the "postulates that limit and control." Federal structure places limits on the Commerce Clause, "but it is difficult to determine what those limits are. We doubt that courts can identify constitutional limitations on the scope of Congress' Commerce Clause powers over the states merely by relying on a priori definitions of state sovereignty." The Constitution limits state sovereignty. For example, Article I, Section 10 withdraws powers from states, and Section 8, Clause 18 gives Congress a great deal of power over state sovereignty (the elastic or Necessary and Proper Clause). Blackmun argued that the internal safeguards of the political process have performed as intended. He concluded: "We do not lightly overrule recent precedent. We have not hesitated, however, when it has become apparent that a prior decision has departed from a proper understanding of congressional power under the Commerce Clause. . . . In sum *National League of Cities* tried to fix what did not need to be repaired."

In a dissenting opinion, Justice Sandra Day O'Connor, joined by Powell and Rehnquist, argued that federalism cannot be reduced to the weak essence that the Court reduces it to here. There is more to federalism than the nature of the constraints imposed on states in "the realm of authority left open to them by the Constitution." The true "essence" of federalism is that states as states have legitimate interests that the national government is bound to respect even though its laws are supreme. The spirit of the Tenth Amendment is that states retain their integrity in a system in which the laws of the United States are supreme. It is not enough that the end be legitimate, but that also the means to that end chosen by Congress must not contravene the spirit of the Constitution. In response to the *Garcia* decision, Congress passed amendments to the FLSA allowing state and local governments to compensate their employees for overtime hours with compensatory time off rather than overtime pay, at a rate of 1.5 hours for each hour of overtime worked.

State Sovereign Immunity and the FLSA

The *Garcia v. SAMTA* decision did not end the debate over federalism and the Fair Labor Standards Act. Presidents Ronald Reagan and George H. W. Bush made appointments to the Supreme Court that altered the political alignments among the justices and reinvigorated a dual federalism philosophy under the doctrine of state sovereign immunity. Sovereign immunity is based on a British common law doctrine that the king (sovereign) can do no wrong; therefore he is immune from lawsuits. Even though the United States is a representative democracy rather than a monarchy, sovereign immunity has been viewed as essential for the fiscal integrity of government. Unlike the deferential approach given to Congress by Democratic appointees to the Court, Republican justices were inclined to use the concept of sovereign immunity to set limits on congressional power.

The new approach was reflected in *Alden v. Maine* (1999). The Eleventh

Amendment states, "The judicial power of the U.S. shall not be construed to extend to any suit in law or equity, commenced or prosecuted against one of the United States by citizens of another state, or by citizens or subjects of a foreign state." The amendment was proposed and ratified after the Supreme Court ruled in *Chisholm v. Georgia* (1793) that Article III of the Constitution authorized a private citizen of another state to sue the state of Georgia without its consent. Officials in Georgia and other states denounced the decision. The Eleventh Amendment reversed the precedent and protected state sovereign immunity. Over the years, however, the Court allowed Congress to make exceptions to this amendment. One such exception includes the FLSA, which enables state employees to bring federal suits against their states. In 1992 five probation officers sued the state of Maine for violating the overtime provision of the FLSA. When a new Supreme Court precedent, *Seminole Tribe of Florida v. Florida* (1996) stopped the suit in federal court, the employees turned to a Maine state court. The state court, however, dismissed the suit based on state sovereign immunity. Maine had not waived its immunity in this policy area.

By a vote of 5 to 4 the Court ruled for the state of Maine. Justice Anthony Kennedy wrote that the original understanding of the Constitution is that no one suggested the document might strip states of immunity. The silence of the document on this issue, Kennedy noted, is instructive. It suggests the sovereign's right to declare immunity from a suit in its own courts. Kennedy asserted that this principle was so well established that the framers did not even conceive of altering it. While sovereign immunity was directed toward federal courts, Kennedy reasoned that it applies with even greater force that states are immune from suits against themselves in their own courts.

Similarly, Kennedy acknowledged that the Eleventh Amendment does not address this issue. But there is nothing in that amendment to suggest that states are not immune from suits in their own courts. Looking to history, Kennedy stated that early congressional practice also suggests states are immune in their own courts. Kennedy claimed there was no instance where Congress purported to allow suits against a nonconsenting state in state court. The FLSA provisions, he argued, are the first to make this assertion.

Justice Kennedy contended that Supreme Court precedent also

recognizes that states retain this constitutional immunity. Our federalism jurisprudence requires Congress to treat states as sovereigns. Private suits against nonconsenting states subject the states to the coercive power of the judiciary. Such power is more offensive in some ways than allowing states to be sued in federal court. In light of the constitutional system within which we live, we are reluctant to conclude that states are not entitled to the sovereignty to which they are entitled—just as the federal government is immune from suits against it in state courts. Kennedy admitted that sovereign immunity does not bar all judicial review. First, it only bars lawsuits in the absence of consent. The Fourteenth Amendment also suggests that states surrendered a portion of sovereignty under the Section 5 enforcement power. Sovereign immunity bars suits against states, but not against lesser entities such as cities, counties, and so on. Finally, Kennedy noted, Maine has not consented to this type of lawsuit. Rather, it has chosen to retain its immunity.

Justice David H. Souter wrote the dissenting opinion, joined by Justice Stevens, Justice Ruth Bader Ginsburg, and Justice Stephen Breyer. Justice Souter argued that states are not sovereign with respect to objects not committed to it (interstate commerce as in *McCulloch v. Maryland*). Thus, under the FLSA the state of Maine is not sovereign given the Court's precedents that this law extends to state employees. Souter pointed out the irony of the Court claiming that the decision is deeply rooted in the Constitution. Justice Souter warned that the decision was as "unrealistic as the laissez-faire doctrine purported to be law in the *Lochner* era." But the damage was done. The impact of the state immunity decisions was that state employees have fewer rights protections under the FLSA than other citizens covered by the law.

From Reagan to Biden: Contemporary Child Labor Issues

After a thirty-year period that saw no major reforms of child labor laws, the issue of working kids returned to the public agenda in the early 1980s. The Reagan administration attempted to weaken child labor restrictions in order to create more employment opportunities for young workers, especially fourteen- and fifteen-year-olds. Proponents of the changes argued that when the child labor standards were established in 1938, fast-food restaurants, retail stores in malls, and other service-oriented establishments were not part of the market. In July 1982, Labor Secretary Raymond Donovan introduced a plan that fundamentally altered child labor policy. The Reagan administration's proposal sought to: (1) open up more opportunities for the employment of children fourteen and fifteen years of age, (2) extend the number of hours per day and per week that children might be employed, (3) revise the standards for child workers in jobs once considered too hazardous, and (4) simplify and broaden the manner in which employers become certified by the Department of Labor to employ full-time students at a substandard minimum wage.

At a hearing held by the House Labor Standards Subcommittee, William Otter, the Labor Department's wage and hour administrator, told the subcommittee that the proposed new regulations "would improve the employment opportunities of young workers without harming their health, well-being, or opportunity for schooling." He read letters from parents, teens, and potential employers that urged a relaxing of regulations to allow fourteen- and fifteen-year-olds to work. Concerned about unemployment for all age groups, Otter stated that "unreasonable and artificial impediments to the employment of all age groups should be eliminated."

The administration's plan for youth work, however, was roundly criticized by witnesses from labor and education groups who denounced the idea as an attempt to "create a kiddy work force" and an act of "insensitivity and stupidity." Thomas Donahue, secretary-treasurer of the AFL-CIO, testified that the proposed rules would "create a pool of cheap, part-time child labor, the beneficiaries of which would be the various industries that already have notorious records for violating and undercutting fair labor standards." Laurence E. Steinberg, an assistant professor at the University of California, Irvine, and a specialist in adolescent development, testified that teens who work more than fifteen to twenty hours a week "spend less time on their studies, receive lower grades, are absent more often, and are less involved in school activities." Other opponents said that teenagers who work increased hours spend less time with their families and friends and tend to use more tobacco, alcohol, and marijuana. Jeffrey Newman, executive director of the National Child Labor

Committee, acknowledged that child labor standards could use some modernization but asserted that during a recession and a period of high unemployment, the proposed changes were in the "wrong context at the wrong time." He described the Reagan administration plan as a "slap in the face for the nation's working class and a pig in a poke for both business and young people." He favored well-designed work and education programs, both public and private, that provided structured training and employment opportunities.

Congressional Democrats introduced a joint resolution to stop Secretary of Labor Donovan from implementing the proposals. Under pressure from Congress and various interest groups, the Reagan administration extended the comment period for the proposed regulations from thirty days to 180 days. Administrators received numerous letters from restaurant owners supporting the new standards, but the plan also generated intense opposition from educational groups, labor unions, and members of Congress who viewed the regulatory plan as a "scheme to enable restauranteurs to exploit school age workers." Public pressure against the changes seemed to have an effect. The regulations remained under review for more than two years. Ultimately, a final rule was never issued.

Congress and the Department of Labor considered additional reforms to child labor standards throughout the 1980s and 1990s, but no major legislation or new regulations were enacted. In April 1986, Senator Dan Quayle (R-IN) advocated that child labor laws be relaxed to allow fourteen- and fifteen-year-olds to work as batboys and batgirls for professional baseball teams, even when the games run late into the evening. Senator Quayle described baseball as the "All-American Sport," and he believed that youth should not have to wait until they were sixteen years old to "associate with players of their home town teams." After a year-long investigation that surveyed 157 sports teams, the Labor Department concluded that "changes in permissible hours and time standards for batboy/girl work would not be detrimental to their health or well-being." Moreover, the department found "no evidence that school grades were adversely affected by such work." Despite these findings, no action was taken on the issue for years.

By the late 1980s, violations of child labor laws were on the rise. The Labor Department reported that it found 22,508 children working in violation of the Fair Labor Standards Act in 1989, twice the rate of the first half of the decade and the highest number of violations since the law was enacted in 1938. Officials attributed the increase to the nation's low unemployment rate, which forced some employers to turn to minors to fill menial jobs, and intensified competition from foreign companies.

With reports indicating widespread levels of illegal child labor across the country, Labor Secretary Elizabeth Dole promised to intensify enforcement efforts and impose stiffer penalties for violations. At the time, fines amounted to just a few hundred dollars and were considered by child employers to be just another cost of doing business. But Labor officials announced plans for a fivefold increase to effectively deter those who might violate child labor laws. Moreover, repeat offenders could face additional penalties. William C. Brooks, assistant secretary for employment standards, also announced plans to establish a working group to explore tougher enforcement practices and a possible revision of job classifications deemed hazardous. Child welfare advocates welcomed the stricter enforcement regime but remained skeptical because the Labor Department was not given additional personnel or funding.

The Clinton administration attempted to improve labor standards by cracking down on child labor law violations. The Labor Department charged Food Lion, one of the nation's fastest growing supermarket chains, with fourteen hundred violations of federal child labor laws. The allegations involved eighty-five stores in twelve states. More than twelve hundred of the alleged violations involved sixteen- and seventeen-year-old minors using meat slicers and power-driven paper balers and children working more hours than federal law allows. Vincent G. Watkins, Food Lion's vice president for projects, disputed the charges, claiming that the company was "the victim of a corporate campaign" by the United Food and Commercial Workers Union. Although the supermarket chain admitted no violations, in August 1993 Food Lion agreed to pay $16.2 million in fines and back wages to settle the allegations. It was the largest settlement ever by the Labor Department with a private company. Publix, another supermarket chain based in Florida and Georgia, also paid a $500,000 fine to settle claims that it violated child labor laws, and the Great Atlantic & Pacific Tea Company, better known as A&P,

paid $490,000 for more than nine hundred alleged violations of child labor laws. Neither company denied or admitted guilt. Commenting on the fines, Labor Secretary Robert B. Reich said his department "will not tolerate companies that seek to gain a competitive advantage" by undermining federal labor standards.

The batboy issue returned with a vengeance during the Clinton administration. Tommy McCoy was hired to be the batboy for the Savannah Cardinals, then a Class A affiliate of the St. Louis Cardinals. A local media outlet ran a story about McCoy's day as a batboy. A Georgia labor official read the story and noticed a problem. McCoy was only fourteen years old, and state child labor laws prohibited fourteen- and fifteen-year-olds from working past 7:00 p.m. on school nights or 9:00 p.m. during the summer. A Labor Department investigator notified the club that the boy's employment violated child labor laws. The team reluctantly dismissed McCoy and replaced him with a sixteen-year-old. The *Savannah Morning News* ran a story about the incident that generated an intense local uproar that was quickly noticed by national media.

Labor Secretary Reich suddenly had a public relations nightmare on his hands. Critics claimed that "insensitive bureaucrats were trampling on the national pastime." Reich did not want to provide ammunition to those who believed that the federal government was out of touch with the American people. On May 13, 1994, the Labor Department proposed a rule "to provide an exception from the permissible hours and time standards for minors 14 and 15 years of age when employed as attendants in professional sports." A total of twenty-six comments were received on the regulatory proposal. Eight minor league baseball teams supported the rule change, arguing that the sports-attendant experience offers young people a chance to interact with role models in a healthy, character-building activity within a family-friendly atmosphere. The National Consumers' League, Child Labor Coalition, National PTA, and a labor organization (Food & Allied Service Trades) opposed the proposed rule based on their concern that "the increased hours and late time of day would be deleterious to the young people's health, safety, and education." Commenters from the restaurant industry complained that it was unfair to exempt the sports industry from child labor regulations while leaving them in place for other industries. Secretary Reich considered all the comments but concluded that the exemption for fourteen- and fifteen-year-old sports-attendants would not constitute oppressive child labor.

Agriculture has always been an area with the weakest child labor protections. Seventeen states exempt farmwork from child labor laws, and the age, hour, overtime, and minimum wage provisions of the Fair Labor Standards Act do not apply to agriculture. For decades, reformers have targeted agricultural work but without much success. For example, during the Obama administration the Department of Labor had to withdraw a proposed rule in 2012 that attempted to protect child farmworkers under age sixteen from dangerous tasks. The Centers for Disease Control's National Institute for Occupational Safety and Health reported that agriculture is the most dangerous work open to children in the United States. Federal law allows sixteen- and seventeen-year-olds to work under hazardous conditions in agriculture while in all other occupations the minimum age is eighteen years.

The proposed rule would have expanded the Hazardous Occupations category to include limits on children under age sixteen operating tractors and using ladders taller than six feet. Although the regulations would not have applied to children working on family farms, there was a political firestorm over the rule. Opponents argued that it would prevent children from learning the basics of farming. Kent Schescke, of the National Future Farmers of America Organization, was concerned about the regulation's student learner exemption. "The proposed rules would severely limit or eliminate opportunities to participate in the experiential learning aspects of our program," Schescke said. "We believe we provide safe learning environments for students that help them succeed in the industry of agriculture."

Opponents of the rule preferred information campaigns and safety training over regulation. Agriculture, however, remains one of the most dangerous occupations for children under age eighteen. Unlike other occupations, in agriculture children can work on any farm at age twelve and at any age on a small farm. The Bureau of Labor Statistics reported that the fatality rate for young agricultural workers is 4.4 times higher than the average for workers in the same age group. Those most at risk are the children of poor migrant farmworkers. Cultural traditions are strong in rural America, and agriculture will continue to be an area targeted for reform.

The 2010 midterm elections were historical. A "Tea Party" wave swept libertarian and conservative Republicans into the majority party in the US House of Representatives, and Republicans made significant gains in state legislatures and governorships. Many "Tea Party" members were hostile to welfare programs and any government regulation of the market. Challenging a long-held societal consensus, some openly questioned the wisdom of child labor laws and argued for their repeal or reform. The attacks on child labor restrictions represented just one front of a broad-based ideological assault on the welfare state and government regulations of the economy that originated during the Progressive, New Deal, and Great Society periods.

At both the federal and state levels, various Republicans argued that the government should stay out of the field of child labor altogether, while others simply wanted to allow kids more freedom to work, often at much cheaper wages than adults. Senator Mike Lee (R-UT), for example, claimed in a video lecture posted to his YouTube channel that the federal government has no authority to regulate child labor. Emphasizing states' rights under the Tenth Amendment, he cited *Hammer v. Dagenhart* to support his position that child labor was an intrastate issue, ignoring the fact that the Supreme Court unanimously overturned the decision in *U.S. v. Darby Lumber*. "This may sound harsh," he admitted, "but it was designed to be that way. It was designed to be a little bit harsh." Maine's Republican governor Paul LePage expressed a desire to lower the legal working age to twelve in his state. Although opposed to permitting twelve-year-olds to work forty hours a week, he said children that age working "eight to ten hours a week . . . is not bad." Maine state representative David Burns criticized child labor regulations, saying, "We have usurped the responsibility of families to make intelligent decisions and transferred that responsibility to school officials and the state." Former Speaker Newt Gingrich called child labor laws "truly stupid" and argued that children should be able to serve as janitors in schools. These comments were part of a widespread campaign to use the crisis of the Great Recession to roll back child labor protections.

Some of the rhetorical broadsides against child labor laws landed nowhere, but several states enacted laws weakening child labor protections. In a report for the Economic Policy Institute, a nonpartisan think tank that focuses on the needs of low- and middle-income workers, political economist Gordon Lafer noted that in 2011 to 2012, four states lifted restrictions on child labor. Idaho was the first state to "make Gingrich's vision reality" when it permitted children as young as age twelve to work up to ten hours a week doing custodial tasks in their schools. Wisconsin abolished all restrictions on the number of hours that minors—age sixteen and over—were permitted to work during the school year. Michigan increased, from fifteen to twenty-four, the number of hours students may work during the school week.

Maine also expanded the number of hours high school students could work each day and week during the school year. Backed by the Maine Restaurant Association, the law expanded the number of hours students can work per school day from four to six and increased total hours for the school week from twenty to twenty-four. One supporter of the legislation expressed the extreme libertarian position that child labor restrictions themselves are wrong. "Kids have parents," argued state representative Bruce Bickford. "It's not up to the government to regulate everybody's life and lifestyle. Take the government away. Let the parents take care of their kids."

Many of these bills were touted as instilling a "work ethic" and discipline in children—the same arguments used a century ago to defend child labor exploitation. Some studies show that learning a work ethic at an early age can teach youth punctuality, frugality, and respect for supervisors. But the attacks on child labor laws were not motivated out of genuine concern for the welfare of teenagers. Looking for a source of cheap labor, all of these measures were pushed by lobbyists for state restaurant and grocer associations, lodging and tourism associations, small business associations, and the chamber of commerce. One lobbyist for the Wisconsin Grocers Association, which successfully worked to repeal child labor restrictions, rejected any comparisons to the days of Upton Sinclair. "Our members are not trying to overwork these kids or create a sweatshop," she stated. "They just want to give kids that first great opportunity you get in a grocery store." Critics, however, warned against weakening protections. "It seems that conservative politicians are trying to take us back to the nineteenth century," said Justin Feldman of Public Citizen, "a time when children went to work instead of school and toiled under dangerous conditions for little pay."

The Aftermath of the Pandemic: Renewed Push
to Weaken Child Labor Laws

As the United States emerged from the Covid-19 pandemic restrictions, a tight labor market, with unemployment at 3.5 percent, created an opening for some states to attack labor protections for minors. Arkansas, Iowa, and at least a dozen other states had introduced or passed legislation to loosen restrictions on child labor by June 2023. Except for New Jersey, which passed legislation in 2022 to allow kids to work longer hours over the summer, these efforts to weaken child labor laws are being led by Republicans. The arguments used to justify undoing child labor protections echoed older arguments made decades ago. Cultural conservatives argue that working has moral value for young people. Libertarians are ideologically opposed to employment regulations, and conservatives say that teens, fewer of whom are in the workforce today than in past decades, could help fill empty jobs in tight labor markets. They also argue that parents should have the authority to make employment decisions for their children.

Opponents of child labor found themselves repeating many of the same arguments used to defend child labor restrictions dating back a century. When kids under age eighteen work long hours or do strenuous jobs, it can disrupt childhood development, interfere with their schooling, and deprive them of the sleep they need. Expanding child labor can encourage kids to drop out of school and threaten their health through injuries and work-related illnesses.

One reason that this new movement to weaken child labor laws is troubling is that it gained traction while blatant violations of laws were on the rise. Child labor violations have increased by 69 percent since 2018, according to the Labor Department. More than eight hundred companies were fined for violating child labor laws just in the 2022 fiscal year—the twelve months that ended in September 2022. Many violations in recent years have involved children who immigrated to the United States without their parents, only to wind up working long hours, sometimes in dangerous jobs, at young ages. Investigative journalists and government regulators have discovered more than a hundred children, some as young as age thirteen, using chemicals to clean meat slicers in slaughterhouses, working at fast-food restaurants until 1:00 a.m., and using dangerous machinery.

The current regulatory regime for child labor is complicated. Both federal and state laws govern the employment of minors. The FLSA sets a floor of regulations in youth employment that cover maximum hours, minimum ages, wages, and protections from hazardous jobs. Federal regulations, however, contain many loopholes and exemptions. If states pass tougher laws, as many have, the stricter standards govern workplace practices. Federal law, for example, does not require minors to obtain "work permits" or "employment certificates," but most states do mandate such documentation. However, some states, primarily those led by Republicans, are trying instead to weaken their child labor rules. Like so many other issues, child labor has become just another front in the partisan battles that divide the nation.

Arkansas governor Sarah Huckabee Sanders signed the "Youth Hiring Act" in March 2023. It eliminated work permits for fourteen- and fifteen-year-olds. Previously, employers had to keep a work certificate on file that required proof of age, a description of the work, and schedule—and written consent of a parent or guardian. Arkansas has scrapped those safeguards against child labor exploitation. Supporters touted the bill as enhancing parental rights, but the law removes any formal role for parents in balancing their kids' education and employment.

Iowa enacted the most radical new law designed to roll back child labor protections. It allows children as young as age fourteen to work in meat coolers and industrial laundries, and teens ages fifteen and older can work on assembly lines around dangerous machinery. Teens as young as age sixteen can serve alcohol in restaurants, provided two adults are present. When Iowa governor Kim Reynolds signed the measure into law on May 26, 2023, the Republican leader described the legislation as "common sense labor provisions that allow young adults to develop their skills in the workforce." US Labor Department officials disagreed. The labor solicitor general argued that several provisions of Iowa's new law violate national child labor standards.

Iowa lawmakers also allowed fourteen- and fifteen-year-olds to work until 9:00 p.m. during the school year with their parents' permission, even though federal regulations prohibit teens that young to work past 7:00 p.m. Labor Department administrators warned Iowa officials that federal regulations would be enforced, but the warnings were ignored. The head of the Iowa Restaurant Association then told its members that they could employ fourteen- and fifteen-year-olds until 9:00 p.m. when school is in session. Some establishments followed the advice but found themselves saddled with thousands of dollars in fines for violating federal child labor provisions. But instead of acknowledging their guilt, government and business leaders complained that they were the victims of heavy-handed federal regulators.

One reform that would strengthen the child labor provisions of the FLSA is to increase the fines for violations. Under current law, the maximum civil monetary fine for a child labor violation is $15,138 per child. There is support in Congress for tougher sanctions. A bipartisan House bill would increase the penalty to nearly ten times the current amount if enacted. Twelve Democratic senators have introduced companion legislation. Representative Dan Kildee (D-MI) has also introduced the Combatting Child Labor Act to strengthen federal child labor restrictions. The bill has dozens of Democratic sponsors. Another bill extends the prohibitions on child labor to independent contractors. However, it is unlikely that any of these measures will pass given the partisan divisions in Congress.

The Federal Minimum Wage and
$15 an Hour Movement

Since the 1980s, conservatives have continued to attack the minimum wage. Congress increased the federal minimum wage to $7.25 an hour in 2007, which became effective in July 2009, but there has been no expansion of the federal minimum since then. It is the longest span without an increase since the Fair Labor Standards Act was passed. The purchasing power of the federal minimum wage, adjusted for inflation, peaked in 1968 and has since lost 31 percent of its value. The House of Representatives has voted several times to increase the minimum rate, but the legislation dies in the Senate under threat of a filibuster. The federal minimum wage has become a victim of the partisan battles in Congress between Democrats and Republicans.

The lack of progress at the federal level in raising the minimum wage has prompted unions and interest groups to press demands for a "living wage" and for a $15 an hour minimum at the state level. Over the past thirty years, referendums and initiatives on increasing the minimum wage have been on the ballot twenty-eight times and have been defeated only twice, and those losses were in Missouri and Montana in 1996. Voters in both states subsequently passed minimum wage initiatives, with Missouri increasing the state minimum wage to $12 in 2023. In 2016, voters in four states—Arizona, Colorado, Maine, and Washington—approved ballot measures that increased the minimum wage by more than $3.75 by 2020.

In the November 2022 midterm elections, voters in Nebraska, Nevada, and the District of Columbia approved ballot measures that raised the state minimum wage. In Nebraska, Initiative 433 incrementally increases the state minimum from $9 an hour to $15 over four years. Nevada voters passed Question 2, which increases the state minimum wage to $12 an hour by July 2024. In the District of Columbia, Initiative 82 passed with 72 percent approval. The measure requires employers to pay $16.10 per hour to tipped employees by 2027, which is the same rate for nontipped workers. In the 2024 election cycle, voters in Alaska approved a ballot measure to increase the state minimum wage to $15 by 2027, and voters in Missouri accepted a ballot initiative that increases the minimum wage to $15 an hour by 2026. Both measures include automatic annual inflation adjustments. As of July 2024, thirty states, plus DC, Puerto Rico, the Virgin Islands, and fifty-six counties and cities, mostly in California, have a minimum wage higher than the federal standard.

The modern FLSA has its share of critics. Some opponents argue that it is a relic of an industrial America that no longer exists and that the law has not adjusted to a high-tech economy with many "gig" employees who are independent contractors or part-time workers. This problem has only been exacerbated with modern work conditions, such as remote and virtual work. When employees are classified as independent contractors, employers are not responsible for minimum wage and overtime protections. Others would like to ease some of the regulations on youth employment by allowing teens to work until 9:00 p.m. during school sessions, and more radical voices would abolish all child labor regulations.

Recent Supreme Court decisions could further weaken the protections of the FLSA. In *Loper Bright Enterprises v. Raimondo* and *Relentless,*

Inc. v. Department of Commerce (2024), the Roberts Court, by a 6 to 3 vote, overruled the landmark 1984 decision in *Chevron U.S.A., Inc. v. Natural Resources Defense Council*, which established what is known as the *Chevron* doctrine. Under the doctrine, if Congress has not directly addressed the administrative question, a court was required to show deference to an agency's interpretation of a statute provided it was reasonable. The *Chevron* doctrine was important for administrative law because it gave federal agencies and departments some discretion in interpretating statutes like the FLSA. Now, judges can possibly intervene and overturn administrative decisions. Employers are already challenging the Department of Labor's expansion of overtime compensation for certain salaried employees, with at least one case questioning the authority of the department to even make such decisions. Judicial activism has the potential to threaten fair labor standards.

Although the Fair Labor Standards Act has areas that can be strengthened, especially the minimum wage and child labor provisions, it still provides employment protections for over 150 million workers. The number of civil lawsuits filed under the FLSA peaked in 2015 at 8,920 but has averaged just over 7,000 in recent years. Those numbers indicate that millions of Americans benefit from the FLSA, but more can be done. From rethinking the forty-hour workweek to indexing the minimum wage to inflation, increasing fines for child labor violations, and extending coverage to independent contractors, a host of reforms have been proposed to reinvigorate fair labor standards, with the goal of improving the quality of life for workers and strengthening the American middle class. Hopefully, this book will help advance and inform that public discussion.

CHRONOLOGY OF FAIR LABOR
STANDARDS

June 2, 1786 — Philadelphia printers agree to a minimum wage of $6 per week following the earliest recorded strike of workers in a single trade.

May 1791 — Philadelphia carpenters strike unsuccessfully for a ten-hour workday and additional pay for overtime. This is the first recorded strike in the building trades.

June 10, 1835 — First general strike in the United States. In Philadelphia, over twenty thousand workers from over forty trades demand a ten-hour workday.

March 31, 1840 — By executive order, President Van Buren introduces ten-hour workday for federal public works projects.

March 1842 — In *Commonwealth v. Hunt*, the highest court of Massachusetts holds that labor has a right to organize in unions, and that a strike for higher wages or shorter hours is "not a conspiracy in restraint of trade" but a legitimate labor activity.

February 1, 1847 — New Hampshire enacts the first state ten-hour-workday law.

August 20, 1866 — A new organization named the National Labor Union asks Congress to pass a law mandating the eight-hour workday. Their efforts fail, but they build support for labor reforms.

May 1, 1867 — The Illinois Legislature passes a law mandating an eight-hour workday. Many employers refuse to cooperate, and a massive strike erupts in Chicago. That day becomes known as "May Day."

May 19, 1869 — President Ulysses S. Grant issues a proclamation that guarantees a stable wage and an eight-hour workday—but only for federal government contract workers. Grant's decision encourages private-sector workers to push for the same rights.

December 28, 1869	Uriah Stephens forms the Knights of Labor in Philadelphia. Initially a secret society, the Knights become an important force in the early days of labor organizing.
May 1, 1886	Labor organizations call for a national strike in support of a shorter workday. More than 300,000 workers turn out across the country.
May 4, 1886	A labor rally at the Haymarket Square in Chicago, called in support of the eight-hour workday, erupts into chaos when an unknown party tosses a bomb at police, who then fire into the crowd. The incident stains labor's image and creates turmoil within the movement. Demonstrators fight with police over the next few days. Many on both sides are wounded or killed in an event that is now known as the Haymarket affair or Haymarket riot.
December 8, 1886	In the wake of the Haymarket affair, labor organizer Samuel Gompers sets up the American Federation of Labor (AFL), a collection of trade unions that will play a major role in the labor movement for decades.
June 29, 1892	Homestead Steel Mill Lockout and Strike begins, resulting in a deadly confrontation between striking workers and Pinkerton agents.
February 24, 1908	In *Muller v. Oregon*, the Supreme Court upholds an Oregon law limiting employment of women in factories and laundries to ten hours a day and sixty hours a week.
June 12, 1912	Massachusetts adopts the first minimum wage law, setting a floor under the pay of women and minors.
February 13, 1913	Oregon passes a minimum wage law. Over the next several months Utah, Washington, Minnesota, Nebraska, Colorado, and California pass minimum wage laws.
April 20, 1914	Multiple deaths occur at the Colorado Fuel and Iron Company when anti-striker militia fire

	upon a miner tent camp. The violent conflict between capital and labor is known as the Ludlow Massacre.
March 6, 1915	Kansas enacts a minimum wage law.
September 3, 1916	Congress passes the Adamson Act, a federal law that establishes an eight-hour workday for interstate railroad workers. The Supreme Court upholds the act in 1917.
September 7, 1916	The Federal Compensation Act provides benefits to workers who are injured or contract illnesses in the workplace. The act establishes the Office of Workers' Compensation Programs.
April 9, 1917	The Supreme Court upholds Oregon's ten-hour law for all workers in *Bunting v. Oregon.*
April 9, 1923	In *Adkins v. Children's Hospital,* the Supreme Court strikes down a minimum wage for women and children in the District of Columbia.
December 13, 1924	Samuel Gompers, the most influential of the early labor leaders, dies at age seventy-four.
September 25, 1926	Ford Motor Company adopts a five-day, forty-hour workweek.
March 3, 1931	The Davis-Bacon Act requires that federal contractors pay their workers the wages and benefits prevailing in the local market when working on a public works project. The law keeps employers from importing cheaper workers from outside the region.
March 23, 1932	The Norris–La Guardia Act proclaims that yellow-dog contracts, which require a worker to promise not to join a union, are unenforceable, settling a long-standing dispute between management and labor. The law also limits courts' power to issue injunctions against strikes.
June 16, 1933	President Franklin D. Roosevelt signs the National Industrial Recovery Act. Over the next two years more than five hundred industry codes establish standards for hours, wages, and child labor.

May 27, 1935	The Supreme Court strikes down the National Industrial Recovery Act in *Schechter Poultry Corporation v. United States.*
June 30, 1936	The Walsh-Healey Act sets minimum wage, overtime pay, and child labor restrictions on federal contracts.
April 12, 1937	The Supreme Court upholds the National Labor Relations Act in *NLRB v. Jones and Laughlin Steel.*
June 25, 1938	Congress passes the Fair Labor Standards Act (FLSA), which limits the workweek to forty-four hours. The FLSA standardizes the forty-hour workweek; codifies paid overtime, minimum wage, and child labor laws; and creates the Wage and Hour Division to enforce the law.
October 24, 1940	As provided for in the FLSA, the forty-hour workweek is established.
February 3, 1941	The Supreme Court upholds the Fair Labor Standards Act in *U.S. v. Darby Lumber.*
May 14, 1947	The Portal-to-Portal Act clarifies issues surrounding compensable hours under the FLSA. Specifically, workers are not compensated for the time it takes to commute to the job or other incidental activities.
June 23, 1947	The Taft-Hartley Act passes over President Harry Truman's veto, drastically amending the Wagner Act of 1935 by reducing the rights of workers to organize labor unions.
October 26, 1949	Amendments to the Fair Labor Standards Act raise the minimum wage to seventy-five cents an hour and extend coverage to air transport workers. Industry committees are eliminated except for in Puerto Rico and the Virgin Islands. The law also authorizes the Department of Labor to sue on behalf of employees for back wages.
June 10, 1963	Congress amends the FLSA with the Equal Pay Act, which prohibits sex discrimination in employment compensation.

September 23, 1966   President Lyndon Johnson signs the 1966 amendments to the FLSA. The law increases the minimum wage to $1.60, extends the minimum wage to farm workers for the first time, repeals numerous exemptions, and expands coverage to state and local government employees in all occupations.

April 8, 1974   Congress extends FLSA coverage to all nonsupervisory employees of federal, state, and local governments and many domestic workers. The minimum wage gradually increases from $2.10 to $2.30 by 1976.

Because this book focuses on the Fair Labor Standards Act and the *Darby Lumber* decision, many aspects of the labor movement are not discussed. However, there are plenty of fine labor studies on the market, including several multivolume works. John R. Commons, an institutional economist and labor historian, co-authored the four-volume *History of Labor in the United States*, which was published between 1918 and 1935. Another multivolume series, Philip S. Foner's *History of the Labor Movement in the United States*, was originally published in 1947 and has been reprinted several times. A popular single-volume text, *Labor in America: A History*, by Melvyn Dubofsky and Joseph A. McCartin, is now in its ninth edition (New York: Wiley, 2017). For coverage of labor strikes that resulted in violence, see Samuel Yellen, *American Labor Struggles 1877–1934* (New York: Pathfinder, 1936, 2004). The decade preceding Franklin D. Roosevelt's first year in office were challenging times for the labor movement. See Irving Bernstein, *The Lean Years: A History of the American Worker 1920–1933* (Cambridge, MA: Houghton Mifflin, 1960).

For an excellent discussion of the early ten-hour and eight-hour workday labor movements, see Brian Greenberg, *The Dawning of American Labor: The New Republic in the Industrial Age* (Hoboken, NJ: Wiley Blackwood 2018). A useful early investigation of the shorter hours' movement is Marion Cahill's *Shorter Hours: A Study of the Movement since the Civil War* (New York: Columbia University Press, 1932). Ira Steward's unsuccessful campaign for a national eight-hour workday in the mid-1800s is described in Hyman Kuritz, "Ira Steward and the Eight Hour Day," *Science and Society* 20, 2 (Spring 1956): 118–134.

Samuel Gompers, longtime leader of the American Federation of Labor, defended the eight-hour movement in *The Workers and the Eight Hour Day* (Washington, DC: American Federation of Labor, 1915). See also Bernard Mandel, *Samuel Gompers: A Biography* (Yellow Springs, OH: Antioch Press, 1963); and Stuart B. Kaufman et al., *The Samuel Gompers Papers* (Urbana: University of Illinois Press, 1991). Terence Powderly, leader of the Knights of Labor, reviewed the efforts of the Knights to promote labor standards in *Thirty Years of Labor, 1859–1889* (Columbus, OH: Excelsior,

1890); see also Melton Alonza McLaurin, *The Knights of Labor in the South* (Westport, CT: Greenwood Press, 1978).

The earliest federal laws restricting work hours are examined in John R. Commons, "Eight-Hour Shifts by Federal Legislation," *American Labor Legislation Review* 7, 1 (1917): 139–154. Professor Commons evaluated the pros and cons of moving toward an eight-hour day from both the employer and worker perspective. A primary source on maximum-hour laws is provided by the Department of Labor, Women's Bureau, The Eight-Hour Day in Federal and State Legislation: Summary of the State and Federal "Eight-Hour Laws" in Effect in the United States: 1920, *Women's Bureau Bulletin, No. 5* (1921). Another discussion of time and work in the early American industrial period is provided by David Brody, *In Labor's Cause: Main Themes on the History of the American Worker* (New York: Oxford University Press, 1993). For a comprehensive contemporary study, see David Roediger and Philip Foner, *Our Own Time: A History of American Labor and the Working Day* (New York: Verso, 1989). The movement toward shorter hours in the first two decades of the twentieth century is covered by Robert Whaples, "Winning the Eight-Hour Day, 1909–1919," *Journal of Economic History* 50, 2 (1990): 393–406. The same author highlighted major historical events in "Hours of Work in U.S. History," EH.Net Encyclopedia, edited by Robert Whaples, August 14, 2001, http://eh.net/encyclopedia/hours-of-work-in-u-s-history/.

Official publication of Supreme Court decisions covering labor issues may be found in *U.S. Reports*. Two early discussions of state police powers include George W. Wickersham, "The Police Power, a Product of the Rule of Reason," *Harvard Law Review* 27 (February 1914): 297–316; and Ernst Freund, *The Police Power: Public Police and Constitutional Rights* (Chicago: Callaghan, 1904). A comprehensive study of the *Lochner* case is provided by Paul Kens, *Lochner v. New York: Economic Regulation on Trial* (Lawrence: University Press of Kansas, 1998). See also Matthew S. Bewig, "Lochner v. the Journeymen Bakers of New York: Their Hours of Labor, and the Constitution: A Case Study in the Social History of Legal Thought," *American Journal of Legal History* 38, 4 (October 1994): 413–451.

Progressive Era critics of the *Lochner* decision took their cue from Justice Harlan's and Justice Holmes's dissenting opinions. For example, Ernest Freund reiterated Justice Harlan's argument that the majority had substituted its view of policy for that of the New York legislature.

Ernest Freund, "Limitation of Hours of Labor and the Federal Supreme Court," *Green Bag* 17 (June 1905): 411. Others repeated Justice Holmes's argument that the Court was enacting Spencer's *Social Statics*; see Learned Hand, "Due Process of Law and the Eight Hour Day," *Harvard Law Review* 21, 7 (May 1908): 495–509; Roscoe Pound, "Liberty of Contract," *Yale Law Journal* 18, 7 (1909): 454–487; and Charles Warren, "The New 'Liberty' under the Fourteenth Amendment," *Harvard Law Review* 39, 4 (February 1926): 431–465. For some scholars in the early 1900s it seemed as though state courts were "illiberal" and blocked needed social and workplace legislation. See William F. Dodd, "Social Legislation and the Courts," *Political Science Quarterly* 28 (March 1913): 1–17.

Prior to the Constitutional Revolution of 1937, the Supreme Court had a mixed record on fair labor standards. Benjamin Wright, in *The Growth of American Constitution Law* (Boston: Houghton Mifflin Co. for Reynal and Hitchcock, 1942), identified nearly two hundred cases where the Court invalidated labor and social welfare legislation. But the Court also upheld many regulatory provisions. For an early analysis of the *Lochner* period that questions whether the courts promoted any uniform economic theory, consult Melvin I. Urofsky, "State Courts and Protective Legislation during the Progressive Era: A Reevaluation," *Journal of American History* 72, 1 (June 1985): 63–91. See also Howard Gillam, *The Constitution Besieged: The Rise and Demise of Lochner Era Police Powers Jurisprudence* (Durham, NC: Duke University Press, 1993); and Michael J. Phillips, *The Lochner Court, Myth and Reality: Substantive Due Process from the 1890s–1930s* (Westport, CT: Praeger, 2001). Phillips concludes that the Court's substantive due process decisions were more Progressive than previously thought and that in some cases, the Court was justified in striking down legislation. For a more nuanced view, see David A. Strauss, "Why Was Lochner Wrong?," *University of Chicago Law Review* 70, 1 (Winter 2003): 373–386. Strauss argues that the Supreme Court was correct to recognize freedom of contract but wrong in elevating it to a fundamental right that can almost never be abrogated.

The case of *Ritchie v. People*, which struck down an eight-hour law for women in Illinois, is analyzed by Andrew Alexander Bruce, "The Illinois Ten-Hour Law for Women," *Michigan Law Review* 8, 1 (November 1909): 1–24. The Supreme Court's decision in *Muller v. Oregon* is examined from a contemporary policy perspective by Nancy Wolloch in *Muller v.*

Oregon: A Brief History with Documents (Boston: Bedford Books, 1996). Felix Frankfurter discussed the Oregon maximum-hours case of *Bunting v. Oregon* in "Hours of Labor and Realism in Constitutional Law," *Harvard Law Review* 29 (1916): 361. Frankfurter's extensive "Brandeis brief" is analyzed by Royal C. Gilkey, "Felix Frankfurter and the Oregon Maximum Hour Case," *University of Missouri Kansas City Law Review* 35, 1 (Winter 1967): 149–157. A critique of the courts and protectionism is offered by Judith A. Baer, *The Chains of Protection: The Judicial Response to Women's Labor Legislation* (Westport, CT: Greenwood Press, 1978).

Women and women's organizations were at the forefront of the social movements for fair labor standards. Emilie J. Hutchinson, a reformer and scholar, published "Women's Wages: A Study of the Wages of Industrial Women and Measures Suggested to Increase Them," in *Studies in History, Economics, and Public Law* (New York: Columbia University, 1919), 1–179. On minimum wage laws, see Vivien Hart, *Bound by Our Constitution: Women, Workers, and the Minimum Wage* (Princeton, NJ: Princeton University Press, 1994). For the role of the National Consumers' League and women in advancing fair labor standards, see Landon R. Y. Storrs, *Civilizing Capitalism: The National Consumers' League, Women's Activism, and Labor Standards in the New Deal Era* (Chapel Hill: University of North Carolina Press, 2000). Other good sources include Julie Novkov, *Constituting Workers, Protecting Women: Gender, Law and Labor in the Progressive Era and New Deal Years* (Ann Arbor: University of Michigan Press, 2001); Holly J. McCammon, "The Politics of Protection: State Minimum Wage and Maximum Hours Laws for Women in the U.S., 1870–1930," *Sociological Quarterly* 36, 2 (Spring 1995): 217–249; and Felice J. Batlan, "Florence Kelley and the Battle against Laissez-Faire Constitutionalism," 2010, http://scholarship.Kentlaw.iit.edu/fac_schol/69.

The early British experience with child labor exploitation is covered by Jane Humphries, *Childhood and Child Labour in the British Industrial Revolution* (Cambridge: Cambridge University Press, 2011). See also Peter Kirby, *Child Labour in Britain, 1750–1870* (London: Palgrave MacMillan, 2003).

The first major work on the subject in America was a treatise by Raymond G. Fuller, *Child Labor and the Constitution*, published in 1923. As former director of research and publicity for the National Child Labor Committee, Fuller drew on his experience in the movement to regulate child labor. While his work discusses two important child labor cases, *Hammer v. Dagenhart* and *Bailey v. Drexel Furniture Company*, and the need for a constitutional amendment, it misses the rest of the story. Another text, *Constitutional Politics in the Progressive Era: Child Labor and the Law*, by Stephen B. Wood, was published in 1968 and, because the focus is on the Progressive Era, ends its discussion of child labor reform in the 1920s. That cutoff date excludes much of the history as well, including two Supreme Court decisions and a proposed constitutional amendment.

Walter I. Trattner's *Crusade for the Children* (Chicago: Quadrangle Books, 1970), provides the best narrative on the struggle over federal child labor legislation and the strategic role played by the National Child Labor Committee. In *Child Labor: An American History* (London: Routledge, 2002), Hugh Hindman uses data from the National Child Labor Committee archives to document the growth of child labor as a social problem. Hindman argues that industrialization both created the problem of child labor and provided the impetus toward its eradication. For a good description of life in the Lowell textile mills, see Chaim M. Rosenberg, *Child Labor in America: A History* (Jefferson, NC: McFarland, 2013). James D. Schimdt, in *Industrial Violence and the Legal Origins of Child Labor* (Cambridge: Cambridge University Press, 2010), argues that there was a large shift in the cultural perception of youthful labor during the late nineteenth and early twentieth centuries. The shift was a product of competing visions of how children would fit into the increasingly dangerous nature of work in industrial America. On one side, young workers and their families sought an industrial childhood because it instilled a strong work ethic and contributed to the household income. In opposition, reformers fought to exclude children from productive life and articulated a new definition of childhood centered on schooling and recreation.

Opposition to the Federal Child Labor Amendment is discussed in Bart Dredge, "David Clark's 'Campaign of Enlightenment': Child Labor and the Farmers' States' Rights League, 1911–1940," *North Carolina Historical Review* 91 (January 2014): 30–62. The most comprehensive and recent exploration of child labor reform is my book *Child Labor in America: The Epic Legal Struggle to Protect Children* (Lawrence: University Press of Kansas, 2018). The study explores the origins of child labor in the United States and the nearly two-century effort to regulate the practice at the state and federal levels. A recent study that emphasizes the sectional conflicts over child labor is provided by Betsy Wood, *Upon the Altar of Work: Child Labor and the Rise of a New American Sectionalism* (Champaign: University of Illinois Press, 2020).

Father John A. Ryan, a Catholic priest who advocated a living wage and child labor restrictions, offered a moral defense of legislative minimum wage laws in *The Living Wage: Its Ethical and Economic Aspects* (New York: Macmillan, 1906). The state minimum wage movement during the Progressive Era was reviewed by Elizabeth Brandeis, daughter of former Supreme Court associate justice Louis D. Brandeis. See "Minimum Wage Legislation," in *History of Labor in the United States, 1896–1932*, vol. 3, Labor Legislation (New York: Macmillan, 1935). Other helpful sources on minimum wage mandates and living wages include Jerold L. Waltman, *The Case for a Living Wage* (New York, Algora, 2004); Steven Epstein, "The Theory and Practice of the Just Wage," *Journal of Medieval History* 17 (1991): 53–71; Willis Nordlund. *The Quest for a Living Wage: A History of the Federal Minimum Wage Program* (Westport, CT: Greenwood Press, 1997); and Valerie Hoekstra, "The Pendulum of Precedent: U.S. State Legislative Response to Supreme Court Decisions on Minimum Wage Legislation for Women," *State Politics and Policy Quarterly* 9, 3 (Fall 2009): 257–283. The landmark decision upholding state minimum wage laws is covered by Helen J. Knowles, *Making Minimum Wage: Elsie Parrish versus the West Coast Hotel Company* (Norman: University of Oklahoma Press, 2021).

The congressional debate over the Fair Labor Standards Act was complex and contentious. For the official records of the hearings and floor debates, see the *Fair Labor Standards Act of 1937, Joint Hearings before Committee on Education and Labor, United States Senate, and the Committee on Labor, House of Representatives, 75th Congress*, Part 1, June 2–5, Congressional Record (Washington, DC: Government Printing Office, 1937). The best secondary source on the five-year struggle to pass federal labor standards is George E. Paulsen's *A Living Wage for the Forgotten Man: The Quest for Fair Labor Standards, 1933–1941* (Selinsgrove, PA: Susquehanna University Press, 1996). Franklin D. Roosevelt's radio address from Albany, New York, known as the "Forgotten Man" speech, can be found online at the American Presidency Project, https://www.presidency.ucsb.edu/documents /radio-address-from-albany-new-york-the-forgotten-man-speech.

Frances Perkins, FDR's labor secretary, offered her perspective on the fight for labor standards in *The Roosevelt I Knew* (New York: Viking Press, 1946). For commentary on the FLSA as it was being debated in Congress, consult "Wages, Hours: Congress Is Stirred by a Contentious Bill," *Pathfinder*, December 18, 1937, 3–7. See also Jonathan Grossman, "Fair Labor Standards Act: Maximum Struggle for a Minimum Wage," *Monthly Labor Review* (June 1978): 24; "The Roosevelt Proposal: President Roosevelt's Message to Congress," *New York Times*, May 25, 1937, 1, 19; also Howard D. Samuel, "Troubled Passage: The Labor Movement and the Fair Labor Standards Act," *Monthly Labor Review* (December 2000): 32–37. Senator Hugo Black's role in supporting labor standards is explored in Virginia Van Der Veer Hamilton, *Hugo Black: The Alabama Years* (Baton Rouge: Louisiana State University Press, 1972). Representative Mary Norton's important role in guiding the Fair Labor Standards Act through the House of Representatives is described in *Mary Norton of New Jersey: Congressional Trailblazer*, by David L. Porter (Vancouver, BC: Fairleigh Dickinson University Press, 2013). Two early discussions of the congressional debate were provided by Paul H. Douglas and Joseph Hackman, "The Fair Labor Standards Act of 1938," *Political Science Quarterly* 53, 4 (December 1938): 491–515; and John S. Forsythe, "Legislative History of the Fair Labor Standards Act," *Law and Contemporary Problems* 6, 3 (Summer 1939): 464–490. The media followed the congressional debate over the FLSA closely. See "Southerners Rake Wage Bill as Evil to the Whole Nation," *New York Times*, July 31, 1937, 1; "Roosevelt Plans Face Fight by King," *New York Times*, November 9, 1937, 5; and "Cotton Mills Call Wage Order Ruinous," *New York Times*, December 4, 1940, 32.

FDR's Court-packing plan is summarized by the National Constitution Center, "How FDR Lost His Brief War on the Supreme Court," February 5, 2024, https://constitutioncenter.org/blog/how-fdr-lost-his-brief-war-on-the-supreme-court-2. An interesting analysis of FDR's efforts to reshape the courts is offered by William E. Leuchtenburg, "FDR's Court-Packing Plan: A Second Life, a Second Death," *Duke Law Journal* (1985): 673–689. For other perspectives on the plan, consult William E. Leuchtenburg, "The Origins of Franklin D. Roosevelt's Court-Packing Plan," *Supreme Court Review* (1966): 347–400; Jeff Shesol, *Supreme Power: Franklin Roosevelt vs. the Supreme Court* (New York: Norton, 2011); and Sheldon Gelman, "The Court-Packing Controversy," *Constitutional Commentary* 28 (2013). Congress passed the Supreme Court Retirement

Act on March 1, 1937, allowing justices to retire at age seventy with a full pension. On August 26, 1937, President Roosevelt signed the Judicial Procedure Reform Act, a compromise on his original reorganization plan.

Child labor reformers were concerned about the limitations of the FLSA with respect to oppressive child labor. For an early discussion, see Katherine Du Pre Lumpkin, "The Child Labor Provisions of the Fair Labor Standards Act," *Law and Contemporary Problems* 6 (1939): 391–405; Courtenay Dinwiddie, "The Present Status of Child Labor," *Social Service Review* 13, 3 (September 1939): 431–439; Note, "Children Still Need Fair Labor Standards," *Social Service Review* 13, 4 (December 1939): 696–698; National Child Labor Committee, "Two Years of Federal Control," *American Child* 22 (December 1940): 2; and Donald Murtha, "Wage-Hour and Child Labor Legislation in the Roosevelt Administration," *Lawyers Guild Review* 5 (1945): 185–191.

Implementation of the Fair Labor Standards Act is reviewed in "Annual Report, Wage and Hour Division, for the Fiscal Year Ended June 30, 1940" (Washington, DC: Government Printing Office, 1941), 91–96; and "Twenty-Seventh Annual Report of the Secretary of Labor" (Washington, DC: Government Printing Office, 1939), 203–206. Both reports can be accessed at http://www.hathitrust.org. Another reference on the implementation of the FLSA is Donald A. Young, "Wage-Hour Law Now in Effect," *Savannah Morning News*, October 24, 1938. Numerous articles on enforcement of the FLSA between 1938 and 1941 are available in the *New York Times* historical database.

The Manuscript Reading Room at the Library of Congress Madison Building houses the public papers (docket sheets, memos, and notes) for several justices on the Hughes Court, including Chief Justice Charles Evans Hughes, Justice William O. Douglas, and Justice Harlan Fiske Stone, the author of the *Darby Lumber* opinion. The Hughes papers contain general correspondence from citizens and a few notes on cases. Memos between Justice Stone and Chief Justice Hughes can be found in the Stone papers. See Harlan Fiske Stone Papers, Library of Congress, Manuscript Reading Room, *U.S. v. Darby Lumber*, memo from Chief Justice Hughes to Justice Stone, January 27, 1941. For a discussion of the docket books in the *Darby Lumber* and *Opp Cotton* cases, see Barry Cushman, "The Hughes Court Docket Books: The Late Terms, 1937–1940," *American Journal of Legal History* 55 (2015): 361–432. Oral arguments in the *Darby Lumber* case are reported in "Wage Act Argued before High Court," *New York Times*, December 21, 1940, p. 22; "Georgian Tells High Court Pay Act, 'Bold, Bad,'" *Atlanta Constitution*, December 21, 1940, 9; "High Court Hears Statesboro Case," *Augusta Chronicle*, December 21, 1940, A3; and "Lovett Attacks Wage-Hour Law," *Savannah Morning News*, December 21, 1940, 12.

Justice Stone's opinion in *Darby Lumber* is discussed in Alpheus T. Mason, *Harlan Fiske Stone: Pillar of the Law* (New York: Viking Press, 1956). Early commentaries on the *Darby Lumber* decision include Robert E. Cushman, "Constitutional Law in 1940–1941," *American Political Science Review* 35, 2 (April 1942): 263–289; Edward R. Rosston, "Constitutional Law: Validity and Scope of the Fair Labor Standards Act," *California Law Review* 29, 5 (July 1941): 615–627; and Robert L. Stern, "The Commerce Clause and the National Economy, 1933–1946," *Harvard Law Review* 59 (July 1946): 883–947.

Most major news outlets recognized the importance of the *Darby Lumber* decision. Notable are "Wage Law Upheld by the Supreme Court; Old Decision Upset," *New York Times*, February 4, 1941, 1; "Wage-Hour Act Is Upheld," *Atlantic News-Telegraph*, February 3, 1941, 1; "Wage-Hour Act Constitutional," *Augusta Chronicle*, February 4, 1941, 1, 3; and "Pay-Hour Law Ruling Curbs Child Labor," *New York Herald Tribune*, February 4, 1941, 1.

The federal prosecution of Fred Darby and his lumber company is based on District Court trial transcripts and supporting documents found at the National Archives and Records Administration in Atlanta, Georgia (atlanta.archives@nara.gov). There is a fee to have the records copied and mailed. A brief history of the lumber company and the *Darby Lumber* case is provided by Patrick Novotny, "United States v. Darby Lumber: Statesboro, Georgia 1939–1941," *Statesboro Magazine* 6, 2 (March/April 2005): 56–61.

The challenges facing the labor movement in the twentieth century are covered by Nelson Lichtenstein, *State of the Union: A Century of American Labor* (Princeton, NJ: Princeton University Press, 2002). The federalism litigation involving the FLSA amendments that extended coverage to state employees is discussed by Lee Epstein, Kevin T. McGuire, and Thomas Walker, *Constitutional Law for a Changing America: Institutional Powers and Constraints*, 11th ed. (Washington, DC: Sage/Congressional

Quarterly Press, 2022). For major amendments to the FLSA, consult Susan Kocin, "Basic Provisions of the 1966 FLSA Amendments," *Monthly Labor Review* 90, 3 (March 1967): 1–4; and US Department of Labor, Wage and Hour Division, "History of Amendments to the FLSA," https:// www.dol.gov/agencies/whd/about/history, accessed July 29, 2024.

The Economic Policy Institute, an independent think tank, produced a useful study of the legislation introduced and passed during the 2022–2023 state legislative sessions that attempted to weaken child labor laws. See https://www.epi.org/publication/child-labor-laws-under-attack/. The Department of Labor also issued a report on its efforts to combat a rise in child labor violations. See https://www.dol.gov/newsroom/re leases/whd/whd20230412. Hannah Dreier of the *New York Times* wrote a scathing expose on how many migrant children are being exploited across the United States; see https://www.nytimes.com/2023/02/25/us /unaccompanied-migrant-child-workers-exploitation.html. Although the article is behind a paywall, it is worth accessing. Another good source on contemporary child labor problems can be found at https://www .newyorker.com/magazine/2023/06/12/child-labor-is-on-the-rise.

The Ballotpedia website has an excellent table listing the twenty-eight voter initiatives to increase the minimum wage from 1996 to 2022, including the election outcomes. Twenty-six of the initiatives passed, usually by wide margins: https://ballotpedia.org/Minimum_wage_on _the_ballot. Useful sources on the challenges facing the modern FLSA include Thomas E. Perez, "The Fair Labor Standards Act at Seventy-Seven: Still Far Reaching, Far-Sighted," *ABA Journal of Labor and Employment Law* 30, 3 (Spring 2015): 299–304; and Kati L. Griffith, "The Fair Labor Standards Act at 80: Everything Old Is New Again," *Cornell Law Review* 104 (2019): 557–603. For an argument on revising child labor standards, see Sarah Clements, "We Need a Federal Young Workers' Bill of Rights," *Georgetown Journal on Poverty Law and Policy*, February 11, 2024, https://www.law.georgetown.edu/poverty-journal/blog/we-need-a-federal-young-workers-bill-of-rights/. Finally, for current standards and regulations under the Fair Labor Standards Act, access the FLSA page at the Department of Labor, https://www.dol.gov/agencies/whd /flsa.

CASES CITED

A. B. Kirschbaum v. Walling, 316 U.S. 517 (1942)

Adair v. United States, 208 U.S. 161 (1908)

Adkins v. Children's Hospital, 261 U.S. 525 (1923)

Alden v. Maine, 527 U.S. 706 (1999)

Bailey v. Drexel Furniture Company, 259 U.S. 20 (1922)

Bunting v. Oregon, 243 U.S. 426 (1917)

Carter v. Carter Coal Company, 298 U.S. 238 (1936)

Champion v. Ames, 188 U.S. 321 (1903)

Chevron U.S.A., Inc. v. Natural Resources Defense Council, 467 U.S. 837 (1984)

Chisholm v. Georgia, 2 Dall. 419 (1793)

Clark Distilling Co. v. Western Maryland Railway Co., 242 U.S. 311 (1917)

Commonwealth v. Hamilton Manufacturing Company, 73 U.S. (6 Wall.) 632 (1867)

Commonwealth v. Hunt, 45 Mass. (4 Met.) 111 (1842)

Darby v. United States, 132 F.2d. 928 (5th Cir. 1943)

Garcia v. San Antonio Metropolitan Transit Authority, 469 U.S. 528 (1984)

Gemsco, Inc. v. Walling, 324 U.S. 244 (1945)

Gibbons v. Ogden, 22 U.S. 1 (1824)

Hammer v. Dagenhart, 247 U.S. 251 (1918)

Helvering v. Davis, 301 U.S. 619 (1937)

Hippolite Egg Company v. United States, 220 U.S. 45 (1911)

Holden v. Hardy, 169 U.S. 366 (1898)

Houston, East and West Texas Railway v. U.S. (a.k.a. Shreveport Rate Case), 234 U.S. 342 (1914)

Inland Steel Co. v. Yedinak, 172 Ind. 423 (1909)

In re Spencer, 149 Cal. 396, 86 Pac. 896 (1906)

Kentucky Whip and Collar Co. v. Illinois Central Railroad Co. (1937)

Lane County v. Oregon, 74 U.S. 71 (1868)

Lochner v. New York, 198 U.S. 45 (1905)

Loper Bright Enterprises v. Raimondo, 603 U.S. 369 (2024)

Maryland v. Wirtz, 392 U.S. 183 (1968)

McCulloch v. Maryland, 17 U.S. 316 (1819)

Morehead v. New York Ex Rel. Tipaldo, 298 U.S. 587 (1936)

Muller v. Oregon, 208 U.S. 412 (1908)

Nash v. United States, 229 U.S. 373 (1913)

National Labor Relations Board v. Jones and Laughlin Steel Corporation, 301 U.S. 1 (1937)

National League of Cities v. Usery, 426 U.S. 833 (1976)

Opp Cotton Mills, Inc. v. Administrator Wage and Hour Division, 111 F.2d 23 (5th Cir. 1940)

Opp Cotton Mills, Inc. v. Administrator Wage and Hour Division, 312 U.S. 126 (1940)

Perkins v. Lukens Steel Company, 310 U.S. 113 (1940)

Relentless, Inc. v. Department of Commerce, __ U.S. __ (2024)

Ritchie v. People, 115 Ill. 98 (1895)

Schechter Poultry Corporation v. United States, 295 U.S. 495 (1935)

Seminole Tribe of Florida v. Florida, 517 U.S. 44 (1996)

Stettler v. O'Hara, 243 U.S. 629 (1917)

Sturges and Burn Manufacturing Co. v. Beauchamp, 231 U.S. 320 (1913)

Swift and Company v. United States, 196 U.S. 375 (1905)

U.S. v. F. W. Darby Lumber Company, 32 F. Supp. 734 (S.D. Georgia 1940)

U.S. v. Darby Lumber Co., 312 U.S. 100 (1941)

U.S. v. Rosenwasser, 323 U.S. 360 (1945)

Warren-Bradshaw Drilling Co. v. Hall, 317 U.S. 88 (1942)

Wenham v. State, 65 Neb. 394 (1902)

West Coast Hotel Co. v. Parrish, 300 U.S. 279 (1937)

Wilson v. New, 243 U.S. 332 (1917)

Wright v. Vinton Branch of Mountain Trust Bank of Roanoke, 300 U.S. 440 (1937)

INDEX

Abbott, Grace, 46, 83
A. B. Kirschbaum v. Walling, 153
Adair v. United States, 26
Adamson Act, 30, 183
Addams, Jane, 42
Adkins v. Children's Hospital, 5, 69–71, 76, 86, 183
administrator, role of, 154–55
agriculture industry, 53, 90–91, 101, 102, 159, 161, 172
Alabama, 41, 53, 75, 85, 105
Alabama (band), 1
Alaska, 178
Alden v. Maine, 165–166
Aldrich, Nelson, 43
Amalgamated Clothing Workers of America, 76–77, 88
American Association for Labor Legislation (AALL), 62, 67
American Association of University Women, 54
American Bar Association, 107
American Bar Association Journal, 123–124
American Child Health Association, 51
American Constitutional League, 54
American Farm Bureau Federation (AFBF), 52–53
American Federation of Labor (AFL)
  child labor bill and, 49
  collective bargaining and, 92
  Congress of Industrial Organizations (CIO) and, 2–3
  Fair Labor Standards Act of 1938 (FLSA) enforcement and, 88, 105
  influence of, 18–19

  on minimum wage, 63
  negotiations of, 2
  opposition from, 94
  origin of, 18, 182
  Ramspeck compromise and, 96
  substitute bill of, 94–95
  thirty-hour workweek drafting by, 30
American Legion, 54
American Newspaper Publishers Association, 111
Andrews, Elmer F., 104–105, 106, 107, 108, 114, 115, 116–117, 118–119
Andrews, John B., 62
A&P, 170–171
Aquinas, Thomas, 57–58
Arena, The (magazine), 42
Arizona, 28, 54, 65, 71, 80, 178
Arizona Republic (newspaper), 134
Arkansas, 53, 54, 65, 67, 71, 175, 176
Arkwright, Richard, 37–38
Australia, workweek hours in, 13

Bagley, Sarah G., 15, 16
Bailey v. Drexel Furniture Company, 5, 50, 126
Ballantine, Arthur A., 123–124
Bankhead, William, 95
Barden, Graham A., 114
Barden bill, 114, 119
Barrett, William H., 122–123, 129–130, 137
baseball, 169, 171–172
battery industry, 106–107
Bernstein, Irving, 5
Beveridge, Albert J., 42–43
Biddle, Francis B., 126–127
Bigelow, Herbert S., 99

in Progressive Era, 57
by state, 62–65
statistics regarding, 80
Statues of Laborers regarding, 58
"switch in time that saved nine"
and, 79–81
variances of, 73
in Victoria, Australia, 60
for women, 5, 75, 105–106
See also wages; *specific laws; specific
states*
mining industry, 23, 41
Minnesota, 45, 65, 67, 182
Mississippi, 85, 105
Missouri, 29, 178
Montana, 28, 178
Morehead v. New York Ex Rel. Tipaldo,
74–76, 79
Muller, Curt, 26
Muller v. Oregon, 27, 133, 182
Murphy, Frank, 128, 129, 153
Myers, Mac, 110, 111
Myrick, Shelby, 138, 139, 141, 143

Nash v. United States (1913), 131
National Association of
Manufacturers (NAM), 54,
87, 96, 102
National Association of Wood
Manufacturers, 87
National Association Opposed to
Woman Suffrage (Woman
Patriots), 54
National Child Labor Committee
(NCLC), 31–32, 41–42,
43–44, 45, 49, 54, 61, 89, 137,
150–151, 159
National Conference of State
Legislatures, 157
National Congress of Mothers, 71
National Consumers' League
(NCL), 26–27, 42, 44, 49,
60–61, 65, 75, 171

National Education Association,
148–149, 150–151
National Farm Bureau Federation,
54, 102
National Federation of Teachers, 54
National Future Farmers of
America Organization, 172
National Governors' Association,
161
National Grange, 52–53, 54, 102
National Guard, 1
National Hardwood Lumber
Association, 107
National Industrial Recovery Act
(NIRA) of 1933
conditions of, 55–56, 73
opposition to, 33–34
origin of, 84
overturning of, 9, 184
overview of, 5–6, 31
signing of, 183
National Institute for Occupational
Safety and Health, 172
National Labor Relations Act of
1935 (Wagner Act), 2, 6, 133,
157, 184
National Labor Relations Board
(NLRB), 94, 124
*National Labor Relations Board v. Jones
and Laughlin Steel Corporation,*
6, 78–79, 86, 135
National Labor Union (NLU), 17,
181
National League of Cities, 161
National League of Cities v. Usery
(1976), 161–165
National League of Women Voters,
71, 89–90
National Negro Congress, 90
National PTA, 171
National Publishers Association, 87
National Recovery Act (NRA), 82,
83

violations of, 112, 121, 138, 141–142, 144, 166

Westinghouse and, 106

Owen, Robert, 13

Panic of 1873, 17

parens patriae (state as parent), 44

Parsons, Herbert, 43

Parton, Dolly, 1

Paul, Alice, 71

Paulsen, George E., 72

Peckham, Rufus, 25

Pennsylvania, 4, 29, 40, 75, 80

Pennsylvania Department of Labor and Industry, 110

Pepper, Claude, 97

Pepper-Hook bill, 156

Perkins, Frances, 30, 82–83, 87–88, 95–96, 117–118, 147, 150–151, 152, 155

Perkins, Fred C., 106–107

Perkins v. Lukens Steel Company, 35

Philadelphia, Pennsylvania, 14, 18, 181

Philadelphia Council for Social Progress, 115

Philip II (king of Spain), 12–13

piece workers, 153

piecework rate, 147–148, 153

Pitney, Mahlon, 47

police, violence by, 1

Pollock, Jackson, 119

Poole, Rufus, 96

Portal-to-Portal Act, 157–158, 184

poultry industry, 33–34

Powderly, Terence V., 18

Powell, Lewis F., Jr., 162, 165

prevailing wage, 83

prison-goods theory of regulation, 90–91, 92

Progressive Era, 4, 19–20, 41–42, 57, 60–61

Progressive Party, 53, 61

progressive reform, stalling of, 5

pro-labor interest groups, political demands of, 4

public education, 164

public employees, 159–161, 164

Puerto Rico, 10, 28, 65, 73, 114, 126, 158, 178

Pure Food and Drug Act, 47

Puritans, 36

Quakers, 36

Quayle, Dan, 169

railroad uprisings, 1, 29–30

Rainey, Henry, 30

Ramspeck, Robert, 96

Rauschenbusch, Walter, 62

Reagan, Ronald, 165, 167–168

Red Scare, 5

Reed, Stanley, 128, 136–137

Rehnquist, William, 162, 163, 165

Reich, Robert B., 171

Reilly, Gerard, 96

Relentless, Inc. v. Department of Commerce, 178–179

Republican Party

child labor restrictions and, 175, 176

Fair Labor Standards Act of 1938 (FLSA) and, 91, 108

federal minimum wage and, 177

as majority, 173

on *Morehead* decision, 76

Taft-Hartley Act and, 156–157

Tea Party and, 173

Twentieth Amendment and, 51, 53

Revenue Act of 1919, 49

Reynolds, Kim, 176

Rhode Island, 39, 40

Ricardo, David, 58

www.ingramcontent.com/pod-product-compliance
Lightning Source LLC
Chambersburg PA
CBHW020114230126
38691CB00015B/152